'At a moment when political economists of global finance are largely preoccupied with, and frustrated by, the post-crisis regulatory response, Chris Clarke's original intervention looks to Adam Smith to bring ethical relations and everyday politics to the centre of critical inquiry.'

Paul Langley, *Durham University, UK*

'Clarke's original and important analysis shows how Adam Smith can help transcend the narrow economistic foundations of not just contemporary financial governance but also much IPE scholarship that overlooks the issues of ethics and moral philosophy that informed classical political economy.'

Eric Helleiner, *University of Waterloo, Canada*

'This major new study demonstrates the richness and complexity of Adam Smith's thought and its relevance to understanding the current problems of our political economy.'

Andrew Gamble, *University of Sheffield, UK*

Ethics and Economic Governance

This book seeks to explore the ethical dimensions of economic governance through an engagement with Adam Smith and a critical analysis of economistic understandings of the global financial crisis. It examines ethical and political dilemmas associated with key aspects of the financialisation of Anglo-American economy and society, including systems of asset-based welfare, modern risk management and debt.

In the wake of the financial crisis, recognition of the way in which everyday lives and life chances are tied into global finance is widespread. Yet few contributions in IPE explicitly tackle this issue as a question of ethics. By developing Adam Smith's under-utilised account of how market-oriented behaviour is constituted through a process of 'sympathy', this book provides an innovative way of understanding contemporary issues of economic governance and the possibilities and limits for intervention within it.

This book turns the common understanding of Smith on its head in order to show the urgency of making better known, or making visible, the ethico-political contestation that lies at the heart of financial market relations. It will be of interest to students and scholars of IPE as well as those across the social sciences who wish to question the foundations of contemporary economy and society.

Chris Clarke is Assistant Professor in Political Economy in the Department of Politics and International Studies at the University of Warwick, UK.

Ripe Series in Global Political Economy

This series, published in association with the *Review of International Political Economy*, provides a forum for current and interdisciplinary debates in international political economy. The series aims to advance understanding of the key issues in the global political economy, and to present innovative analyses of emerging topics. The titles in the series focus on three broad themes:

- the structures, processes and actors of contemporary global transformations
- the changing forms taken by governance, at scales from the local and everyday to the global and systemic
- the inseparability of economic from political, social and cultural questions, including resistance, dissent and social movements.

The *RIPE Series in Global Political Economy* aims to address the needs of students and teachers. Titles include:

Transnational Classes and International Relations
Kees van der Pijl

Globalization and Governance
Edited by Aseem Prakash and Jeffrey A. Hart

Nation-States and Money
The Past, Present and Future of National Currencies
Edited by Emily Gilbert and Eric Helleiner

Gender and Global Restructuring
Sightings, Sites and Resistances
Edited by Marianne H Marchand and Anne Sisson Runyan

The Global Political Economy of Intellectual Property Rights
The New Enclosures?
Christopher May

Global Political Economy
Contemporary Theories
Edited by Ronen Palan

Ideologies of Globalization
Contending Visions of a New World Order
Mark Rupert

The Clash within Civilisations
Coming to Terms with Cultural Conflicts
Dieter Senghaas

Capitalist Restructuring, Globalisation and the Third Way
Lessons from the Swedish Model
J. Magnus Ryner

Transnational Capitalism and the Struggle over European Integration
Bastiaan van Apeldoorn

World Financial Orders
An Historical International Political Economy
Paul Langley

Global Unions?
Theory and Strategies of Organized Labour in the Global Political Economy
Edited by Jeffrey Harrod and Robert O'Brien

Political Economy of a Plural World
Critical Reflections on Power, Morals and Civilizations
Robert Cox with Michael Schechter

The Changing Politics of Finance in Korea and Thailand
From Deregulation to Debacle
Xiaoke Zhang

Anti-Immigrantism in Western Democracies
Statecraft, Desire and the Politics of Exclusion
Roxanne Lynn Doty

The Political Economy of European Employment
European Integration and the Transnationalization of the (Un) Employment Question
Edited by Henk Overbeek

A Critical Rewriting of Global Political Economy
Integrating Reproductive, Productive and Virtual Economies
V. Spike Peterson

International Trade and Developing Countries
Bargaining Coalitions in the GATT and WTO
Amrita Narlikar

Rethinking Global Political Economy
Emerging Issues, Unfolding Odysseys
Edited by Mary Ann Tétreault, Robert A. Denemark, Kenneth P. Thomas and Kurt Burch

Global Institutions and Development
Framing the World?
Edited by Morten Bøås and Desmond McNeill

Contesting Globalization
Space and Place in the World Economy
André C. Drainville

The Southern Cone Model
The Political Economy of Regional Capitalist Development in Latin America
Nicola Phillips

The Idea of Global Civil Society
Politics and Ethics of a Globalizing Era
Edited by Randall D. Germain and Michael Kenny

Global Institutions, Marginalization, and Development
Craig N. Murphy
Governing Financial Globalization

International Political Economy and Multi-Level Governance
Edited by Andrew Baker, David Hudson and Richard Woodward

Critical Theories, International Relations and 'the Anti-Globalisation Movement'
The Politics of Global Resistance
Edited by Catherine Eschle and Bice Maiguashca

Resisting Intellectual Property
Debora J. Halbert

Globalization, Governmentality, and Global Politics
Regulation for the Rest of Us?
Ronnie D. Lipschutz, with James K. Rowe

Neoliberal Hegemony
A Global Critique
Edited by Dieter Plehwe, Bernhard Walpen and Gisela Neunhöffer

Images of Gramsci
Connections and Contentions in Political Theory and International Relations
Edited by Andreas Bieler and Adam David Morton

Global Standards of Market Civilization
Edited by Brett Bowden and Leonard Seabrooke

Beyond Globalization
Capitalism, Territoriality and the International Relations of Modernity
Hannes Lacher

Global Public Policy
Business and the Countervailing Powers of Civil Society
Edited by Karsten Ronit

The Transnational Politics of Corporate Governance Regulation
Edited by Henk Overbeek, Bastiaan van Apeldoorn and Andreas Nölke

Critical Perspectives on Global Governance
Rights and Regulation in Governing Regimes
Jean Grugel and Nicola Piper

National Currencies and Globalization
Endangered Specie?
Paul Bowles

Conflicts in Environmental Regulation and the Internationalization of the State
Contested Terrains
Ulrich Brand, Christoph Görg, Joachim Hirsch and Markus Wissen

Beyond States and Markets
The Challenges of Social Reproduction
Edited by Isabella Bakker and Rachel Silvey

Governing International Labour Migration
Current Issues, Challenges and Dilemmas
Edited by Christina Gabriel and Hélène Pellerin

The Industrial Vagina
The Political Economy of the Global Sex Trade
Sheila Jeffreys

The Child in International Political Economy
A Place at the Table
Alison M. S. Watson

Capital as Power
A Study of Order and Creorder
Jonathan Nitzan and Shimshon Bichler

Global Citizenship and the Legacy of Empire
Marketing Development
April Biccum

The Global Political Economy of Intellectual Property Rights,
Second Edition

The New Enclosures
Christopher May

Corporate Power and Ownership in Contemporary Capitalism
The politics of Resistance and Domination
Susanne Soederberg

Savage Economics
Wealth, Poverty and the Temporal Walls of Capitalism
David L. Blaney and Naeem Inayatullah

Cultural Political Economy
Edited by Jacqueline Best and Matthew Paterson

Development, Sexual Rights and Global Governance
Resisting Global Power
Amy Lind

Cosmopolitanism and Global Financial Reform
A Pragmatic Approach to the Tobin Tax
James Brassett

Gender and Global Restructuring
Second Edition

Sightings, Sites and Resistances
Edited by Marianne H. Marchand and Anne Sisson Runyan

Variegated Neoliberalism
EU Varieties of Capitalism and International Political Economy
Huw Macartney

The Politics of European Competition Regulation
A Critical Political Economy Perspective
Hubert Buch-Hansen and Angela Wigger

The Political Economy of Global Remittances
Gender and Governmentality
Rahel Kunz

A Critical History of the Economy
On the Birth of the National and International Economies
Ryan Walter

The International Political Economy of Transition
Neoliberal Hegemony and Eastern Central Europe's Transformation
Stuart Shields

The Global Political Economy of Trade Protectionism and Liberalization
Trade Reform and Economic Adjustment in Textiles and Clothing
Tony Heron

Transnational Financial Associations and the Governance of Global Finance
Assembling Wealth and Power
Heather McKeen-Edwards and Tony Porter

The Capitalist Mode of Power
Critical Engagements with the Power Theory of Value
Edited by Tim Di Muzio

The Making of Modern Finance
Liberal Governance and the Gold Standard
Samuel Knafo

The State of Copyright
The Complex Relationships of Cultural Creation in a Globalized World
Debora J. Halbert

Transnational Financial Regulation after the Crisis
Edited by Tony Porter

The Political Economy of Global Capitalism and Crisis
Bill Dunn

Global Capitalism
Selected Essays
Hugo Radice

Debtfare States and the Poverty Industry
Money, Discipline and the Surplus Population
Susanne Soederberg

Currency Challenge
The Euro, the Dollar and the Global Financial
Miguel Otero-Iglesias

Fringe Finance
Crossing and Contesting the Borders of Global Capital
Rob Aitken

Asymmetric Crisis in Europe and Possible Futures
Critical Political Economy and Post-Keynesian Perspectives
Edited by Johannes Jäger and Elisabeth Springler

Hybrid Rule and State Formation
Public-Private Power in the 21st Century
Edited by Shelley L. Hurt and Ronnie D. Lipschutz

Global Economic Governance and the Development Practices of the Multilateral Development Banks
Edited by Susan Park and Jonathan R. Strand

Ethics and Economic Governance
Using Adam Smith to Understand the Global Financial Crisis
Chris Clarke

Ethics and Economic Governance

Using Adam Smith to understand the global financial crisis

Chris Clarke

Routledge
Taylor & Francis Group
LONDON AND NEW YORK

First published 2016 by Routledge

2 Park Square, Milton Park, Abingdon, Oxfordshire OX14 4RN
52 Vanderbilt Avenue, New York, NY 10017

Routledge is an imprint of the Taylor & Francis Group, an informa business

First issued in paperback 2020

British Library Cataloguing in Publication Data
A catalogue record for this book is available from the British Library

Library of Congress Cataloging-in-Publication Data
Clarke, Chris, 1985– author.
Ethics and economic governance : using Adam Smith to understand the global financial crisis / Chris Clarke.
pages cm. — (RIPE series in global political economy)
Includes bibliographical references and index.
1. Smith, Adam, 1723–1790. 2. Economics—Moral and ethical aspects. 3. Finance—Moral and ethical aspects. 4. Financial crises. 5. Global Financial Crisis, 2008–2009. I. Title.
HB103.S6C53 2016
330.9'0511—dc23
2015025490

ISBN: 978-1-138-84034-8 (hbk)
ISBN: 978-0-367-59776-4 (pbk)

Typeset in Times
by Apex CoVantage, LLC

Contents

Acknowledgements

While writing this book I was fortunate enough to work within an especially strong and supportive community in the Department of Politics and International Studies at the University of Warwick. I would like to acknowledge the contribution that members of the International Political Economy research cluster have made to the development of my work, especially André Broome, Ben Clift, Juanita Elias, Simon Glaze, Christopher Holmes, Shirin Rai, Lena Rethel, Ben Richardson, Chris Rogers, Timothy Sinclair and Lauren Tooker. I reserve special thanks to Matthew Watson and James Brassett for their supervision of my doctoral thesis out of which this book grew. Their friendship, support and intellectual prowess meant that I enjoyed an incredibly rewarding PhD experience for which I am very grateful. Charis Blythe was also critical in providing the support that led to my successful completion. Over the years, numerous PAIS colleagues past and present have engaged me in stimulating discussion and debate that contributed to the development of my work. For this, among many others, I am very grateful to Ben Braun, Renske Doorenspleet, Andrew Hammond, Charlotte Heath-Kelly, Edward Page, Ben Rosamond, Leonard Seabrooke, Alex Sutton, Nick Vaughan-Williams and Simon Willmetts. In the development of the manuscript André Broome, Ben Clift, Chris Rogers, Michael Saward and Alex Sutton also deserve special thanks for reading early drafts and providing insightful comments on all or parts of the book.

Numerous friends and colleagues beyond Warwick have helped develop my thinking while writing this book. I thank in particular Rob Aitken, Philip Cerny, Randall Germain, Paul Langley, Bill Maurer and Johnna Montgomerie. Mark Blyth deserves special thanks for hosting me during a period of study at the Watson Institute for International Studies, Brown University. The UK Economic and Social Research Council made both this visit and my entire doctoral study possible by providing financial support for which I am very grateful. I also thank Jacqueline Best, as editor of the *RIPE Series*, Lydia de Cruz at Routledge, and two anonymous reviewers for excellent guidance on the development of the manuscript.

I consider myself very lucky to have such a supportive family who have helped me at every stage. I am especially grateful to my parents, who have been unwavering in their encouragement and devotion to me. Finally, the biggest thanks of all are reserved for Adrienne Roberts.

Introduction

The global financial crisis (GFC) of 2007–2008 resulted in the unprecedented bailout of finance undertaken in the name of protecting ordinary people. National governments took extraordinary action to save the banking system – an act that would have been unimaginable only a few months before. Stakes were taken in huge financial institutions to protect depositors, while coordinated interest rate cuts followed by extensive quantitative easing programmes became the order of the day to keep the financial system 'working'. Rather than rethink the foundations of the system that produced the crash, Western states and international economic institutions essentially resolved to restore the status quo operations of finance (Helleiner 2014). The claims made to justify this action were inflated, hugely contestable and depended on rendering the crisis as 'governable' in a particular way. Finance simply had to be saved to protect *our way of life* (Brassett and Clarke 2012).

Underpinning the argument that the global financial system *had* to be rescued is a widely accepted account of economic governance that ought to be challenged. Without fundamental rethinking, the economic and financial status quo that brought about the crisis in the first place will continue unabated. The GFC showed how destructive it can be when lives and life chances are tied ever closer to financial markets, but little has changed in the post-crisis era (Crouch 2011; Mirowski 2013). For the most part, states and international economic institutions continue to operate on the assumption that financial markets are benevolent forces serving the interests of everyone. It is commonly held among them that the more that people are tied into these markets the better. This is particularly astonishing in the wake of such an enormous financial crisis hitting the Anglo-American 'heartland' of capitalism (Gowan 2008). In short, the idea is that if people live as financial citizens – internalising the ethos of finance into their own lives – they are more likely to flourish in today's world. This worldview is hugely influential throughout Anglo-America and dominates much thinking in contemporary economic governance.

Many of the assumptions on which this form of governance rests are 'economistic' in nature. That is, they delimit understandings of life in contemporary society principally in terms of the narrow pursuit of 'self-interest' or its more abstract synonym 'utility maximising behaviour' (Force 2003: 8). This set of ideas is not new and has been critiqued from a wide variety of approaches in the social sciences. It dates back to at least the formation of the notion of 'utility' in the eighteenth century, finds new expression and purpose with the rise of marginalist analysis in the nineteenth century and is often considered to be a defining feature of 'neoliberalism' that has dominated the latter part of the twentieth and early twenty-first centuries. The economistic essence of governance today can be most readily identified in those arenas of national, regional and global governance that assume market behaviour to be a *natural* facet of life. Often this is discussed in terms of neoliberalism, the well-known legacies of Thatcherism in the United Kingdom and Reaganism in the United States, and the intellectual outlook of the major international economic institutions, such as the International Monetary Fund (IMF). To be sure, though, the neoliberal worldview is not necessarily the same as that of an economist (Fourcade-Gourinchas and Babb 2002: 570; Mirowski 2013: 10). The more general *economistic* outlook to which I refer is that which ostensibly views markets as natural and made up of politically and ethically neutral 'self-interested' interactions guided by the 'invisible hand of the market'.

This book goes back to the thinker most associated with the invisible hand – Adam Smith – in order to challenge this economistic worldview and rethink how to understand the GFC. One of the more pervasive characteristics of the avalanche of commentary on the crisis by opinion leaders around the world has been ubiquitous reference to Smith's intellectual legacy. He has been invoked as an authority on why the crisis occurred, as a ghost commentator on the follies of big banks and even as a champion of neoliberalism who has now definitively been proven wrong. The major claim of this book is that by turning the common understanding of Adam Smith on its head, it is also possible to turn accepted wisdom about economic governance on its head as well. By combining Smith's under-utilised ethical theory and political economy with analysis of finance in crisis, this book challenges the status of contemporary economic governance and the limits of its ethical imagination. The ever-deeper enmeshing of financial market life and everyday life is a failed experiment; one which many states, international economic institutions and indeed ordinary people have not yet fully recognised.

This book provides a renewal of Smith that draws attention to his understanding of market-oriented behaviour constituted by 'sympathetic' interpersonal relations. The notion of sympathy here is not the same as a modern-day definition in terms of feeling sorrow for someone's suffering. Rather, on Smith's account, sympathy refers to a psychological device most people hold, or can learn, for negotiating and regulating moral instincts through the activation of fellow-feeling. By paying attention to a sensibility to sympathy in political economy theory and practice, it is possible to develop a sympathetic political economy that provides a direct challenge to economic governance as it currently stands.

The remainder of the introduction proceeds as follows. First, I demonstrate why it is politically urgent to engage with economic governance by mobilising a sympathetic political economy. While many accounts of the GFC offer cutting critiques of finance, they do not go far enough in tackling the ethical dimension of the crisis in order to challenge the status of contemporary economic governance that lies at its heart. Second, I explain why it is productive to engage with Smith's concept of sympathy when attempting to remedy this dilemma. Finally, I provide an overview of the book.

Global finance in crisis

Few accounts explicitly tackle the GFC as a *crisis of ethical imagination*. By this is meant there is lack of attention given to how much of the contemporary governance implicated in the crisis is built on an economistic worldview that marginalises meaningful ethical deliberation. A variety of perspectives engaged in political economy analysis, broadly defined, can be shown to leave this aspect of economic governance under-examined, including scholars in international political economy (IPE), heterodox economics, economic sociology and political theory. In replicating an economistic worldview when seeking to understand the crisis, questions of interpersonal ethics are relegated to the sidelines. The consequences of this, in short, are that it becomes next to impossible to find alternatives that transcend the conjuncture that brought about the crisis. It limits the ethical and political imagination to one of *enabling* or *disabling* certain types of behaviour, at the expense of reimagining how market-oriented behaviour could be constituted *differently*. To illustrate this point, I briefly survey approaches to the crisis found in the IPE literature at the level of regulation and governance of finance, on the one hand, and the level of everyday life of finance, on the other.

At the regulatory level the crisis was one brought about by the failures of deregulation, whether at the level of the state or the institutions of global economic governance. Consider Anastasia Nesvetailova's (2010: 4 emphasis in original) argument that 'the key cause' of the crisis was the 'pervasive and dangerous myth . . . that by inventing novel credit instruments and opening up new financial markets, today's financiers *create money and wealth*'. For those interested in the regulatory mismanagement of finance, there is every reason to expect that looking at 'modern financial alchemy' offers fruitful answers to what went wrong and how to fix it (Nesvetailova 2010: 1). For instance, Randall Germain (2010: 2) calls for the reinforcement of the regulatory capacity of nation states and new restrictions on financial institutions so as to push back at the 'liberalization and globalization of financial markets'. In global governance, the crisis was also one of the consequences of deregulation. As Eric Helleiner (2014: 11) shows, throughout 2008 there were significant calls for a radical rethinking of the 'market-friendly' international financial standards that led to the crisis. However, he suggests, such calls were not met as the level of regulatory reform that has been undertaken is 'remarkably tame' (Helleiner 2014: 12). At the institutional level as well, while the IMF has rethought the norm of capital freedom, much of the discussion still centres on the issue of whether *more* or *less* regulation is desirable (Gallagher 2015).

By focusing on the problems of the era of deregulated finance, such accounts can successfully explain in what ways regulation served to encourage or enable the types of market-oriented behaviour that proved so unsustainable as markets began to collapse from 2007 onwards. Yet, in the main, they are less concerned with the *constitution* of that market-oriented behaviour in any significant ethical sense. This means the place of the implied ethics of economistic liberalism and their role in the GFC is not adequately unpacked.

Engaging with the constitution of market-oriented behaviour more directly, everyday and cultural political economy engagements with the crisis complicate the view of the deregulatory era by offering more from of a 'bottom-up' perspective on finance. For instance Paul Langley (2008b: 10) explains that 'the mundane and routine practices of saving and borrowing are themselves of great constitutive significance in contemporary finance'. This analysis is part of work that attempts to demystify the totalising place of global finance on the imagination of those who study financial practice (Aitken 2007; Seabrooke 2006; Watson 2007). In these perspectives the constitution and 'performance' of market-oriented behaviour is taken much more seriously.

Concerning the crisis specifically, Langley (2008b: 233) claims that the sub-prime mortgage crisis was 'profoundly related to the wider transformations that have created unprecedented relationships between Anglo-American everyday borrowing, on the one hand, and the capital markets of global finance, on the other'. He further claims that 'risk technologies' were at the heart of the crisis, given that 'risk-based pricing failed, on its own terms, to effectively price risk in US sub-prime mortgage networks' (Langley 2008b: 236). While an important contribution to understanding the place of everyday saving and borrowing in the crisis, a tendency to emphasise the deregulatory period that *enabled* certain types of financial behaviour can still be detected in this and other important contributions.

For instance, Herman Schwartz (2009: 201) similarly explains how the crisis 'marks the high tide of the neoliberal erosion of the institutional structure of the Bretton Woods-era Keynesian welfare state'. He argues that 'the bursting of the housing bubble revealed that the entire global financial system had also mortgaged itself to the fortunes of the housing market' (Schwartz 2009: 200). Elsewhere, Schwartz and Leonard Seabrooke (2009: 1) have detailed the need to explore how '[d]ifferent kinds of housing finance systems . . . produce different political subjectivities influencing the core issues' of IPE. On their terms, study of the 'varieties of residential capitalism' is important for understanding 'national economic systems and stability and order' (Schwartz and Seabrooke 2009: 2). Even in everyday and cultural political economy perspectives, then, there is still an emphasis on how the experiences of people in their everyday lives should be understood and theorised in relation to some broader 'system', usually conceived within the context of the deregulation of global finance, which is a key explanatory factor in *enabling* the market-oriented behaviour that is presumed to have caused the crisis.

Smith's concept of sympathy provides an alternative lens through which to rethink how to understand the GFC. It provides a way of exposing and challenging the implicit economism of such discussions concerned with enabling behaviour. The economism here involves leaving the category of the individual market agent as one that can be *expected* to perform the role that contemporary economic governance prescribes to them. The concept of sympathy refocuses analysis around the *constitution* of market-oriented behaviour in a more thoroughgoing way. It unpacks what ethical contestation must be shut down under economic governance in order to produce financialised societies.

Michel Foucault's genealogy of liberal government has often been mobilised to better understand the character of neoliberalism in the world economy and to cast critical scrutiny on its potentially constitutive effect on the individual subject (e.g. Aitken 2005; Amoore 2004; Best 2005; Langley 2008a; 2008b; Vestergaard 2009). Jacqueline Best's (2007: 92) suggestion that the 'liberal individual is not born but is made' is one that chimes particularly well with the perspective developed in this book. However, Foucault's (2008: 278) genealogy of modern neoliberalism imposes upon Smith a generative role in producing the theories that subsequently construct the modern neoliberal subject. As will become clear in this book, Smith had very little to do with the historical trajectory that led to the central importance of *homo economicus* in liberal governance. Ironically, then, not only do I position a more robust historiographical account of Smith against an economistic 'Smith', but I do so, in part, in a way that turns this more robust historiographical Smith against Foucault's own critical genealogy of liberalism.

The result is that economic governance can be critically engaged through a perspective that does not necessarily rely on the governmentality tradition, while sharing some complementarities in opening up the status of the liberal 'subject'. This is beneficial because it retains some of the routes to a sympathetic political economy, inspired by Smith, but does not have to accept the disciplinary effects of economic governance as totalising, or even successful. Indeed, this has to be the case, given that Smith did not write at a time of a liberal state. This is important, as will become apparent, in that my approach insists on the contestability of interpersonal ethics, which was available in Smith's time and arguably can be again today.

Adam Smith in question

Appeals to the intellectual authority of Adam Smith abound in discussions of the GFC. Former Chairman of the US Federal Reserve Alan Greenspan (2011) suggests that 2008 marked a 'rare exception' to how Smith's invisible hand operated worldwide. Former Vice Chairman of the Federal Reserve Alan Blinder (2010) also appeals to the invisible hand as 'one of history's great ideas' in his response to the crisis. Another former Chairman Paul Volcker (2010) invokes Smith, albeit in different terms, to lend support to his banking reforms: apparently Smith 'advocated keeping banks small'. A leading figure in global financial reform and winner of the Sveriges Riksbank Prize in Economic Sciences in Memory of Alfred Nobel, Joseph Stiglitz (2010a), suggests that recent problems in the world economy are down to the fact that Smith's invisible hand 'did not hold': 'Few today would argue that bank managers, in their pursuit of their self-interest, had promoted the well-being of the global economy'. Another winner of the Nobel Memorial Prize in Economic Sciences, Paul Krugman (2010), argues that Smith 'called for a ban on high-risk, high-interest lending, the 18th-century version of subprime'.

Another Laureate, Gary Becker (2011), in his discussion of 'government failure' in the crisis, suggests that the 'traditional case for private competitive markets goes back to Adam Smith'. Yet another Laureate writing on the crisis Robert Shiller (2009) claims that Smith held the 'standard "classical" theory' that 'people rationally pursue their own economic interests in free markets'. This roll call could continue; but clearly, in discussions of the GFC, what Smith said appears to be of great significance.

However, exactly what Smith did or did not say is subject to substantial dispute. There is a highly complex and extremely contested historiography of Smith (Kennedy 2005; Muller 1995; Tribe 1999). Thus appeals to his intellectual authority ought to be viewed as appeals to one 'Adam Smith' among many. Despite some slight differences in emphasis, the accounts noted above present a very *specific* image of Smith. It is a depiction of him which is based on an 'economistic' historiography of his work. Notably, this image drawn from an economistic historiography of Smith is used in support of a particular mode of analysis. It is a form of study which itself, put simply, takes a markedly 'economistic' view of market-oriented behaviour. Whether implicitly or explicitly, historiographical matters always play a pivotal role in the formation and debate of matters of contemporary political economy.

This book draws upon an historicised interpretation of Smith. It provides a novel account of sympathy and its implications for conceptualising market-oriented behaviour and in turn understanding the crisis itself. In brief, Smith's concept of sympathy can be thought of as an imaginative 'procedure' through which people come to assess the actions, circumstance and suffering of others and themselves (Force 2003; Peil 1999). This is not simply an 'other-directed' ontology of the individual. It refers to a continual balancing act and negotiation between an individual 'self' principally concerned and broader societal norms and values, the 'other', which are potentially encountered and internalised through the activation of what Smith termed an 'impartial spectator' (*TMS* I.i.5.4). Taking the concept of sympathy seriously, then, means the constitution of market-oriented behaviour is understood through reference to fundamental interactivity between an individual and society in terms of ethico-political questions (Vaggi 2004). This could be thought of in terms of Smith providing a 'relational self', as opposed to the 'atomised self' imputed onto Smith by the economistic historiography of his work (Weinstein 2006: 82). Thus, on one level, a recovery of the notion of sympathy is important because it represents a crucial aspect of his thought that is currently almost completely overlooked by scholars operating with an economistic historiography of Smith.

On another level, the concept of sympathy provides a route to thinking about how to understand the GFC and rethinking finance in light of the crisis. This book stages an encounter, or dialogic conversation, between key aspects of a sympathetic political economy, on the one hand, and central features of 'economistic liberalism' of economic governance today, on the other. The latter features are chosen because they are widely recognised as fundamental sites of the financialisation of Anglo-American economy and society in recent decades. They are also those aspects of financialisation deeply implicated in the crisis: (1) systems of asset-based welfare (Finlayson 2009; French *et al.* 2011; Hay 2009; Langley 2006; 2007; Watson 2009a; 2010); (2) modern risk management (Froud and Johal 2008; Nesvetailova 2010; Warwick Commission 2009); and (3) indebtedness (Montgomerie 2006; 2009; Roberts 2013; Schwartz 2009).

The conceptual and empirical debates engaged with in this book largely centre on Anglo-American finance, along with some broader appeals to issues of global financial governance in a wider sense. This draws limits around the scope of the book, but in many ways global crisis governance *is* primarily Anglo-American in nature given the continued global dominance of the US dollar and the global reach of Wall Street and the City of London (Langley 2015: 1). Certainly in the context of the GFC, the argument of this book is most telling in terms of the way it sheds light on the economistic essence of Anglo-American finance, even though the corrosive effects on human wellbeing produced by this financial structure are often felt most acutely elsewhere.

In this book I argue the following. Many existing understandings of and responses to the GFC are subject to a crisis of ethical imagination. This is because economistic liberalism largely denies a place for contestable interpersonal ethics, which places severe limits around how market-oriented behaviour can be conceived. A sympathetic political economy provides a route out of this dilemma because a sympathetic sensibility recognises that ethical negotiation is central to the constitution of market-oriented behaviour. On this account a challenge can be mobilised to: (1) individualised notions of responsibility embedded within systems of asset-based welfare; (2) disembodied accounts of risk in modern risk management; and (3) depoliticised understandings of indebtedness. Radical responses that mobilise an ethos of sympathy can then be imagined through ways of coming to know finance differently. Practically speaking, this points to a fundamental overhaul of finance to make the social relations that underpin finance more 'knowable' and not just assume that market outcomes are the result of some unknowable 'invisible hand'.

Outline of the book

Chapter 1 is about why there is a need to engage with Adam Smith's work in an historicised way. The intellectual historian Quentin Skinner is appealed to as providing key principles to successfully analyse readings of Smith. Chiefly engaging with IPE literature, it is demonstrated that many of these uncritically reproduce a number of Skinnerian 'mythologies of interpretation'. The payoff of this examination is that IPE scholars are shown to often directly imitate a problematic 'economistic' historiography of Smith. This matters because of the lasting disciplinary effects for political economy of reading Smith, and those in the 'canon' that follow and respond to him, in an economistic way.

A more historiographically robust interpretation of Smith that closely maps his intentions in writing his texts is provided in Chapter 2. The location of his texts within their historical and intellectual context allows for attention to be drawn to Smith's central concept of sympathy. This was developed as part of an effort to move debates about the rise of commercial society *away* from understandings based on notions of 'self-interest'. Instead, a sensibility to sympathy gives an account of how the constitution of market-oriented behaviour involves contestable interpersonal ethics at the individual level.

Then Chapter 3 stages an encounter between Smith's sympathetic political economy, on the one hand, and the economistic liberalism of today on the other. The themes Smith uses right at the beginning of *The Theory of Moral Sentiments* (*TMS*) to set out the concept of sympathy are juxtaposed with three significant sites of finance implicated in the GFC. As mentioned, these are systems of asset-based welfare, modern risk management and personal indebtedness in Anglo-American societies today. The central conceptual argument made is that there is a crisis of ethical imagination in economistic liberalism because contestable interpersonal ethics tend to be denied altogether.

Chapter 4 builds on these points to analyse the 'regulatory level' of Anglo-American finance. The proposition that the GFC can be understood as a crisis based on the denial of contestable interpersonal ethics is interrogated. It is illustrated how at the regulatory level: (1) asset-based systems of welfare enjoy a largely unquestioned position, even though issues of access to homeownership and financial security fall right at the heart of the crisis; (2) credit risk management practices persist largely unchallenged and, in fact, along with the securitisation model, are further normalised based on continued faith in the 'science' and 'perfectibility' of risk management; and (3) the view of debt appears to continue to depoliticise creditor-debtor relations by insisting on the normalisation of financial services and working to articulate model financialised citizens.

Finally Chapter 5 explores whether interventions into the 'everyday politics' of the GFC provide a challenge to the regulatory level of finance more congruent with an ethos of sympathy. The analysis illustrates: (1) how certain parts of the everyday politics of the crisis articulate a complex and variegated attitude with regard to systems of asset-based welfare, which offers a sharp critique of homeowner ideology and state restructuring towards individualised notions of responsibility; (2) how elements of the everyday agenda present an interesting challenge to both existing understandings of credit risk management and uses of structured finance; and (3) how some everyday interventions provide an unforgiving repoliticisation of credit-debt relations by drawing attention to the sizable power of banks and other financial institutions in a financialised economy, the redistributive politics of credit-debt relations and the underlying material or capacity struggles that personal debt might conceal. The book concludes with how these interventions help in efforts to 'rethink' finance along more sympathetic lines.

1 Engaging Adam Smith

There are at least two images of Adam Smith that sustain opposing approaches to understanding the social world. The first more dominant image depicts him as the originator of a liberal tradition of political economy and, subsequently, economics more narrowly defined. This image is mobilised in economistic accounts of the global financial crisis (GFC), and associates Adam Smith with ideas about how instrumentally rational behaviour, guided by an invisible hand, leads to the greater good of society. A second image of Smith situates his political economy within the broader context of his moral philosophy and, as he did, attaches greater significance to his concept of sympathy.

The first image might appeal to Smith as an intellectual authority on how market-pricing dynamics ought to work, such that the crisis can be narrated as a temporary breakdown in the ordinary workings of global finance. The second might appeal to a more historiographically robust account, drawing on his understanding of 'sympathetic' market relations, such that the crisis can be interrogated as an important signifier of the limitations of the ethics of economic governance. This book mobilises this second image to provide an alternative way of understanding and responding to the crisis.

Direct invocations of Smith are not the only reason to go back and engage with his work in order to analyse how the GFC is and should be understood. Scholars such as Smith cast a large shadow over scholarly study in political economy. To be sure, the term 'political economy' here is used in a broader sense than the study of contemporary comparative or international political economy (IPE). The political economy endeavour itself is also often pursued, albeit in radically different forms, across a range of disciplines including economics, sociology, political science and political theory (Clift 2014: 6). Yet it is precisely in the politics of the disciplinary boundaries between and across these subjects where the thought of scholars such as Smith becomes so pivotal. As William Tabb (1999: 31) argues:

> The reason Adam Smith and other canonical writers are open to multiple and conflicting readings is that the interpretation of these texts is a struggle over the construction of the discipline. The canon defines what a field is "legitimately" about. Practitioners outside the mainstream needing to redirect the discussion can do worse than to reread important contributions and attempt to reorient their accepted meaning.

Thus the study of the history of political economy is essentially a creative and critical endeavour. At once it provides alternative ways of reflecting on the contemporary social world *and* new ways of analysing how existing understandings of the contemporary social world are themselves derived. A notion of 'pragmatic historiography' is developed in this chapter from the work of Quentin Skinner and located within discussions of 'historicising' contemporary IPE, a field of study built on the foundations of political economy (Watson 2005a). Some of Skinner's key principles are then used to dispel various mythologies that currently surround Smith's name in IPE and related fields so that a more productive reading of his work can be built in the next chapter.

Pragmatic historiography

Historicising political economy

There are a multitude of possible meanings for what it means to 'historicise' social study. This ranges from an 'awareness-of-history' type grounding for the conventional subject matter found in introductory texts to fields such as IPE (e.g. O'Brien and Williams 2007; Strange 1994) through to explicit calls for a 'thick' historicisation study that stresses the situated position of the scholar and the necessarily reflexive aspects of scholarly inquiry (Burch 1997; Germain and Kenny 1998; Amoore *et al.* 2000). Compared in such a way, the most significant and convincing accounts of historicisation are those that suggest a 'thicker' approach. These can be built upon to develop a notion of pragmatic historiography.

Conventionally, at least in the sense of its institutionalisation as a formal academic subject field, IPE locates its 'birth' in the 1970s (Blyth and Spruyt 2003: 608; Higgott 1994: 157; Ravenhill 2005: 15; Strange 1994: 18; for a critique see Clift and Rosamond 2009). These types of contributions historicise IPE in the sense that they attempt to locate the development of the subject field as a whole in some kind of historical context. They also echo tendencies in international relations scholarship where the prevalent approach employed to explain theoretical developments is based on a form of external explanation. That is, scholars place a considerable degree of emphasis on the ways in which change in political conjunctures outside the subject field play a role in bringing about theoretical and conceptual change within it (Jørgensen 2000: 10). For many, then, the breakdown of the post-war Bretton Woods system was the originating point for contemporary IPE.

However, such perspectives have a weak appreciation for the role of historical *situation* in IPE scholarship. That is, although they recognise the importance of placing ideas and the authors of those ideas in historical context, such scholars cannot be said to be responding fully to the implications of this historical awareness. This is because they do not allow the importance they attach to the role of history in theoretical development to be carried through into an histori*cised* approach to IPE. Rather, the tendency is to see history, understood as a sequence of distinct 'past' events, as important because it can be shown to have influenced particular scholars and modes of thought at a particular time and then 'move on' from history to the more pressing concerns of 'current' IPE analysis. As such this thin form of historicisation incorporates into IPE a sense of history and a sense of historical specificity, but where that specificity refers to the comprehension of events rather than to the ideas, language and meanings which are used in order to frame attempts to derive such comprehension.

A 'thicker' form of historicisation takes the implications of recognition of the situated position of the scholar as a central starting point for IPE. By problematising the notion of reflexivity, it challenges the core positivist assumption of 'orthodox' IPE that 'social action can be understood universally over time and space and therefore objectively' (Murphy and Tooze 1991b: 19; see also Amoore *et al.* 2000: 54). This thicker form of historicisation might be said to share similarities with those strands of critical theory that attempt to present alternative methods for understanding the social world (Germain 1996: 202). Indeed the reflexivity present in critical theory, broadly understood, appears to hold significant sway for some IPE scholars (Murphy and Tooze 1991a; Cox 2000; Abbott and Worth 2002; Murphy and Nelson 2002). Randall Germain (2000: 68) suggests that an historical mode of thought 'takes its starting point to be the historicity and transformability of all human practice, including the way in which it is embedded in layers of patterned collective activity'. For him (Germain 2000: 70; see also Germain 1997), then, the 'social world is a historically constructed environment rather than a given one, and our representations of it provide a powerful point of entry into considering how and where its relationships might be challenged'.

By embracing post-positivist accounts of the philosophy of social science, associated with forms of feminist, constitutive and critical IPE, those that have called for this thicker form of historicisation have been able to show the political possibilities opened up by adopting an historicised approach. By recognising the contextual and situated nature of the scholarly endeavour, this form of historicisation has as a key component an engagement with disciplinary histories (Holden 2002: 255; Little 1999: 297; Tooze 1997: 208). This is why it is useful to consider ways of historicising political economy in relation to the intellectual historian Quentin Skinner.

Quentin Skinner

In his influential article 'Meaning and Understanding in the History of Ideas', Skinner makes an important statement about the purpose of studying intellectual history. He claims that the fact that texts from earlier eras deal with 'their own quite alien problems' is 'the key to the indispensable value of studying the history of ideas' (Skinner 1969: 52). For Skinner (1969: 52), therefore:

> The classic texts, especially in social, ethical, and political thought, help to reveal – if we let them – not the essential sameness, but rather the essential variety of viable moral assumptions and political commitments.

On this account, the fact that past texts deal with their own questions and are not necessarily a source of direct 'answers' to questions of a later era can serve to expose the multiplicity of possible ethico-political commitments across time. In other words, past texts do not simply contain 'timeless' truths that can be applied to understanding today's world, yet the very *act* of seeking to interpret them is an important part of coming to terms with the situated and provisional nature of scholarly endeavour. This is no less true for the history of political economy and IPE than it is for any other area of concern (Rosow 1997).

Skinner's approach is based on the idea that viewed pragmatically, linguistic activities comprise at least two kinds of action: first, putting forward 'locutionary' meaning and, second, doing so with a 'point' or intended 'force' (Tully 1988: 8). The former refers to the idea that a writer is saying or writing something with 'propositional' meaning. The latter, of more importance for Skinner, refers to the idea that a writer will be *doing something in writing* – words, sentences and arguments will contain what J.L. Austin (1975) calls an 'illocutionary force'. Using this distinction Skinner (1988b: 283) argues that in order to understand a particular idea or concept it is necessary to grasp not just the meanings of the terms used to express it but also the 'range of things that can be done with it'. This leads him to suggest that successful interpretation is dependent on the recovery of a particular writer's 'intentions' (Skinner 1988a: 74–76). In one key statement he suggests that successful interpretations involve:

> limiting our range of descriptions of any given text to those which the author himself might in principle have avowed, and . . . recovering the complex intentions of the author in writing it.
>
> (Skinner 1974: 283)

Thus it is possible to identify two principal themes in Skinner's approach (Pocock 1985: 4–5). The first is the importance of the 'intention' of a writer in the act of writing. From this perspective, the task of negotiating meaning is an attempt to recover intentions and there is usually some evidence for all writers that can be mobilised to this effect. This implies that any particular writer inhabits an historically given world that is only apprehensible in the ways rendered available by historically given languages. This leads John Pocock (1985: 5) to suggest that Skinner's approach compels the intellectual historian to recover both a writer's language and their intentions.

The second theme of Skinner's approach is that of 'performance'. In pursuing his studies, Skinner (1988b: 279) came to stress the importance of what a particular writer was *doing* when they wrote: as he puts it, 'texts are acts'. Crucially, the types of utterance with which Skinner is concerned are arguments in a situated context, not just strings of propositions. The concept of intention is not undermined, therefore, but complemented by the notion of the act of writing as a performative 'move' (Pocock 1985: 5). In this way, 'any act of communication always constitutes the taking up of some determinate position in relation to some pre-existing conversation or argument' (Skinner 1988b: 274). Therefore Skinner's approach entails treating texts in a self-consciously historical manner by locating them in time and place and examining them in their linguistic context. I will pursue this endeavour with regard to Smith in the next chapter.

Skinner has been subjected to a number of critiques from those assessing his methodological contribution to the study of intellectual history (e.g. Mew 1971; Parekh and Berki 1973; Keane 1988). By far the most devastating criticism and the one most relevant for use here is centred on the actual *purpose* of reading historical texts. In Skinner's (1969: 50) provocative argument:

> [T]he classic texts cannot be concerned with our questions and answers . . . There is in consequence simply no hope of seeking the point of studying the history of ideas in the attempt to learn directly from the classic authors by focusing on their attempted answers to supposedly timeless questions.

This idea builds on Austin's theory that illocutionary force cannot easily 'carry' across time and space (Graham 1977: 109). However, Skinner's position here has led some to suggest that it undermines the reading of historical texts entirely: if nothing can be extrapolated from them in order to illuminate contemporary scholarly debates, the value of their study is seemingly lost (Parekh and Berki 1973: 180; Tarcov 1988: 194–195). On this view, the study of past texts becomes 'little more than a sterile celebration of intellectual pedigree' (Femia 1988: 158). This is not how I want to approach Adam Smith.

Nevertheless, the Skinnerian approach can be defended on the grounds that its important ideas about interpreting past text can be accepted as guiding principles, without the need to subscribe to steadfast assumptions that might appear to collapse into relativism (Minogue 1988). They are guidelines to enable the reader to avoid overly 'textual' or overly 'contextual' interpretations, not a barrier to all interpretation and position taking. Skinner (1969: 7 emphasis added) suggests that his procedures should be used 'to uncover the *extent to which* the current historical study . . . of ideas is contaminated by the unconscious application of paradigms whose familiarity to the historian disguises an essential inapplicability to the past'. Indeed his focus on authorial intent ultimately speaks to the question of how much emphasis should be placed on certain features found in a text given the contingent relationship between text and context (Skinner 1974: 281). It offers guidance concerning the importance of the linguistic context of a text, but it does not entail a relativism that might ultimately undermine studying the text in the first place (Taylor 1988). Following Skinner's pragmatic attitude, any ambiguities left between the two forms are essentially creative: a space for potential further performative intervention on behalf of the interpreter.

This stance accepts that past texts, such as Smith's, are concerned with their own questions and are not necessarily a source of direct 'answers' to questions of a later era. Rather than undermining the purpose of the study of intellectual history altogether though, Skinner celebrates this as an invitation to expose the multiplicity of viable ethical and political commitments across time and space. In his terms, the study of past texts helps learning about 'our own contingent arrangements', which is 'to learn the key to self-awareness itself' (Skinner 1969: 53). Skinner (1988b: 286) thus suggests that the 'anthropological' justification for studying intellectual history is that it allows the contemporary scholar to stand back from 'our own prevailing assumptions and structures of thought', to reveal that 'our own descriptions and conceptualizations are in no way uniquely privileged'. In other words, through the study of intellectual history 'we can hope to acquire a perspective from which to view our own form of life in a more self-critical way, enlarging our present horizons instead of fortifying local prejudices' (Skinner 1988b: 287). This anthropological justification for the study of intellectual history, based on what I have termed here an attitude of pragmatic historiography, therefore directly complements those thick accounts of historicising IPE outlined above.

From this perspective, conversation and debate in intellectual history, including contestation over the history of its central concepts and the construction of theoretical lineages, is itself foundational to what it means to be *doing* critical inquiry in political economy. This is important in Smith's case because, as Rosow (1997: 55) argues, mainstream IPE tends to interpret liberalism from Smith as something 'between a conservative celebration of a global commercial society and a utilitarian managerialism'. The next section provides an account of Smith in IPE, identifying how many interpretations pay little or no attention to Skinnerian interpretive principles, so that his work can then be studied as part of a more historicised IPE in the following chapter.

Skinnerian mythologies about Adam Smith

> Histories of economics are generally written by economists for other economists. They use the language and analytical approaches with which they are familiar, and in so doing convert past theories into variants of those with which they are already familiar.
>
> (Tribe 1999: 615)

For the most part, IPE scholars tend to rely on an overtly economistic historiography of Smith. That is, they are inclined to follow in the footsteps of Keith Tribe's economists who write histories of economics for other economists, as opposed to using the what he calls the 'approach of an historian' to arrive at an appropriately historicised understanding of his work. In turn, this helps explain why IPE scholars provide such a poor account of Smith in terms of failing to employ some of Skinner's most basic principles for interpreting past texts. This section offers a typological characterisation of Smith in IPE based on four 'mythologies' of interpretation Skinner identifies: (1) 'doctrine', (2) 'prolepsis', (3) 'parochialism' and (4) 'coherence'.

The precise ways in which IPE interpretations of Smith tend to uncritically replicate these mythologies are highly significant in two key respects. First, on issues of 'doctrine', 'prolepsis' and 'parochialism', on the whole, they can be shown to quite clearly succumb to Skinner's mythologies. Here IPE scholars tend to directly imitate a markedly economistic historiography of Smith, almost entirely replicating the interpretation of his work to be found in histories of economics written by economists. Specifically, with respect to each issue, this means: construing an 'invisible hand' doctrine from his text, characterising Smith as the 'father of economics', and reading concepts such as 'laissez-faire' and 'capitalism' back into his work. Second, on the issue of 'coherence', IPE scholars have next to nothing to say on a topic fervently disputed by intellectual history scholars: the Adam Smith Problem. This debate centres on whether or not Smith's *The Wealth of Nations* (*WN*) is 'consistent' with his earlier *The Theory of Moral Sentiments* (*TMS*), but what IPE interpretations tend to do is ignore parts of his work altogether so as to present a consistent image based on a small section of *WN* alone. The suspect economistic historiography of Smith in IPE is therefore a foundational problem with which to engage in order to begin to problematise constructions of contemporary political economy and the ethics of economic governance today.

The invisible hand doctrine

According to Skinner, the mythology of 'doctrine' tends to come in two main forms. The first, considered in this section, consists in various ways of assuming that incidental remarks found in a text are somehow representative of a writer's doctrine on one of the themes that the reader is *expecting* to find (Skinner 1969: 12). In this way, the reader has a 'set' expectation that a 'classic' writer will put forward some coherent doctrine on their given subject (Skinner 1969: 7). This is extremely problematic because a given writer could erroneously be 'discovered' to have held a view on a subject to which they might not have even meant to contribute often due to some chance similarity of terminology (Skinner 1969: 7). In other words, there is a danger of misreading back into a past text a coherent account of a doctrine that was no part of the author's original intention, but has come to be associated with them only *after* they wrote the texts.

This first textual mythology is particularly relevant to those interpretations of Smith that assimilate his work to a doctrine of the 'invisible hand' of the market. On these readings, Smith is said to believe that whenever individuals are left alone to pursue their interests an invisible hand will ensure that they will benefit society as a whole (Fleischacker 2004: 138). The concept is in fact seen by many as foundational to the whole discipline of economics (Samuels *et al.* 2011). For example, James Tobin (1996: 205) claims that the invisible hand is 'one of the Great Ideas of intellectual history' because it explains how 'market competition transmutes selfish and myopic individual actions into the wealth of nations'. Certainly, from the nineteenth century onwards, the 'invisible hand' became synonymous with the 'price mechanism' in economics (Peil 1999: 157). As such, quite unambiguously, in an economistic historiography of Smith there is an overwhelming tendency to suggest that he advocated an invisible hand doctrine. In fact it is celebrated as one of the crowning achievements of his work.

This is also the well-known reading of Smith in IPE that holds his name almost synonymous with the invisible hand of the market (e.g. Burchill 2005; Crane and Amawi 1997; Dunne 2005; Isaak 1995; Rupert and Solomon 2006; Woods 2001). The invisible hand doctrine is then thought to explain, in a rather simplistic state-market construction, how he was against a role for the state in economic activity and for letting market dynamics operate as much as possible. The invisible hand is presumed to represent the coordinating logic of the price system.

Typically Smith is said to have argued against the idea of the state having a role to play in economic growth and development because 'the role would be performed much more effectively by markets guided by the invisible hand of self-interest' (Panić 2003: 72). This interpretation is one of Smith as the originator of a 'liberal' tradition (e.g. Balaam and Veseth 2008; Kirshner 2009; Miller 2008; Payne 2005; Pettman 1996; Ravenhill 2005) or even an early precursor of 'neoliberalism' (e.g. Bukovansky 2006; Steger 2002; Swift 1993). Smith's 'liberal' position supposedly suggests removing 'the state' from 'the economy' in order that the free market should be left alone to automatically allocate resources to their most efficient use – a '*depoliticization* of production and well-being' (Nitzan and Bichler 2000: 67 emphasis in original).

How does the invisible hand doctrine operate according to this account of Smith? The familiar depiction is the 'notion that markets and the pursuit of self-interest [will] lead, as if by an invisible hand, to economic efficiency' (Stiglitz 2007: xiv). This understanding appears, at least in general terms, again and again in IPE. For instance, an invisible hand supposedly: 'guides the economy and promotes the common good' (Balaam and Veseth 2008: 39); 'translates individual pursuit of self-interest into optimal public benefit' (Steger 2002: 9); 'turns self-seeking individual behaviour into socially beneficial outcomes' (Ravenhill 2005: 19–20); leads 'self-interested individuals to produce socially useful goods and services in the most efficient possible way' (Rupert and Solomon 2006: 56); steers 'private self-interest to the public good' (Isaak 1995: 99); 'intervenes between the motives of the individual and the "ends" of society as a whole' (Dunne 2005: 190); guarantees 'that economic choices made by individuals in the pursuit of their personal interests and preferences [will] have a beneficial effect for society as a whole' (Acocella 2005: 10); and 'ensures an efficient and equitable distribution of goods and services across the world economy' (Woods 2001: 285). Thus, in this widespread doctrinaire reading of Smith, the invisible hand metaphor is used repeatedly to make the claim that the 'self-interest of one becomes the general interest of all' (Burchill 2005: 73).

For those who celebrate this account from a 'liberal' perspective, Smith is credited with 'inventing the concept of the self-regulating market' (Miller 2008: 9) and the invisible hand is identified as a 'metaphor for a coordinating mechanism of the activities of individuals who, apart from their own production and consumption, know very little of the wider economy' (Sally 1998: 19). His invisible hand is essentially thought of as a 'benevolent' force (McWilliams and Piotrowski 2001: 484), which creates 'an overall benefit to society' (Hite and Roberts 2007: 5). In making the suggestion that 'the "invisible hand" of the market naturally ensures that the pursuit of self-interest, in and of itself, will lead to the public good', Smith is credited with founding a 'new line of IPE theory' (Crane and Amawi 1997: 6).

While a handful of IPE scholars recognise that Smith's use of the term in *WN* actually refers to a 'preference for domestic over foreign produce' (Dunn 2009: 28), the metaphor is also readily associated with a conception of international trade in which 'the law of supply and demand [can] work unhindered' (Palan and Cameron 2003: 115). Smith's defence of international free trade is said to even take on a religious dimension in the sense that he offers 'a theology of the global market' guided by the invisible hand (Beard 2007: 21). Based on this faith in the operation of free markets, it is further suggested that the invisible hand by the end of the nineteenth century had become 'global' in reach (Hoogvelt 2001: 15). Likewise, Kenichi Ohmae's 'borderless world' is also associated with the workings of an invisible hand on a global scale (Schrecker 1997: 2). These interpretations of the doctrine of the invisible hand at the international level certainly point to how it has become a 'powerful and enduring metaphor' for IPE scholars (Dunn 2009: 14).

The lasting significance of the invisible hand metaphor is also evident in the work of those scholars who are more critical of Smith's ostensible doctrine in defence of the price mechanism. Certainly his invisible hand is said to occupy 'an important position' to Marx among others (Dasgupta 1998: 50). From this more critical perspective, the invisible hand is understood as a convenient way of abstracting away from 'asymmetric social relations' (Agathangelou 2004: 83), it is almost ridiculed as a 'magic unseen hand' (Prestowitz 2005: 210), and takes on a somewhat more sinister tone in the form of a 'hidden hand' for others (Balaam and Veseth 2008: 12; Pettman 1996: 11; Woo-Cumings 2003: 215). Elements of these critiques of the doctrine also take further dimensions, discussed below, when the invisible hand metaphor is associated with later developments in economic thought that came after Smith's time, such as general equilibrium theory (Boyer 1996: 86; Foster 2001: 113), 'First Welfare Theorem' (Carter 1997: 123), and 'utilitarian' outcomes (Lipschutz 2005: 45; Kline 2005: 40).

However, in *stark contrast* to this reading of Smith in IPE, many scholars in the specialist Smith studies literature tend to represent voices that might challenge this canonical and ultimately misleading understanding of his work. From within such literature, a strict invisible hand interpretation of Smith is actually viewed on the whole with equal wonder and disdain. Perhaps most forcefully, Emma Rothschild (2001: 116) has suggested that 'Smith did not especially esteem the invisible hand' and thus it is best interpreted as a 'mildly ironic joke'. Remarkably, for Smith scholars at least, he only used the term *three* times in the entirety of his published output and none of these usages point towards the construction of a coherent 'doctrine'. In brief, Rothschild (2001: 116) shows how his first use in *History of Astronomy* is clearly sardonic as Smith is highlighting the naivety of polytheistic societies. The second use, in *TMS*, describes the way in which rich proprietors – by employing a great number of poor workers to produce luxury commodities to some extent and in a particular sense – advance a larger interest than their own. The third and final use, in *WN*, concerns the issue of international trade, where Smith argues that if restrictions are removed, merchants tend to prefer to support domestic industries, in the interest of their 'own security' (Rothschild 2001: 117). Nathan Rosenberg (1979: 24) calls this final use 'unfortunate' because of the way in which 'it has been so totally misinterpreted'. Likewise, Samuel Fleischacker (2004: 139) stresses that Smith's use of the term here is in the making of a relatively small point that merchants will tend to base their trade in home ports: he does not claim that an invisible hand *always* guides individual economic decisions toward the 'good' of society.

Interestingly, while agreeing with Rothschild that the focus on the invisible hand is significantly overplayed, Matthew Watson (2005a) has a somewhat different interpretation of Smith's distinct use of the term in *TMS*. For him, rather than suggesting that in some way the landowning classes inadvertently promote the interests of the landless labourers, Smith is actually appealing to the invisible hand as something 'akin to a trick in nature . . . which overrides the price system' and prevents the former from consuming 'the vast majority of the earth's natural resources . . . because their consumption is limited by a finite ability to consume' (Watson 2005a: 174–175). Significantly, for Watson (2005a: 175), this means that despite their desire to revel in and means to satisfy 'gratuitous displays of opulence', put simply, 'the landowning classes can eat only what they are capable of eating'. This interpretation – exceptional in light of the vast majority of readings in IPE – supports the important point that, for Smith, 'the mere existence of a price system to guide exchange relations does not necessarily lead to socialization into purely self-interested forms of behaviour, and neither does it explain how market relations are constituted in practice' (Watson 2005a: 175). I return to this point in the next chapter.

Despite such disagreements over precise interpretation, most serious Smith scholars also take direct issue with the recasting of a supposed doctrine of an invisible hand to general equilibrium theories that were to come *after* his time. Donald Winch (1997: 399), for example, points to how general equilibrium theorists often erroneously speak of a 'pure theory of the invisible hand' as a 'theory that will explain how an anarchistic society based on self-interest alone is capable, under fairly restrictive conditions, of achieving an optimal allocation of resources judged in terms of Pareto optimality'. Winch (1997: 399) disparagingly compares this understanding to a 'useful mental gymnasium for economists and a self-consistent agenda for dealing with the inevitable impurities of the real world', but in actuality, it was clearly *not* intended by Smith to represent a 'mechanical model of market operation'.

Overall the notion that Smith advocated an invisible hand doctrine represents a rather simplistic misinterpretation of his work that can be understood in terms of a Skinnerian mythology of doctrine. To read Smith in such a way is to erroneously construct a doctrine, which was no part of his intention, on his largely incidental three usages of the term 'invisible hand'. Drawing from the specialist Smith studies literature though, this mythology can be easily discarded because his work tends not to be approached in such a doctrinaire manner by historians of thought. As Alec Macfie (1967: 54) argues, Smith's invisible hand also 'had a good smack of cynicism in its composition', which indicates how it did not represent a coherent doctrine for Smith, nor should such a doctrine be read back into his work. Somewhat unfortunately IPE scholars, from a 'liberal' perspective or otherwise, tend to reproduce a flawed doctrinaire reading in this regard because they appear to import their understanding directly from an economistic historiography of Smith.

The 'father' of economics

Skinner's (1969: 22) mythology of 'prolepsis' occurs when a reader prioritises the ostensible *significance* of a given text over its actual meaning. This occurs when the reader is more interested in the 'retrospective significance' of a given work rather than its original meaning for the writer themselves (Skinner 1969: 22). In this way, historical significance becomes conflated with an account of what the writer was doing in writing the text, which often in principle cannot be accurate (Skinner 1969: 23). Of course, a text can only gain accepted historical significance *after* it has been written, which produces considerable interpretive dilemmas when readers later attempt to recover the author's actual intentions in writing their text.

In this sense, the very way in which Smith is widely regarded as the 'founding father' of economics seems to involve the distorting effect of this form of mythology. Certainly, in both IPE and mainstream economics, Smith is commonly described as the 'founder' of economics (e.g. Acocella 2005: 10; Brown and Ainley 2009: 154; Miller 2008: 11; Rupert and Solomon 2006: 11; Shaw 2000: 231; Stiglitz 2007: 66; Williamson and Milner 1991: 19). In IPE, Robert Gilpin (1987: 26) makes the influential claim:

> Liberalism, which emerged from the Enlightenment in the writings of Adam Smith and others, was a reaction to mercantilism and has become embodied in orthodox economics. It assumes that politics and economics exist, at least ideally, in separate spheres; it argues that markets – in the interest of efficiency, growth, and consumer choice – should be free from political interference.

On this reading, his work represents a decisive moment at which a 'scientific' conception of the self-regulating 'economic' realm assumed dominance over what had until that time been an exclusively 'moral' and 'political' domain (Winch 1978: 7). In the IPE literature, he is said to have understood economic and political matters to be 'largely separable' (Steger 2002: 9) because he 'clearly believes that economics has a logic distinct from politics and should not be unduly hampered by political machinations' (Crane and Amawi 1997: 7). Along these lines, one interpretation holds that 'from Smith onward' there was a split in understanding human action between the 'vertical dimension' of power and the 'horizontal axis' of 'well-being, free choice, exchange and equilibrium' (Nitzan and Bichler 2000: 67). The former refers to the 'political', the latter to the 'economic' realm of social life. In short, this means that Smith is supposed to represent a 'depoliticization of resource allocation and [a] devaluation of place and social solidarity' in society (Agnew 1994: 94). On this reading, the publication of *WN* thus marks the all-important 'separation between public and private in economic affairs' (Haufler 2006: 89).

These readings are noticeably derived from an economistic historiography of Smith. As Jan Peil (1999: ix) suggests, the generally accepted understanding of Smith's 'contribution' to economic analysis is exemplified by Joseph Schumpeter's claim that he is best understood as providing a Walrasian general equilibrium theory *in nucleo*. In other words, from this perspective, '[m]uch of the history of neoclassical economics can be read as a mediation on Adam Smith's "invisible hand theorem"' (Carter 1997: 122). *WN* is thus understood as the origin of the 'ideal of markets of pure and perfect competition', which is later 'elaborated by

Alfred Marshall and generalized by Leon Walras' (Boyer 1996: 100). This interpretation is very much mirrored in the IPE literature. As a supposed forerunner to economic 'science', it is emphasised how Smith was 'concerned with the natural laws of wealth' (Isaak 1995: 117), the 'laws governing the wealth of nations' (Gilpin 1987: 44), and how he understood economics as an 'imaginary machine' in the 'spirit of Newton' (Gill 1997: 53–54), which can be conceived of as the 'science' of the wealth of nations (Carlsson *et al.* 1994: 12). In this way, the claim is often made that *WN* is 'the foundation for modern economics' (Hite and Roberts 2007: 5).

From this perspective, Smith is also associated with the interrelated ideas of the self-interested individual and of the price mechanism that coordinates the actions of these individuals in accordance with public interest (Peil 1999: 37). In both IPE and mainstream economics, Smith is often said to have put forward the 'famous "economic man" dictum' (Miller 2008: 20). On this reading, he had a 'thin' ethical notion of the self 'as a short-term interest maximizer' (Isaak 1995: 99) and he 'embraced . . . self-interest and greed' (Martinez 2009: 4). Associated claims are typically that Smith thought that human beings 'are by nature economic animals' (Gilpin 1987: 27) and that 'the objective of economic activity is consumption' (Prestowitz 2005: 177). Although his conception of the individual is discussed more fully in the next chapter, in IPE Smith is very much associated with a *homo economicus* understanding of man against which a number of critical IPE scholars position themselves, particularly from a Gramscian or feminist perspective (Beiler and Morton 2006: 164; Griffin 2007). Ironically, of course, the 'economic man' construction is actually one of J. S. Mill's and is unrelated to Smith because it post-dated him by the best part of one hundred years (Morgan 2006: 5).

Nevertheless, further illustrative of an economistic historiography of Smith, George Stigler (cited in Force 2003: 1) characterises *WN* as 'a stupendous palace erected upon the granite of self-interest'. Stigler (1976: 1201 emphasis added) claims:

> Smith had one overwhelmingly important triumph: he put into the center of economics the systematic analysis of the behavior of individuals pursuing their self-interest under conditions of competition. This theory was the *crown jewel* of *The Wealth of Nations*.

In a similar reading, Samuel Hollander (cited in Recktenwald 1978: 62) suggests that '[t]he whole Walrasian, Marshallian, and Hicksian price theory . . . is clearly implicit in Adam Smith's concept of natural price'. For him, Smith showed how the price mechanism can be relied upon to clear product and factor markets, which leads him to believe it is justified to use 'the current state of knowledge regarding the general equilibrium process' in a study of Smith's work (Hollander 1973: 13). Likewise this economistic position is also reflected in Maurice Dobb's (1937: 5) suggestion that Smith's theory of value was of utmost importance because of its role as a unifying quantitative principle that enabled the production of postulates in terms of the general equilibrium of the economic system. Such readings are representative of an economistic historiography of Smith that, on the whole, seems to suggest that there are few problems involved in reading modern economic analysis into his work.

However, problematically from the perspective of a Skinnerian mythology of prolepsis, many of these economistic interpretations of Smith rely on a focus on the first part of *WN* to the detriment of the rest of his work (Coats 1975: 221). Indeed, the most prominent nineteenth-century revisionist of Smith's work, J. R. McCulloch, as an admirer of 'economic science' in the modern sense is said to have 'boiled Smith's life work down to Book One of *The Wealth of Nations*' (Fitzgibbons 1995: 149–150). Stemming from this account, the economistic historiography of Smith thus has an extremely selective focus on his arguments about natural liberty, self-interest and the beneficial outcomes of market forces; which necessarily excludes the ethics, moral psychology, jurisprudence, rhetoric and belles lettres contained within his work as a whole (Tribe 1999: 609–610; Griswold 1999: 9).

Interpretations of Smith that hold him up as the forerunner to general equilibrium theory and the application of a utility maximisation postulate are reflective of a flawed usage of his work that is at least in part predetermined by an expectation that such themes can be read into his work. In actuality, it relies on a *narrow* interpretation of Smith as the founder economics, which can be usefully remedied through recourse to the history of thought historiography of Smith. For instance, Donald Winch (1992: 92) correctly identifies the way in which increasingly since the nineteenth century a number of influential schools of thought in social science have shared the belief that the advancement of economics as a science requires the separation of its subject matter from moral considerations. Yet, crucially, to read this separation in Smith is deeply problematic in Skinnerian terms because it involves a process of extrapolation from Smith's actual texts and even contradicts his intentions in writing them (Macfie 1967: 13). As Stephen Rosow (1997: 45) argues, the separation of the economy from its embeddedness in social and political practice was a 'foreign thought to Adam Smith and his contemporaries'. Indeed, an economistic depiction of Smith does not adequately characterise the larger social and political dimensions of his enquiry (Winch 1978: 70). Put simply, Smith does not apply a universal 'economic' approach as 'sub-rational' instincts play a crucial part in both his *WN* and *TMS* (Winch 1978: 167). He was also aware that a simple economistic model of interaction is lacking because it does not take into account, among other things: the way (mis)perceptions are formed; social setting; interdependence between individuals and groups; and unintended consequences (Winch 1978: 167).

In his consideration of Smith's philosophy of science, Fleischacker (2004: 33) suggests that Smith was not presenting principles that he expected to hold as economic 'facts' available to every generation in history. As such, this implies that those who use Smith's principles to explain every economic phenomenon today are betraying their master's legacy rather than preserving it (Fleischacker 2004: 33). Likewise, Anthony Endres (1991: 94) argues that given the concepts that Smith sets out in his *Lectures on Rhetoric and Belles Lettres*, the chapter on 'bounties' in *WN* 'is best viewed as a disciplined exercise in advocacy rather than as a crude polemic or an illustration of applied economic analysis or "science"'. As Pierre Force (2003: 101) suggests, 'attempts to translate the language of economic science and rational choice theory into the language of early modern moral philosophy (and vice versa) should be carried out with caution'.

Interestingly, some areas of the IPE literature are rather more robust on this issue than others, at least in terms of not separating the economic and the political in Smith. They thus avoid uncritically accepting a mythology of prolepsis. For instance, the claim is made that Smith would have been 'surprised' at the differentiation of the social sciences into separate spheres of study (Brown and Ainley 2009: 18). As Andrew Gamble (1983: 66) points out, for Smith 'the purpose of political economy was to provide guidance to the statesman', which in turn is picked up in the suggestion that for Smith 'the economy was eminently political and politics was obviously tied to economic phenomena' (Frieden and Lake 2000: 3). Smith is also understood to have recognised 'the interconnections of the political and the economic inherent within a conception of capital as a set of social relations of production' (Clift and Rosamond 2009: 99) and thus is part of a tradition that highlights the 'importance of treating markets as arenas of governance and decision-making arenas in their own right' (Baker 2005: 104–105).

Moreover, there is a degree of recognition that Smith understood political economy to be 'closely linked to the study of moral philosophy' (Cohen 2008: 17) – the practical aspect of the study of moral philosophy' (Mittelman and Pasha 1997: 16) – and that he places his work 'within a moral and historical context' (Crane and Amawi 1997: 7). He is also recognised to be concerned with theorising the 'moral sentiments of economic actors' (Santiso 2003: 2) and the philosophical quandary of the 'relationship between individual self-interest and the collective needs of the community' (Underhill 2000: 17). Indeed this is often accepted as part of his 'ultimate concern' for 'fostering human dignity and the ethical life' (Murphy and Tooze 1991b: 27).

Overall, read through the lens of a concern with issues related to a potential mythology of prolepsis, the historiography of Smith in IPE is somewhat complex. On the one hand, there are a number of interpretations that follow an economistic historiography of his work by understanding him as the father of economics, which often includes situating a 'break' between the economic and the political in his work, and attributing the economic man construction to Smith. Such readings clearly reproduce a mythology of prolepsis that can be countered through appeal to a history of thought historiography of Smith. Indeed it is pointed out that 'the view held by most serious Smith scholars [is] that Smith was *not* an incipient neoclassical economist' (Fitzgibbons 1995: 171 emphasis in original). Vivienne Brown (1994: 22) uses the Baktinian notion of 'canonisation' to criticise economistic readings of Smith that reduce the 'dialogic complexity of the past to a single voice for consumption in the present'.

Nevertheless, on the other hand, other more subtle interpretations of Smith in IPE recognise that he does not separate the economic from the political and the ethical in his work. Notably, such contributions follow more closely a history of thought historiography of Smith. This tendency might be attributed to how the discipline of IPE tends to work at the intersection of the political and the economic (e.g. Strange 1994), and so it suits IPE scholars to claim that Smith was undertaking a similar scholarly endeavour by invoking the authority of his name. However, this position sits rather uncomfortably alongside how IPE tends to follow an economistic historiography of Smith when it attempts to interpret other more specific aspects of his work.

Laissez-faire capitalism

Skinner's (1969: 24) mythology of 'parochialism' relates to interpretive attempts to understand an unfamiliar conceptual scheme found in a past text in terms that are more familiar to the current day. Such attempts are potentially problematic because they present the distinct possibility of 'misdescribing' the sense and intended reference of a text through a suspect process of 'historical foreshortening' (Skinner 1969: 24). As such, even when attention is seemingly focused entirely on a text itself, the 'very familiarity of the concepts that the historian uses may mask some essential inapplicability to the historical material' (Skinner 1969: 28). On the one hand, to an extent, the very process of interpreting past texts necessarily involves the reconceptualising of themes and concepts into terms and categories that are more familiar today. On the other hand, though, it is possible to identify a number of readings of Smith's texts that clearly approach them in such a way as to significantly underplay, or simply ignore, the historicised meanings of the concepts he used. In tending to follow this latter route, the economistic historiography of Smith in IPE appears to reaffirm this mythology.

First and foremost, this is evidenced in many interpretations of Smith that directly 'translate' his work into contemporary political concepts and terminology. As Fleischacker (2004: 19) points out, it is indeed possible to use Smith's work to support views of government from both the political left and right in terms of wealth redistribution, but even though both are plausible, they require considerable extrapolation from his actual work. This is because, for one thing, Smith was writing at a time when *production* was above all the central concern of political economy, not the issue of *distribution*, which later assumed such pivotal importance (Fleischacker 2004: 19). As such, it is imperative to be aware of context when attempting to view Smith's 'individualism' in a modern sense (Clark 1989: 54). Indeed even Hollander (1987: 3–4), a historian of thought who tends to use a distinctly economistic historiography, claims that Smith represents one of 'the masters' whose work has been misused by politicians and 'others with an axe to grind' for their own ends and indeed 'possibly without having read them'. He claims that Smith's work contains sustained arguments for a moderate kind of interventionism, harsh criticisms of capitalist institutions and, equally plausibly, the roots of early British socialism (Hollander 1987: 4). Hollander (1987: 4) thus finds it entirely inappropriate that conservatives 'sporting Adam Smith neckties' frequently cite Smith as the champion of an extreme form of 'laissez faire'.

This attribution of a laissez faire policy prescription to Smith is most problematic in terms of reproducing an interpretive mythology of prolepsis. Yet more often than not in IPE, Smith is quite simply the 'alleged father of laissez faire' (Diaz-Alejandro 1978: 92). On many accounts, Smith is said to have '*of course*, generally advocated laissez-faire policies' (Balaam and Veseth 2008: 104 emphasis added). 'Laissez faire' – as both a policy prescription (e.g. Cohen 1974: 23; Mittelman 1997: 80; O'Brien and Williams 2007: 83; Pettman 1996: 196; Steger 2002: 10; Swift 1993: 67; Versluysen 1981: 242) and as a normative or ideological liberal argument for free trade (e.g. Aggarwal 1985: 10; Isaak 1995: 4–5; Lal 2006: 48; Miller 2008: 245; Sally 1998: 17) – is in fact widely understood to be central to his work. These IPE readings echo Paul Samuelson's (1969: 4) economistic interpretation in which Smith is said to 'extol the role of *laissez-faire*'.

Notably, however, Smith *did not ever* use the phrase. This is the case even though it was popularised in 1750's France and thus could have been employed systematically by him if it was part of his intention to do so. As Jakob Vestergaard (2009: 185) correctly highlights:

> Recent work in the history of economic thought has challenged the widespread notion that Adam Smith may be considered the founding father of *laissez-faire* liberalism . . . Smith's views on the proper role of government in a market society have been severely misrepresented.

He suggests that '[f]rom the perspective of this body of research [Smith studies], it would be a gross mistake to extrapolate from Adam Smith's critique of mercantilism to a general "anti-government" or laissez-faire stance' (Vestergaard 2009: 186).

As well as concepts he did *not* use, it can still be difficult to appropriately interpret some of the specific concepts Smith *did* in fact use without succumbing to a mythology of parochialism. Of particular concern here is his use of the phrase 'the system of natural liberty'. Notably, writing in the mid-to-late eighteenth century, Smith did not refer to a system of free enterprise as 'capitalism', but as 'the system of natural liberty' in which 'things were left to follow their natural course, where there was perfect liberty' (Smith cited in Cropsey 1975: 148). As Winch (1978: 142) argues, although this point is often ignored, the rapid translation of Smith's use of the term 'commercial society' into 'capitalism' is flawed for the simple reason that the latter term was not available to him. Crucially, the relationship between capital and wage labour was not central to Smith's society, which means that the relationship between the two was merely one of a whole range of market relationships (Winch 1978: 142). Nor, incidentally, is Smith's 'system of natural liberty' interchangeable with the term 'free trade' because the former term has 'jurisprudential' connotations that the latter does not (Fitzgibbons 1995: 172). Smith's criticisms of the prevailing economic order, mercantilism, were that it did not work in accordance with the principles of natural liberty, not based on some ultimate evaluation of an idealised structure such as the perfect competition paradigm (Buchanan 1979: 120).

In the IPE literature, however, there tends to be a straightforward link made between Smith's work and capitalism. Typically, Smith is understood as 'the first to develop a comprehensive portrait of capitalism' (Balaam and Veseth 2008: 40) and to have provided the 'era's best description of what was the emerging capitalist system' (Hite and Roberts 2007: 4–5). On such readings, his work: explains how capitalism 'creates the wealth of nations' (Bonefeld 2006: 45), describes how 'capitalism and markets came into existence' (Harrod 2006: 32–33), and on the whole 'celebrated' capitalism (Walker 2010: 231). For Smith's critics, Mark Martinez's (2009: 8–9) comments on the association between his work and capitalism are typical:

> Adam Smith, the intellectual godfather of capitalism, argued that greedy people in competitive environments could become good and even lead moral lives. Smith argued that, freed from abusive feudal authority and stifling traditions, greed in the pursuit of profit could be transformed into a quest to please and serve others. Simply put, customers would not return to a merchant if they were treated rudely or received a shoddy product. Merchants would be forced to produce quality goods and treat people well if they wanted to succeed. Hard work and moral lives would be the end result, and society would be the beneficiary. Freedom and the pursuit of profit would replace feudal customs and traditions that obligated subservience and duty. And, 'like an invisible hand,' the moral and material needs of society would be met.

Together with the other simplistic treatments of the relationship between Smith and 'capitalism', this attribution of a 'consumer is king' in a capitalist economy idea to Smith (Balaam and Veseth 2008: 42) clearly replicates a Skinnerian mythology of parochialism. Put simply, it can be shown through recourse to a history of thought historiography of Smith that he did not provide an 'ideology' of capitalism as some in IPE claim (e.g. Panić 2003: 14–15).

Notably, as a useful corrective, Gavin Kennedy's (2005: *ix*) central argument is that Smith wrote for *his* times, when religious superstition dominated the beliefs and attitudes of individuals to a degree not easily comprehended today. Moreover, Edward Harpham (1983: 766) suggests that in order to grasp the political significance of the historical arguments that Smith develops, it is necessary to situate them within his broader economic arguments and his specific critique of the mercantile system. In this endeavour, moreover, scholars must be wary of transposing nineteenth-century analytical meanings onto the less familiar eighteenth-century concepts that make up Smith's work (Winch 1978: 142). In fact, Winch (1978: 165) successfully demonstrates that applying what are basically nineteenth-century perspectives to what is 'quintessentially' a work of the eighteenth century not only introduces artificialities but also obscures some of the essential features of Smith's work. Reading Smith's texts through the lenses of a 'laissez faire' policy position and an ideology of 'capitalism' poses exactly these sorts of problems. Overall, rather than blindly following an economistic historiography of Smith that does not attend to issues of historicised meaning, IPE scholars might look to this history of thought literature – *and his texts themselves* – in order to provide their own more accurate historiography of Smith.

The Adam Smith Problem

Finally, Skinner's (1969: 16–19) mythology of 'coherence' concerns the ways in which readers attempt to find in past texts a level of *consistency* that is essentially unfounded. This flawed procedure attributes coherence to writers based on the suggestion that they present a 'closed system', even though they may have never even attempted to provide such a system (Skinner 1969: 17). In turn, problematically, this may involve discounting the actual stated intentions of a writer and even ignoring whole texts that are presumed not to fit in with an overall body of work. Also, it might include readers taking it upon themselves to demonstrate that any contradictions within or between texts are not real barriers to a coherent system because there cannot *really* be any genuine contradictions in a single author's work: the reader just has to search a little harder. At first glance, this mythology of coherence is similar to the above mythology of doctrine, and indeed clearly all the interpretive mythologies can overlap and appear at the same time. However, rather than the issue of whether or not a writer is putting forward a single overarching doctrine, it is much more concerned with issues of 'coherence' and 'consistency'.

In the Smith studies literature, this particular mythology has had a significant and lasting impact in the form of a debate that came to be known as the Adam Smith Problem. On one rather simplistic level, the debate revolves around the proposition that *TMS* and *WN* fundamentally contradict each other because of the way in which the former seems to recommend and endorse 'benevolence' while the latter 'self-interest' (McLean 2006: 82). *TMS* is said to be aligned with the 'benevolent' moralists Francis Hutcheson and Anthony Ashley-Cooper Shaftesbury whereas, by contrast, the proper working of the economic order set out in *WN* is thought to be closer to the 'egoistic' ethics of Thomas Hobbes and Bernard Mandeville (Viner 1989: 130). In Jacob Viner's (1989: 126) terms, at least with respect to the character of the natural order, there is thus a 'substantial measure of irreconcilable divergence' between *TMS* and *WN*. He points to the way in which, first, a benevolent deity who is author and guide of nature is part of the former book but almost entirely missing from the latter; and second, that the novel feature of human nature presented in *TMS* – benevolence – is not relied upon in the proper working of the economic order set out in *WN* (Viner 1989, 126; 130).

Notably, in the IPE literature, the vast majority of interpretations of Smith are derived almost exclusively from his *WN*, while *TMS* is largely ignored. This means that the question of whether the two texts form a coherent whole is rarely even acknowledged, let alone examined. One exception is Razeen Sally (1998: 75–76; 87) who picks up on Viner's suggestion that Smith 'alternates between "partial models" applicable to different compartments of human action' and therefore argues that *WN* and *TMS* deal with what are essentially different 'spheres' of the social world, rather than being contradictory. Others recognise how in *TMS*,

Smith 'avers that the power and wealth created by the division of labour is quite "contemptible and trifling"' such that the text presents at least some sort of challenge to the optimism of a wealthy society in *WN* (Blaney and Inayatullah 2010: 37). Along these lines, it is pointed out that in *TMS* he 'also stressed that in civil society, social propensities constrain egoism and help to avert discord' through a 'discussion of "fellow feeling", personal conduct, rules of justice and morality' (Mittelman 1997: 80).

However, despite these notable exceptions amongst others (e.g. Watson 2005a; 2013), *TMS* is rarely given the same amount of attention as *WN* so any discussion of the potential Adam Smith Problem is largely absent. On the one hand, it is potentially beneficial for IPE interpretations of Smith that scholars tend *not* to succumb to this Skinnerian mythology of coherence: how can they have a misplaced concern for consistency between *WN* and *TMS* if the latter tends to be entirely overlooked? However, on the other hand, much more problematically, IPE scholars tend to ignore *TMS* while, perhaps unknowingly, routinely accepting the interpretation of *WN* that underpins many flawed accounts of one half the Adam Smith Problem. In other words, as discussed above in the section concerning the invisible hand, most IPE scholars understand *WN* to be all about how the 'self-interest of one becomes the general interest of all' (Burchill 2005: 73).

In a sense then, the way in which *TMS* is overlooked by the vast majority of IPE scholars serves to demonstrate the way in which IPE tends to follow an economistic historiography of Smith that emphasises the invisible hand doctrine to the detriment of a robust interpretation of his actual texts. Even on those occasions when *TMS* is discussed in the IPE literature, the general tone of these discussions tends to echo more mainstream economic interpretations in which his 'other', less important text is referred to occasionally to make the point that Smith was more than just an economist. This mirrors, for example, Joseph Stiglitz's (2007: 189–190) suggestion that in 'Smithian economics, morality played no role', but at the same time he 'was intensely concerned about moral issues' in *TMS*. Yet, perhaps unsurprisingly, the problem of consistency between Smith's two major published works has not been readily considered by most working in the economics mainstream either because *TMS* is considered to be 'psychological' or 'ethical' rather than an 'economic' text (Peil 1989: 280–281). On such readings then, the inconsistencies result in Smith's first major publication – and the one he gained fame for writing during his lifetime – being ignored.

By contrast, the Smith studies literature takes *TMS* much more seriously and so discussions of coherence and consistency often come to centre stage. In light of ideas about the mythology of coherence, though, the *problem* with the Adam Smith Problem is not so much its identification in Smith's work. There may well exist subtle differences in various areas of his work that do not in any way undermine his intention. More problematic is the response of those who then attempt to find coherence, in order to solve the contradiction, where perhaps there is none or even where the subject matter itself is inherently contradictory. Indeed there are various accounts in the Smith studies literature that have suggested that the Adam

Smith Problem is in fact not really a contradiction at all. Most influentially D. D. Raphael and Alec Macfie (1982: 20), the editors of the Glasgow edition of *TMS*, have called it 'a pseudo-problem based on ignorance and misunderstanding' of the relation between the two books.

Indeed the general trend in the literature is now to seek ways of synthesising his work through appeal to how *TMS* provides a moral basis on which to ground the chiefly economic ideas contained within *WN*. For example, Glenn Morrow (1989: 177) argues that Smith does not consider the individual as an absolute and irreducible entity existing prior to social existence, as could be interpreted from *WN*, but as a product of their social environment, clearly evidenced in *TMS*. In a similar way, Winch (1992: 105) reconciles a renowned passage on self-interest with Smith's concern for sympathy:

> We may have no need of the benevolence of the butcher when we appeal to his self-interest in selling us meat, but that does not mean we have no imaginative sympathy, no capacity to understand and approve or disapprove of his behaviour.

In all, as Horst Claus Recktenwald (1978: 56) and Jan Peil (1999: 7) have identified, viewing his work as a comprehensive whole is one of the key features in the renaissance of interest in Smith over the last thirty years. As a result, recent trends might produce readings of Smith that in attempting to solve the Adam Smith Problem actually reproduce a mythology of coherence by reading back into his work a level of consistency that might not be supported by his actual texts.

However, there are other Smith scholars who have suggested that the Adam Smith Problem – perhaps in a modified form that moves away from its rather crude 'benevolence' versus 'self-interest' exposition – constitutes an important part of Smith's work and as such should not be explained away. For instance, Laurence Dickey (1986: 582) argues that the Adam Smith Problem has too readily been dismissed and that this dismissal serves to obscure some of the deeper issues it raises. Similarly, Richard Teichgraeber (1981: 111) suggests that the Adam Smith Problem can only be so easily rejected if it is understood in its original and somewhat oversimplified form. He points to the work by Joseph Cropsey and Robert Cumming who have considered the problem in a 'revamped form' in order to describe the 'very complex task of establishing Smith's intentions as a moral and social theorist' (Teichgraeber 1981: 111).

Thus, perhaps in order to avoid the mythology of coherence in this instance, it is possible to agree with Vivienne Brown (1994: 24) who suggests that the identity of each text is not reducible to the issue of authorial coherence or consistency; and further, despite very different rhetorical styles, it does not need to be. Rather than ignoring such questions, then, IPE scholars could engage with an historiography of Smith that recognises the existence of a *potential* Adam Smith Problem. At the very least, this would avoid unconsciously replicating the simplistic and erroneous economistic historiography of Smith, which reduces his thought to the *WN* side of the debate.

Concluding remarks

> Against the idea of atomistic individuals acting like calculating machines driven by price signals, more recent readings typically place an emphasis on understanding behaviour in relation to its concrete socio-historical context. This means that in the new readings of Smith's economic analysis, individuals are still considered as economic agents, but their agency is no longer interpreted as atomistic, mechanistic and rationalistic. Instead, recent scholarship on Smith pays far greater attention to the ways in which his individuals act according to prevailing social values and rules.
>
> (Peil 1999: 9)

Jan Peil summarises superbly the way in which recent specialist work on Smith has shaped current understandings of him as a thinker. By contrast, in the main, IPE scholars fail to produce appropriately historicised interpretations of his texts, which, among other things means they tend to fail to adequately understand Smith's 'individual' in the way Peil describes. In this chapter, I have used some key interpretive mythologies identified by Quentin Skinner to map out representations of Smith in IPE and expose some of the widespread problems of interpretation surrounding his work. In terms of issues of doctrine, prolepsis and parochialism, IPE interpretations of Smith, on the whole, quite clearly succumb to Skinner's mythologies. While the instructive interpretive debates about the Adam Smith Problem in the history of thought literature are, for the most part, not even noticed as issues to be debated in IPE. Scholars tend to directly imitate a markedly economistic historiography of Smith, almost entirely replicating the interpretation of his work to be found in histories of economics written by economists. This has huge ramifications given Smith's foundational role in defining what it means to be 'doing' political economy in the first place. In a sense the entire politics of the disciplinary boundaries of IPE rest on his name.

The second image of Smith outlined at the start of this chapter draws from a more robust 'history of thought' historiography of Smith, which at present does not figure predominantly in IPE (for notable exceptions see Dunn 2009; Gamble 1983; Glaze 2008; 2015; Watson 2005a; 2013). Intellectual history scholars take the broader context of Smith's moral philosophy much more seriously by approaching his oeuvre in a way that has been described as 'comprehensively, as an integrated *whole*' (Recktenwald 1978: 56 emphasis in original). In other words, they read his *WN* through the perspective of his *TMS* and take each book to be of equal importance. In so doing, put briefly, they pick up on a fundamental concern in his texts for questions about the cultivation of standards of ethical behaviour in the emerging commercial society of his time (Fitzgibbons 1995; Fleischacker 2004; Force 2003; Rasmussen 2008; Teichgraeber 1986). In the next chapter, I provide a more successful account of Smith drawn from this second image. That IPE holds such a suspect economistic historiography of Smith makes this task all the more pressing. It is not just 'what Smith said' that is at stake, but the character of political economy as a subject field and how its scholars can even begin to comprehend the GFC.

2 Adam Smith's sympathetic political economy

> Retrospection, literally the act of looking back, is an intellectual exercise that is in some sense similar to Smith's sympathy. For Smith, sympathy is not simply fellow feeling, as it demands a process of assessing circumstances.
>
> (Montes 2004: 2)

Leonidas Montes draws an interesting parallel between the task of the intellectual historian, who might seek to interpret meaning and understand intention in past texts, and Smith's concept of sympathy because they both involve an imaginative change of place and situation. In this chapter, I make the case that Smith's sympathy should be understood centrally as an imaginative ethical procedure, through which people come to assess the actions and circumstance of others and themselves. A sensibility to sympathy dynamics offers a route to bringing questions of ethics right back into the heart of discussions of economic governance. In turn a sympathetic political economy provides new ways of understanding the GFC.

As I explored in the previous chapter, interpretations of Smith tend to be derived from an economistic historiography of his work. This is problematic because it in part serves to draw boundaries around what constitutes 'legitimate' contemporary political economy using Smith as a foundational scholarly authority. At the same time, the same particular delimitation of political economy also tends to exclude or at least marginalise questions of ethical contestation at the individual level. Both of these problematic tendencies can be productively engaged through a return to Smith's sympathy. This chapter shows how Smith's sympathy concept, almost completely overlooked by IPE scholars, can provide a complex and compelling perspective on contemporary market-oriented behaviour while still remaining attentive to the historicised meaning of his work.

The first section considers Smith's eighteenth-century context and his intellectual influences. How did the context in which Smith wrote help to produce the meaning and significance of his ideas? With which other moral philosophers was Smith engaged when writing his work? This is essentially a Skinnerian attempt to locate Smith in his socio-linguistic context in order to gain a deeper understanding of his thought. The second section studies some aspects of Smith's work that might help shed light on his intervention into debates of his time. Both Smith's 'intentions' and his 'politics' are understood in relation to his immediate socio-linguistic context. Finally, drawing on the contextual claims made in the first two sections, a more detailed account of Smith's concept of sympathy is offered. A thorough reading of sympathy is vital to understanding Smith's conception of market-oriented behaviour. This idea is further developed in the next chapter as it provides a key way to conceive of the individual in a distinctly different way than the economistic understandings of market-oriented behaviour that prevail today.

Smith's context

Eighteenth-century commercial society

The most significant aspect to note of Smith's time was its *pre-industrial* character. It is easy to succumb to a Skinnerian mythology of parochialism and overlook the fact that the supposed 'father of capitalism', when he was writing in the mid-to-late eighteenth century, was living in and writing about a world that was only just starting to assume those features and would *later* be designated as 'capitalist'. Indeed it has been suggested that it was only in the last decade of the eighteenth century or so that existing forms of economy and society in lowland Scotland started to break up under the changes brought about by industrial capitalism (Teichgraeber 1986: xvii).

In Smith's (*WN* I.iv.1) own terms, the 'commercial society' of his time is to be thought of as an outgrowth of an advancing level of the division of labour, not necessarily a particular mode of production:

> When the division of labour has been once thoroughly established, it is but a very small part of a man's wants which the produce of his own labour can supply. He supplies the far greater part of them by exchanging that surplus part of the produce of his own labour, which is over and above his own consumption, for such parts of the produce of other men's labour as he has occasion for. Every man thus lives by exchanging, or becomes in some measure a merchant, and the society itself grows to be what is properly a commercial society.

As was customary in eighteenth-century scholarship Smith refers to 'man' here as a synonym for 'people', which I do not reproduce unless making direct use of his work. This quotation shows how Smith's 'commercial society' does not necessarily designate a society based on industrial capitalist relations of production and exchange. He is interested in the emerging social transformations that are occurring around him, particularly those brought about by societies choosing to advance their division of labour, but in no proper sense can Smith said to be studying the onset of capitalist market relations.

However, many commentators have criticised Smith for failing to anticipate how radically economy and society would be transformed after the onset of the industrial revolution. Athol Fitzgibbons (1995: 11) points out that despite all its institutional detail, *WN* 'did not mention power-driven methods of production, and it made almost no reference to the cotton industry, which was about to become the leading edge of British industrial growth'. Meanwhile Charles Kindleberger (1976: 1–6) makes the convincing case that as a 'literary economist', Smith did not have a thorough understanding of the industrial revolution, the onset of which many date to be contemporaneous with his writing of the *WN*, because he primarily drew his examples from books published in the first quarter of the eighteenth century. 'Smith's discussion of the allocation, distribution, and the division of labour through the market', he continues, 'was largely related to what is now called "proto-industrialization", rather than the industrialization into large factories of the industrial revolution' (Kindleberger 1976: 24). Conceivably, then, the pre-industrial and pre-capitalist nature of Smith's time might present a key limiting factor on the extent to which it is possible to invoke his ideas in any meaningful sense in the industrial, or post-industrial, economy and society of today.

Nevertheless, from a pragmatic historiographical perspective the very notion that his ideas are in some sense 'of another time' and can only be understood through undertaking an historicised process of interpretation allows them to hold a certain promise. They constitute different frames of understanding market-oriented behaviour compared to what would follow and thus an alternative mode of thought compared to the capitalist, and later economistic, individual. Indeed, along these lines, Mary Morgan (2006: 2) argues that Smith's 'portrait' of market-oriented behaviour acts 'as a foil to give a sharper focus to the model man constructions that come in later economics'. While Smith did not live under 'capitalism', part of the argument of this book is that an ethos of sympathy can be mobilised as a form of analysis and critique of capitalist social relations. I return to this problematic issue below.

Smith's insights are particularly notable given that he was writing at the time of the onset of important world-historical developments that he was one of the first to identify as the transition from feudal society. As Jan Peil (1999: 49) suggests, the 'commercialization and liberalization of society' were leading moral philosophers to discuss moral problems from something of a 'new economic point of view' because it was now possible to give accounts of *everyday* people 'successfully making an independent living outside the traditional constraints of the feudal hierarchy'. Of course, not everyone benefitted equally from the downfall of feudalism, which is one of the foundational points in Marx's much later account of the new position of the wage labourer. For moral philosophers a century earlier though, such changes were less apparent and their focus was on the broader ethical effects of commercialisation on society, rather than on class relations per se. This led them to a new focus, as Watson (2013: 10) points out, on the 'existence of increasingly institutionalised commercial relations . . . deemed to be symbolic of an economy capable of producing surplus', which were understood 'to require new political and moral structures in order to contain likely flashpoints'. Within such structures, eighteenth-century moral philosophers became interested in how people came to embody new subjectivities, as part of efforts to guard against, rather than embrace, struggles over surplus and apparent increases in possessive individualism (Watson 2013: 10).

The evolving nature of inquiries undertaken by moral philosophers at this time could be located within debates about whether Smith fits into a 'jurisprudential' or a 'civic humanist' tradition of thought (Hont and Ignatieff 1983). While Smith clearly had a central concern for questions of justice as well, he pays close attention to questions about commercial society that seem to have distinctly civic humanist undertones. Such questions were not new to Smith's time, but they did take on new weight and meaning, especially with regard to the constitution of ethical behaviour. In particular, debates about the social desirability of wealth and commercial values were becoming highly relevant in eighteenth-century Britain because they were seen to threaten traditional social norms and culture (Fitzgibbons 1995: 12).

Smith (*TMS* I.iii.3.1) sought to directly contribute to this conversation when he considered the double-edged nature of the admiration of the rich:

> This disposition to admire, and almost to worship, the rich and the powerful, and to despise, or, at least, to neglect persons of poor and mean condition, though necessary both to establish and to maintain the distinction of ranks and the order of society, is, at the same time, the great and most universal cause of the corruption of our moral sentiments.

Given the prominence of the concept of 'self-command' in his work, the debates surrounding civic humanism in the latter half of the eighteenth century were a powerful influence on Smith's thought (Montes 2004: 57). At the very least, it means that his conception of the individual is likely to contain a specific concern for the cultivation of ethical behaviour between people and groups that conforms to civil society. This process of cultivation is closely linked to his concept of sympathy as a generator of standards of interpersonal ethics at the individual level discussed below. Moreover, such a conception is in direct contrast to the asocial individual of economistic understandings both of his work – often derived from an erroneous economistic historiography – and of liberal perspectives on governance today.

Hutcheson, Hume and the Scottish Enlightenment

Smith was in many ways directly influenced by his immediate predecessors and by a number of other eminent moral philosophers writing at a similar time. Notably, Francis Hutcheson played an important role in the development of certain ideas that helped to set the terms of debate for moral philosophers of the Scottish Enlightenment. Hutcheson's notion of 'moral sense', which held that moral judgements were not primarily matters of 'reason' or 'self-love' as commonly supposed, was a key concept on which Smith and others could develop their views about individual moral behaviour (Teichgraeber 1986: 29–30). Richard Teichgraeber (1986: 36) compares Hutcheson's moral sense argument to the idea that 'moral judgements are products of a human faculty distinct from reason and analogous to the ordinary five senses', such that people are 'moved by certain feelings that in turn prompt judgements of approval or disapproval'. Rather than in some way *consciously* deciding to approve or disapprove, for Hutcheson (2002: 175–176 emphasis in original), such moral judgements are the result of an *instinctive* sense:

> If one asks 'how do we know that *our Affections are right when they are kind?*' What does the Word [right] mean? Does it mean *what we approve?* This we know by *Consciousness* of our *Sense*. Again, how do we know that our *Sense* is right, or that we *approve our Approbation?* . . . To answer this, we must first know that the *same Constitution* of our *Sense* shall always remain: And again, that we have applyed our selves carefully to consider the *natural Tendency* of our Actions.

Hutcheson was himself perhaps indebted to John Locke for the way in which he adapted his understanding of the workings of the five senses to the human world. As Locke had put forward the view that knowledge of the external natural world must have its origins in the working of the five senses, Hutcheson suggested that much the same was true of moral senses. He attempted to demonstrate that judgements regarding appropriate behaviour must also derive from the operation of a 'sense' that 'instinctively comes into play when we observe the conduct of others' (Teichgraeber 1986: 40).

Thus Hutcheson in many ways allowed Smith to move away from a 'predetermined ideal vision' of morality towards a conception of what Teichgraeber (1986: 47) calls an 'internal process'. This is supported in Smith's (*TMS* VII.iii.3.6) claim:

> That faculty, which Mr. Locke calls reflection, and from which he derived the simple ideas of the different passions and emotions of the human mind, was, according to Dr. Hutcheson, a direct internal sense. That faculty again by which we perceived the beauty or deformity, the virtue or vice of those different passions and emotions, was a reflex, internal sense.

As will become apparent, this had clear ramifications for Smith in his *internal* mental device, the 'impartial spectator'. If it is possible to identify an important conversation that Smith contributed to in response to lines of argument about moral sense, Hutcheson helped him to move away from those values and concepts articulated by natural law theorists towards a distinctly different interest in the role of sentiments, passions and feelings in human conduct. Such an interest is in contrast to the almost un-feeling, un-sentimental as it were, economistic understanding of the individual in contemporary liberalism from which sentiments and passions, especially those of ethico-political nature, are expunged.

David Hume also represents a central Scottish Enlightenment philosopher who built on Hutcheson's ideas and was in conversation with Smith on significant points. As Teichgraeber (1986: 89) explains, Hume's theory of justice can be 'understood as an explanation of Hutcheson's account of non-rational psychology of moral judgement [turned] into a broader theory of social and political relationships among men'. For Hume, building on Hutcheson, moral judgements could not be reduced to either self-love or reason, as moral judgement was more the outcome of certain sentiments that were distinct from both. As Hume (1751: 8 emphasis in original) writes:

> We shall consider the Matter as an Object of Experience. We shall call *every Quality or Action of the Mind*, virtuous, *which is attended with the general Approbation of Mankind*: And we shall denominate vicious, *every Quality, which is the Object of general Blame or Censure.*

Hume thus constructed a critical response to a key premise in existing natural law philosophy: rather than obligations directed by 'right reason', ethical and legal codes must be explained in terms of elementary passions and instincts (Teichgraeber 1986: 101).

On the one hand, there are important points of agreement between Hume and Smith. As a 'progressive' philosopher in the eighteenth-century European Enlightenment sense, Hume saw an historic opportunity to establish society on 'science' as opposed to religious superstition. In this light, Hume can be viewed as a thinker who contributed to a gradual move away from the idealist philosophy of the Greeks towards humanism and an image of society that 'by rejecting religious superstition, would be enriched by trade and informed by science' (Fitzgibbons 1995: 27). Along these lines, it would appear that Smith followed Hume to the extent that he recognised the promise of Britain moving away from 'its medieval mire of backwardness and superstition' (Fitzgibbons 1995: 29). For instance, Smith (*TMS* III.6.1) writes:

> Religion affords such strong motives to the practice of virtue, and guards us by such powerful restraints from the temptations of vice, that many have been led to suppose, that religious principles were the sole laudable motives of action . . . It may be a question, however, in what cases our actions ought to arise chiefly or entirely from a sense of duty, or from a regard to general rules; and in what cases some other sentiment or affection ought to concur, and have a principal influence.

On the other hand, Smith disagreed with Hume's view that this new society emerging in eighteenth-century Britain had to start from a sceptical rejection of *all* moral values. Fitzgibbons (1995: 15) argues that as 'Hume's scepticism effectively undercut the traditional rationalization for a moral and political élite, it further implied that there was no ultimate justification for any social rules at all'. Smith countered this 'nihilistic version of liberal society' by constructing arguments that rejected extreme scepticism (Fitzgibbons 1995: 15). Essentially, Smith made the case that if Hume's theory of morals and psychology involved reducing everything to 'feelings and sensations' then it is possible to turn science against Hume by suggesting that these very feelings and sensations themselves have to be explained (Fitzgibbons 1995: 93).

Smith's concept of sympathy is precisely the device he suggests can explain these sensations. Although he acknowledges that imagined experience cannot be the same as that of immediate experience, Smith argues that it is possible to gain some kind of insight into the feelings and sensations of others through an imaginative procedure:

> Though our brother is upon the rack, as long as we ourselves are at our ease, our senses will never inform us of what he suffers. They never did, and never can, carry us beyond our own person, and it is by the imagination only that we can form any conception of what are his sensations. Neither can that faculty help us to this any other way, than by representing to us what would be our own, if we were in his case. It is the impressions of our own senses only, not those of his, which our imaginations copy. By the imagination we place ourselves in his situation, we conceive ourselves enduring all the same torments, we enter as it were into his body, and become in some measure the same person with him, and thence form some idea of his sensations, and even feel something which, though weaker in degree, is not altogether unlike them.
> (*TMS* I.i.1.2)

Given that Smith's sympathy is based on ideas about the operation of moral insight, there is therefore a fundamental difference between Smith and Hume because the latter, for the large part, rejected the notion that there could even be moral insights of this kind.

The distance between the two thinkers has implications for Smith's understanding of the individual moral agent. Fitzgibbons (1995: 28–29) argues that 'Smith rejected every one of Hume's major philosophical propositions, including utility, scepticism, the relativity of values, radical individualism, and the rigorous distinction between positive and normative ideas'. Smith in fact fervently scorned the 'rational utility maximiser' who was Hume's 'alternative ideal to the ancient philosopher who had perceived the higher world through contemplation and the mind' (Fitzgibbons 1995: 52). Smith rejected a theory of utility on a number of grounds. For a start, as has been noted, he opposed the nihilism of Hume that such a theory seemed to imply.

Perhaps more importantly for Smith, a theory of utility could not even provide a proper explanation of sensations themselves. In his eyes, although there may be a certain level of admiration attached to the apparent convenience of utility in terms of means fitting ends, there is no suggestion that it can be regarded as part of an explanation of sensation or moral agency. Indeed there are comments made by Smith (*TMS* I.i.4.4) to suggest that the idea of utility is not much more than a post-hoc rationalisation of action: for instance, he calls such explanations 'plainly an after-thought'. Referring to Hume directly, Smith (*TMS* IV.2.3) writes:

> The same ingenious and agreeable author who first explained why utility pleases, has been so struck with this view of things, as to resolve our whole approbation of virtue into a perception of this species of beauty which results

> from the appearance of utility. No qualities of the mind, he observes, are approved of as virtuous, but such as are useful or agreeable either to the person himself or to others; and no qualities are disapproved of as vicious but such as have a contrary tendency . . . But still I affirm, that it is not the view of this utility or hurtfulness which is either the first or principal source of our approbation and disapprobation. These sentiments are no doubt enhanced and enlivened by the perception of the beauty or deformity which results from this utility or hurtfulness. But still, I say, they are originally and essentially different from this perception.

The intellectual relationship between Smith and Hume is complex with regards to their understanding of the individual moral agent. There are clear points of agreement: both thinkers wrote in conversation with Hutcheson's ideas about moral sense in order to move away from the idealist philosophy of the Greeks and natural law philosophy towards a humanism based on understanding feelings and sensations. However a key point of divergence turns on their response to this move. For Hume, it led to scepticism and the adoption of a theory of utility. For Smith, by contrast, there was still a role for moral insight, which required an understanding of moral judgement that went beyond the misleading concept of utility. The stark contrast between the position that Smith took in conversation with his contemporaries and the importance that would subsequently be attached to the concept of utility, albeit in a distinctly modified form, in later economistic understandings of market-oriented behaviour is notable here. It is even more ironic that a theory of 'utility-maximisation' then gets erroneously imputed onto Smith himself. Reading Smith in a new light here can provide escape from some of the narrowness of much political economy analysis that is imbued with a degree of economism by bringing *his* concerns back into view.

Rousseau, Mandeville and 'self-love'

Alongside utility contemporary economistic conceptions of market-oriented behaviour typically rely on some understanding of an individual's pursuit of 'self-interest', narrowly understood. Following Pierre Force (2003: 1), it is important to note that the *specific* term 'self-interest' occurs only *once* in *WN*. Even this single usage seems to be rather different to the common perception of what self-interest means in Smith's supposed 'system'. It appears in the context of a discussion about education where Smith points to the problem of clergy members not being responsive to their students' needs. He writes: 'In the church of Rome, the industry and zeal of the inferior clergy is kept more alive by the powerful motive of self-interest, than perhaps in any established protestant church' (*WN* V.i.g.2). Thus, this solitary use in *WN* does not really have anything to say about economic coordination and certainly does not suggest that the self-interest of one leads to the good of all.

Rather than the term self-interest, Smith makes much more use of the term 'self-love' in *TMS*. Crucially, for Force (2003: 1–2), self-love should be understood both as a term used by moral philosophers throughout the seventeenth and eighteenth centuries carrying with it a specific tradition of thought and as the 'translation of a technical term used by Renaissance humanists, *philuatia*'. Thus the meaning of self-love needs to be negotiated in the context of its philosophical lineage rather than simply translated into ideas about self-interest. Rather than *amour-propre*, the French translation, Smith's use of the term self-love appears to carry a meaning which is closer to Jean-Jacques Rousseau's *amour de soi*: an instinct for self-preservation and immediate gratification in the Stoic sense, which in itself is 'neither vicious nor virtuous' (Force 2003: 42).

In this way, Smith's (*TMS* II.ii.2.1) understanding of self-love refers to a basic care of oneself, which is not at odds with broader societal norms and values:

> Every man is, no doubt, by nature, first and principally recommended to his own care; and as he is fitter to take care of himself than of any other person, it is fit and right that it should be so. Every man, therefore, is much more deeply interested in whatever immediately concerns himself, than in what concerns any other man . . . But though the ruin of our neighbour may affect us much less than a very small misfortune of our own, we must not ruin him to prevent that small misfortune, nor even to prevent our own ruin. We must, here, as in all other cases, view ourselves not so much according to that light in which we may naturally appear to ourselves, as according to that in which we naturally appear to others.

In this Stoical sense, as opposed to a seemingly ruthless selfish or purely self-interested action, this understanding of self-love sheds a rather different light on Smith's oft-cited, and almost always misinvoked, passage about the butcher, the brewer and the baker. The earlier part of the paragraph containing this line has one of his few mentions of self-love in the *WN* (as much of the discussion of self-love occurs in *TMS*). It reveals that even though an individual's most basic concern may simply be care for oneself, Smith's (*WN* I.ii.2 emphasis added) stress on the interdependence and cooperative nature of people in society is still notable:

> But *man has almost constant occasion for the help of his brethren*, and is in vain for him to expect it from their benevolence only. He will be more likely to prevail if he can interest their self-love in his favour, and shew them that it is for their own advantage to do for him what he requires of them . . . *Give me that which I want, and you shall have this which you want.*

The point of the butcher-brewer-baker passage, according to Samuel Fleischacker (2004: 91 emphasis in original) is that the butcher's customer can appeal to someone else's needs and thus, regardless of whether or not the butcher is self-interested, 'the argument depends on the butcher's *customer* being able to perceive, and address himself to, *other people's interests*'. In this sense, rather than 'an almost Ayn Randian exaltation of self-love', the passage emphasises the capacity to be '*other*-directed' (Fleischacker 2004: 91 emphasis in original).

Stephen McKenna (2006: 134) also notes the other-directed intentions of the passage by drawing attention to the way in which immediately before and after in the text Smith is not discussing the subject of benevolence per se, but 'discussing the centrality of persuasion as a means of achieving the cooperation necessary in a civil society'. In support of this more linguistic reading of the passage, McKenna refers to how in his *Lectures on Jurisprudence* Smith argues that moves towards commercial society depend on people's inclination to *persuade* rather than a natural inclination to trade (McKenna 2006: 134). On such an account, the idea that someone is 'more likely to prevail if he can interest their self-love in his favour' is understood through the prism of communicative action rather than physical action. Either way, the passage should clearly be understood as making reference to 'other-directed' intentions.

Moreover, as Fleischacker (2004: 90) further points out, in the butcher-brewer-baker passage, Smith would surely have used a less obvious example if he were attempting to show that people are *always* motivated by self-interest. Smith could, for example, have used Mandeville's suggestion that charitable actions are really motivated by self-interest. Yet because he does not intend to advance this Mandevillian thesis he appeals to one of the paradigmatic ways in which most people already expect self-interest, or perhaps more accurately in Smith's terms, self-love, to work (Fleischacker 2004: 90).

Others have sought to suggest that Smith worked with a 'compartmentalised' understanding of human life such that people can occupy different roles in different areas of life (Otteson 2002: 193). On this reading, the butcher-brewer-baker passage in *WN* is an instance of Smith working on an assumption of self-interest as the source of motivation, but in an arena of 'specifically economic relations' rather than implying that 'all interactions between people should be predicated on self-interest' (Otteson 2002: 193). While this interpretation serves to avoid a simplistic reduction of the account of motivation in such passages to pure self-interest, read alongside Smith's account of self-love and in the context of his response to Mandeville, a rather different understanding can be discerned that does not 'compartmentalise' in this way.

In fact a notable point of convergence between Smith and Rousseau is that they both felt compelled to write in response to Mandeville's work on what might be termed 'the interest doctrine', or alternatively 'the selfish hypothesis' (Force 2003: 43). Mandeville's (1732: 39) distinctly self-interested understanding of human nature might be summed up in his statement that:

> Man is so Selfish a Creature, that, whilst he is at Liberty, the greatest Part of his Time will always be bestow'd upon himself . . . It is obvious likewise, that he neither loves nor esteems any Thing so well as he does his own Individual; and that there is Nothing, which he has so constantly before his Eyes, as his own dear Self.

The key idea of the interest doctrine was that self-interest could act as a general explanatory principle for *all* human behaviour and action, much like the way in which economic science attempts to colonise all aspects of human understanding today. Although Smith and Rousseau essentially disagree with the interest doctrine, rather than simple censure, they agree with Mandeville as a starting point in order to refute him (Force 2003: 43). On the one hand, their response to Mandeville consists in acknowledging that the description of human behaviour in the interest doctrine *appears* in many ways to be accurate. Smith (*TMS* VII.ii.4.6) writes:

> Though the notions of this author [Mandeville] are in almost every respect erroneous, there are, however, some appearances in human nature, which, when viewed in a certain manner, seem at first sight to favour them.

Smith and Rousseau agree with Mandeville (1988: 64) to the extent that 'the true Object of Pride or Vain-glory is the Opinion of others' and this concern for the opinion of others often drives what people do in society.

On the other hand, both Smith and Rousseau are highly suspicious of a theory of behaviour such as the interest doctrine that at least appears to claim to explain *all* human action (Boltanski 2004: 37; Force 2003: 261; Otteson 2002: 193). Indeed Smith (*TMS* VII.ii.4.12 emphasis added) is deeply critical of Mandeville on this point:

> It is the great fallacy of Dr. Mandeville's book to represent every passion as wholly vicious, which is so in any degree and in any direction. It is thus that he treats every thing as vanity which has any reference, either to what are, or to what ought to be the sentiments of others: and it is by means of this sophistry, that he establishes his favourite conclusion, that *private vices are public benefits*.

Smith is here explicitly rejecting the idea that is commonly attributed to *him*. Even more productively, through the act of rejecting the interest doctrine Smith develops an account of moral sentiments that provides a very different basis for social analysis that can be mobilised in political economy today. A sensibility to sympathy is so far removed from a notion of self-interest that it can provide a new lens to analyse and critique those very approaches built on the latter.

Both Smith's and Rousseau's reply to Mandeville is at once psychological and historical. For Rousseau, people in a commercial society tend to be driven by amour-propre, 'a passion that has little to do with natural selfishness, and much to do with reason, reflection, and our ability to identify with the feelings of others' (Force 2003: 261). For Smith, in commercial society 'vanity' takes centre stage, 'a passion that does not originate in self-love (in the Stoic sense of concern for one's preservation) but rather in sympathy and the desire for sympathy' (Force 2003: 261). Thus for Smith and Rousseau, people in commercial society do not continually pursue the satisfaction of material wants as ends in themselves as the interest doctrine might suggest. Rather individuals are seemingly driven by amour-propre or vanity, as they increasingly become predominant in commercial society, to 'seek wealth and material goods only as a means towards an infinitely more elusive goal: praise and approbation from others' (Force 2003: 45).

Smith (*TMS* III.4.7) views the constant drive to impress upon the opinion of others in the following way:

> Our continual observations upon the conduct of others, insensibly lead us to form to ourselves certain general rules concerning what is fit and proper either to be done or to be avoided. Some of their actions shock all our natural sentiments. We hear every body about us express the like detestation against them. This still further confirms, and even exasperates our natural sense of their deformity. It satisfies us that we view them in the proper light, when we see other people view them in the same light . . . Other actions, on the contrary, call forth our approbation, and we hear every body around us express the same favourable opinion concerning them. Every body is eager to honour and reward them. They excite all those sentiments for which we have by nature the strongest desire; the love, the gratitude, the admiration of mankind. We become ambitious of performing the like; and thus naturally lay down to ourselves a rule of another kind, that every opportunity of acting in this manner is carefully to be sought after.

A crucial part of Smith's response to Mandeville therefore is remarkably similar to that of Rousseau, rightfully understood as one of the fiercest critics of commercial society. In fact, Smith provides a laudatory account of Rousseau's work in his 'Letter to *The Edinburgh Review*', which reveals something of the proximity of their perspectives. Smith actually offers Rousseau's *Discourse on Inequality* as an example of one of the reasons why the coverage of the periodical should be extended to include more works from the Continent (Rasmussen 2008: 59–60). Smith (1982b: 250) writes:

> Whoever reads this last work [*Discourse on Inequality*] with attention, will observe, that the second volume of the Fable of the Bees has given occasion to the system of Mr. Rousseau, in whom however the principles of the English author are softened, improved, and embellished, and stript of all that tendency to corruption and licentiousness which has disgraced them in their original author.

The notable implication of this proximity for an understanding of Smith's individual is that, as with Rousseau, he clearly rejected the interest doctrine as holding any significant promise in terms of understanding individual moral agency. Likewise, as with Rousseau, Smith saw the historically conditioned nature of behaviour in his argument that it is essentially the development of 'vanity' as a driving motive, rather than naturally ingrained self-interest, which influences people in commercial society. As Force (2003: 47) surmises:

> When authors like [Alfred] Hirschman or [Amartya] Sen propose to discard the theoretical parsimony advocated by their fellow economists, they follow

> the path opened by Rousseau and Smith, who both believed that the 'selfish hypothesis' was too clever to be truth, and proposed systems based on principles other than self-interest. On the other hand, we have seen that Rousseau and Smith shared another belief: although it is true that the 'selfish hypothesis' cannot explain human nature, human behavior in civilized society can be described in very large part as a search for wealth and material goods. In other words, the ultimate goal of economic activity is something symbolic and intangible: approbation from others. At the same time, for historical reasons, the search for praise and approbation now manifests itself almost exclusively as a search for wealth.

This picks up on the way in which both Smith and Rousseau understood economic agency to be an 'historicised phenomenon' (Watson 2013: 16). By this is meant that, on both of their accounts, the assumption of transcendent behaviour at the individual level is to be rejected in favour of giving attention to the cultural norms that influence conceptions of appropriate behaviour. Proper and improper action is therefore derived from the interaction between the individual and a structured system of manners at a particular time (Watson 2013: 16). Significantly, any degree of recognition on Smith's behalf of the historically and socially conditioned nature of economic agency seems to be in direct contrast to those later economistic understandings of market-oriented behaviour which, building on the premises of the interest doctrine, are noticeably ahistorical. Mobilising Smith then becomes a useful means of developing a political economy that can more adequately engage with the constitution of market-oriented behaviour in a more thoroughgoing sense.

There are also similarities between Rousseau's analysis of 'pity' and Smith's account of sympathy that both take Mandeville as an important starting point. For Rousseau pity 'is a pre-rational faculty, made weaker by the full use of human reason' (Force 2003: 27). Building on Mandeville, François de La Rochefoucauld and Shaftesbury, the key intellectual move that Rousseau makes is to base pity on his concept of 'identification': the process by which people put themselves imaginatively 'in the place of the person who is suffering' (Force 2003: 25; 31). Rousseau (1997: 153) writes:

> [B]enevolence and friendship, properly understood, are the products of a steady pity focused on a particular object . . . commiseration is nothing but a sentiment that puts us in the place of him who suffers . . . Indeed commiseration will be all the more energetic in proportion as the Onlooking animal identifies more intimately with the suffering animal.

As will become clear, there are striking similarities between Rousseau's 'identification' and Smith's sympathy. At this point it is worth considering in detail one of Smith's key statements regarding his thoughts on sympathy and self-love as it reveals his distance from Mandeville and his proximity to Rousseau. Smith (*TMS* VII.iii.1.4 emphasis added) writes:

> Sympathy, however, cannot, in any sense, be regarded as a selfish principle. When I sympathize with your sorrow or your indignation, it may be pretended,

> indeed, that my emotion is founded in self-love, because it arises from bringing your case home to myself, from putting myself in your situation, and thence conceiving what I should feel in the like circumstances. But though sympathy is very properly said to arise from an imaginary change of situations with the person principally concerned, yet this imaginary change is not supposed to happen to me in my own person and character, but in that of the person with whom I sympathize. When I condole with you for the loss of your only son, in order to enter into your grief I do not consider what I, a person of such a character and profession, should suffer, if I had a son, and if that son was unfortunately to die: but *I consider what I should suffer if I was really you, and I not only change circumstances with you, but I change persons and characters*. My grief, therefore, is entirely upon your account, and not in the least upon my own. *It is not, therefore, in the least selfish* . . . That whole account of human nature, however, which deduces all sentiments and affections from self-love, which has made so much noise in the world, but which, as far as I know, has never yet been fully and distinctly explained, seems to me to have arisen from some confused misapprehension of the system of sympathy.

As this passage attests, a focus on the relationship between Smith and Rousseau highlights their remarkably similar engagement with concepts relating to questions of individual behaviour, action and suffering. Their common response to Mandeville and their specific interpretation of self-love provides a cutting critique of the interest doctrine and those later perspectives that build upon its premises. As Vivienne Brown (1994: 99) points out, Smith uses a distinctly Stoic understanding of self-love in *TMS*, which means it is 'hazardous' to read it in search of moral categories that can be used as validating devices for the economic development of a commercial society. The irony, of course, is that in holding up Smith as its intellectual forebear, the economistic understanding of the individual in many contemporary liberal perspectives takes as its first principle the interest doctrine, or the 'selfish hypothesis', which originated in its current form largely in Mandeville, whom Smith and Rousseau were in fact adamantly refuting in their work. Those readings of Smith, which largely depend on an economistic historiography of his work (Chapter 1), in making claims like 'self-interest leads as if by an invisible hand to the good of society' are actually exposing a doctrine much closer to Mandeville than to Smith. Rather ironically, Smith (*TMS* III.2.27) was incredibly critical of the interest doctrine and, in his terms, considered Mandeville a 'splenetic' philosopher. An emulation of his critique of the state of theorising in his day might be a useful way of mobilising an historicised account of Smith's intentions today in political economy.

Smith's intervention

Smith's intentions

Rather than present an interest-based account of liberalism, one of the primary aims of Smith's work appears to be to offer new ethical insight into early commercial society and the character of the values that might underpin such a society (Fitzgibbons 1995: 193). Yet, as mentioned, the suggestion is often made that Smith must have in some sense 'compartmentalised' his 'ethics' and his 'economics' in order to do so (Otteson 2002: 193). On this argument, his thoughts on self-love in commercial society and his virtue ethics appear to apply to two separate spheres: that of what 'actually happens' and that of 'what should be' (Fitzgibbons 1995: 3). In response to these accounts, Fitzgibbons (1995: 4 emphasis in original) suggests that 'the more intriguing possibility is that Smith wanted to *integrate* economics and morals, by developing a philosophy that would harness the force of self-love without being dominated by it'. On this interpretation Smith saw himself as working within the framework of Hutcheson's and Hume's 'highest ambitions', which were to contribute to moral philosophy as broadly conceived in both its classical humanist and natural law senses (Teichgraeber 1986: 122).

However, it is necessary to proceed with caution when attempting to give a complete account of Smith's overall intentions along these lines. Jerry Evensky is particularly illuminating on this issue. In essence, Evensky (1987: 175–176) suggests that there are 'two voices' in which Smith writes: Smith as moral philosopher, on the one hand, and Smith as historian, contemporary observer and social critic on the other. In the former, 'Smith sees the world as the Design of the Deity, a perfectly harmonious system reflecting the perfection of its designer' (Evensky 1987: 176). In the latter, by contrast, Smith sees the world not in the Design of an ideal vision because 'human frailty leads to distortions in the Deity's Design' (Evensky 1987: 176). For Evensky (1987: 184), then, Smith intentionally makes a clear distinction between an 'ideal world' of the Design and the 'real world' for which he offers a 'practical-prescriptive perspective'. What is particularly worthy of note is that there may be an alteration in Smith's approach concerning this distinction as his thought developed over time. Evensky (1989: 378) suggests that 'in Smith's early work his moral philosophical voice represented humankind as evolving in spite of its flaws toward an approximation of an ideal society'. By contrast, in his later work, Smith 'took on the new role of social critic' as he realised that the power of factions and monopolies were not just historical artefacts, but actually continuously detrimental to the progress of commerce (Evensky 1989: 379).

There is no need to impose on Smith a level of consistency that is unwarranted or to suggest that he ought to be criticised if his thoughts altered due to the adoption of a different 'voice' over time. To do so would be to succumb to Skinner's mythology of coherence and might involve discounting parts of his work. What is more interesting from the perspective of recovering Smith's understanding of the individual is that if it is possible to identify a shift in his thought, or simply the presence of two voices in his work, his conception of the individual moral agent might not be completely static and unified either. If Smith was operating as both a moral philosopher and as a social critic, as Evensky suggests, he may have included a level of malleability into his conception of the individual that depended on historical circumstance. In other words, the particular social rules and values of the society become central. Smith (*TMS* III.4.11) writes:

> When these general rules [formed through attempting to impress upon the opinion of others], indeed, have been formed, when they are universally acknowledged and established, by the concurring sentiments of mankind, we frequently appeal to them as to the standards of judgment, in debating concerning the degree of praise or blame that is due to certain actions of a complicated and dubious nature. They are upon these occasions commonly cited as the ultimate foundations of what is just and unjust in human conduct; and this circumstance seems to have misled several very eminent authors, to draw up their systems in such a manner, as if they had supposed that the original judgments of mankind with regard to right and wrong, were formed like the decisions of a court of judicatory, by considering first the general rule, and then, secondly, whether the particular action under consideration fell properly within its comprehension.

This has important implications for considering individual behaviour as the outcome of a sympathetic procedure that takes place in society, discussed below, as opposed to a transcendental standard of moral judgement. As Smith (*TMS* VII. iv.6) himself writes, ethics is 'a science which . . . does not admit of the most accurate precision'. Indeed this leads Vivienne Brown (1994: 75 emphasis added) to make the argument that in *TMS* Smith's 'ideal moral agent . . . is not the unified, integral moral agent such as we see in the case of the ideal Stoic man, the "fully furnished and completed being" of the monologic hero, but in some respects is *a more fractured and struggling moral being*'. This is a point to which I return, for it alludes to how Smith's individual might be understood as *a site at which* judgement and standards of ethics come to be interactively formed and contested. A sensibility to sympathy might be developed as a form of analysing and providing alternatives to existing understandings of market-oriented behaviour in political economy.

Smith's 'politics'

An attempt to get a grasp of Smith's intentions does not become that much more straightforward by considering his 'politics' in the narrow sense of the term. Yet, as Donald Winch (1978) shows, a consideration of his thought along these lines can be very revealing in terms of locating it in its linguistic and historical context. Winch (1978: 141) claims that Smith's many criticisms of all 'interest groups' in society make it extremely difficult to categorise his politics: he could be construed as anything from a 'nostalgic Tory' to 'a pioneer theorist of labour exploitation along Marxian lines'. Indeed, as Fitzgibbons (1995: 70) points out, it is possible to identify Smith as a 'revolutionary', but the issue with this is that at his time 'collectivism was a right-wing doctrine that favoured the social and religious power structure, whereas liberalism meant subverting that structure and introducing radical social change'. In any case, for Winch (1978: 142), one must not, as many economists and historians of economic thought tend to do, place meanings developed in the nineteenth century and after to the less familiar eighteenth-century concepts that make up Smith's work.

Striking examples of this kind can be discerned in Michael Fry's (1992) edited collection *Adam Smith's Legacy: His Place in the Development of Modern Economics*, which contains a significant number of Nobel Laureates in Economics reflecting on the 'relevance' of Smith to modern economics to mark the bicentenary of his death. For instance, Paul Samuelson attempts to 'test' the 'findings' of the classical political economists 'with the aid of modern techniques' and discovers that Smith emerges with 'flying colours'; Richard Stone writes about Smith's ideas on 'public economic policy and its limits', claimed to be a 'subject of self-evident interest even two hundred years later'; and James Tobin sets out 'to trace the presence or otherwise of the invisible hand in modern macroeconomics' (Fry 1992: xi–xiii). In light of a Skinnerian perspective, the general tone of this whole collection as a celebration of Smith as the founder of modern economics appears to submit to a mythology of prolepsis. More problematically, picking up on Winch's critique, these contributions tend to fall foul of a mythology of parochialism in the sense that they engage in a process of historical foreshortening whereby ideas and concepts are deemed applicable to the contemporary world at the expense of historicised meaning.

A further problem identified by Winch (1978: 23) is that there is apparent 'underlying agreement' about situating Smith's politics within arguments about an emerging 'liberal capitalist context'. This interpretation of Smith's politics locates him as part of 'a much larger story in which the strength and autonomy of a socio-economic realm variously threatens, limits, or deflects the realm of the political' (Winch 1978: 23). However, in response to this line of thinking, Winch's (1978: 26) central argument is that Smith's style of political analysis cannot be located within the language and categories of the liberal capitalist perspective. Indeed, on his reading, Smith's politics are far more 'problematic than it has been made to appear' (Winch 1978: 26). Most firmly, Winch (1978: 180–181) suggests that:

> Smith did not advocate the establishment of a particular economic order called capitalism; nor did he prize what he set out to analyse, namely commercial society, for the sake of its benefits in the form of democratic freedoms.

In many ways, perhaps the value of Winch's work comes from the way in which he demonstrates exactly who and what Adam Smith *was not*. At the very least, he shows that it is possible to read into Smith's politics elements of a number of positions (Winch 1978: 182). Yet, in doing so, Winch also serves to distance Smith from those interpretations that suggest that he was essentially arguing for a capitalist system as part of a larger liberal capitalist or bourgeois 'tradition' of thought.

On Winch's (1978: 184) reading, there is a significant gulf between Smith's endeavour and those who are commonly regarded as his successors. Put simply, there is not an unbroken tradition of liberalism, or bourgeois ideology, stretching from Locke through Smith and Hume to John Stuart Mill and on to present-day economic science. What is important for my consideration of Smith's understanding of the individual in this regard is that this distances him from any form of Benthamite utilitarianism. Such a position would ignore Smith's understanding of the individual and his conception of sympathy. For instance, a sympathetic sensibility draws attention to how the pursuit of material possessions has less to do with an innate drive to accumulate and more to do with the cultural and ethical construction of vanity in commercial society. This section has indicated what Smith clearly does not stand for, while the final section of this chapter presents a more constructive account of his concept of sympathy.

Smith's sympathy

Understanding sympathy

Building on the account of Smith's socio-linguistic context and intentions given above, I now focus on his understanding of the individual in a more direct sense through his concept of sympathy. In many ways, Smith's use of the term is a reinterpretation of existing uses by his immediate predecessors. In particular, it relates to a transformation of Hutcheson's ideas about moral sense as a mechanism of approbation and disapprobation to a wider theory concerning the individual in society (Peil 1999: 58). In Hutcheson's (2002: 178 emphasis in original) terms:

> If any say, 'this *moral Sense* is not a *Rule*:' What means that Word? It is not a *strait rigid Body*: It is not a *general Proposition, shewing what Means are fit to obtain an end*: It is not a *Proposition, asserting, that a Superior will make those happy who act one way, and miserable who act the contrary way*. If these be the Meanings of *Rule*, it is no *Rule;* yet by reflecting upon it our Understanding may find out a *Rule*. But what *Rule* of Actions can be formed, without Relation to some *End* proposed? Or what *End* can be proposed, without presupposing *Instincts, Desires, Affections*, or a *moral Sense*, it will not be easy to explain.

In many ways Hutcheson uses a 'traditional' conception of sympathy, which is based on a medical account in which it is a sort of 'emotional contagion, whereby the feelings of one individual are transmitted to others' (Force 2003: 31). By contrast Smith thought that people cannot directly access the feelings of others in this way, so he placed a greater emphasis on the role of a 'mental representation of what others are feeling' (Force 2003: 31). Thus Smith moved the concept of sympathy away from an almost chance 'contagion' of feeling, as in Hutcheson, towards a conception of a more active, process-driven mechanism involving the mental representation of another's position and circumstance. As Smith (*TMS* I.i.1.2 emphasis added) writes, 'it is by the *imagination only* that we can form any conception of what are [another person's] sensations'.

Smith's use of the concept of sympathy is also 'significantly more complex than the analogical inference Hume had posited' (Teichgraeber 1986: 135). Indeed in Hume's (1751: 144) understanding, sympathy appears to be a more straightforward sharing of sentiment:

> From this Influence of Cheerfulness, both to communicate itself, and to engage Approbation, we may perceive that there are another Set of Virtues, which, without any Utility or any Tendency to farther Good, either of the Community or of the Possessor, diffuse a Satisfaction on the Beholders, and conciliate Friendship and Regard. Their immediate Sensation, to the Person possessed of them, is agreeable. Others enter into the same Humour, and catch the Sentiment, by a Contagion or natural Sympathy: And as we cannot forbear loving whatever pleases, a kindly Emotion arises towards the Person who communicates so much Delight and Satisfaction.

One way to understand this altering of Hume's understanding is to consider that rather than as the starting point of moral judgement, Smith saw sympathy as 'its very essence' (Teichgraeber 1986: 135). For Smith, an expression of sympathy is not only to *respond* to a particular situation in Hutcheson's sense but also, and more significantly, to enter a process of *judging* what passions and feelings *ought* to be in play in that given situation. What this means, and what is not straightforward to appreciate from a present-day perspective, is that for Smith sympathy is not limited to pity and compassion for the misfortune of others (Peil 1999: 84). Rather, it has a wider meaning expressing the possibility of fellow-feeling with *any* sentiment (*TMS* I.i.1.5).

The contemporary reader might understand Smith's sympathy as something closer to the term 'empathy' or Rousseau's 'identification' highlighted above. As Luc Boltanski (2004: 37 emphasis in original) points out:

> With this premise Smith places himself in the current of Scottish moral philosophy which, in reaction against anthropologies based on selfish interest, especially those of Hobbes and Mandeville, and also in seeking to overcome interpretations of Lockean sensualism which lead towards sceptical subjectivism, makes the 'moral sense' (Shaftesbury) a 'faculty of the human mind' (Hutcheson). *Sympathy* is the natural faculty without which an individual could not know or be interested in someone else.

It is also crucial to recognise that Smith's sympathy does not refer to specific 'motives' of behaviour or action: the fellow-feeling expressed in the term is of a different *kind* to concepts such as altruism or egoism. By contrast, it is a great deal closer to the 'intersubjective grounds' on which assessments of behaviour and action are considered in terms of *ideas about* benevolence, prudence, justice, self-control and so on (Peil 1999: 59). Indeed the intersubjective nature of sympathy is made clear by Smith (*TMS* II.ii.2.1) when he emphasises the dynamics of the relationship between a concern for oneself and a concern for others:

> There can be no proper motive for hurting our neighbour, there can be no incitement to do evil to another, which mankind will go along with, except just indignation for evil which that other has done to us. To disturb his happiness merely because it stands in the way of our own, to take from him what is of real use to him merely because it may be of equal or of more use to us, or to indulge, in this manner, at the expence of other people, the natural preference which every man has for his own happiness above that of other people, is what no impartial spectator can go along with.

Thus, Smith's sympathy seems to have built into it recognition of the interactivity between concern for oneself and concern for others. In other words, Smith views sympathy as a potential principle in people that 'fosters a continuous relationship between spectators and agents, a natural interdependence among social beings . . . [It] not only accounts for moral judgement, but more importantly perhaps, it influences human behaviour *ex ante*' (Montes 2004: 55). Another way of expressing this is that Smith provides an account of the 'macro-foundations of microeconomics' (Vaggi 2004: 27). People tend to be guided and constrained by a particular social or macro-structure such that, in certain important ways, 'rules and norms of human conduct derive' from society (Vaggi 2004: 27). This relationship might be understood as an interactive process between the individual, on the one hand, and broader social groups and systems, on the other, in which sympathy comes to generate both a matrix of judgement and standards of ethics at the individual level.

The individual in society

That sympathy can be understood as an interactive process also highlights the way in which Smith conceived of the individual not in an atomistic sense, but as an individual in society. According to Andrew Skinner (1996: 59 emphasis added), in *TMS*, 'Smith's argument is in large measure designed to explain the manner in which we form judgements as to the propriety or merit of actions taken by ourselves or others, *and that such judgements always have a "social" reference*'. On Smith's account, then, 'man experiences himself as an individual in relation to society' and, at the same time, 'society itself is experienced as a whole comprised of social processes which – by means of social values and rules – give sense, meaning and guidance to the feelings, thoughts, and behaviour and actions of its individual members' (Peil 1999: 58). From this sympathy perspective, the individual and society in some sense presuppose each other as individuals experience and understand themselves only against a background of interaction with other people and society more generally (Peil 1999: 64).

However, an important question this begs is where the boundaries of any particular society lie: who is to be included and excluded? For Smith, on the one hand, there is clearly a sense that a person's sympathy can only extend so far because there are certain 'distance-decay' dynamics that limit the ability to sympathise with others. Smith writes (*TMS* III.3.4):

> Let us suppose that the great empire of China, with all its myriads of inhabitants, was suddenly swallowed up by an earthquake, and let us consider how a man of humanity in Europe, who had no sort of connexion with that part of the world, would be affected upon receiving intelligence of this dreadful calamity. He would, I imagine, first of all, express very strongly his sorrow for the misfortune of that unhappy people, he would make many melancholy reflections upon the precariousness of human life, and the vanity of all the labours of man, which could thus be annihilated in a moment. He would too, perhaps, if he was a man of speculation, enter into many reasonings concerning the effects which this disaster might produce upon the commerce of Europe, and the trade and business of the world in general. And when all this fine philosophy was over, when all these humane sentiments had been once fairly expressed, he would pursue his business or his pleasure, take his repose or his diversion, with the same ease and tranquillity, as if no such accident had happened. The most frivolous disaster which could befal himself would occasion a more real disturbance. If he was to lose his little finger to-morrow, he would not sleep to-night; but, provided he never saw them, he will snore with the most profound security over the ruin of a hundred millions of his brethren, and the destruction of that immense multitude seems plainly an object less interesting to him, than this paltry misfortune of his own.

On the other hand, as this passage continues, Smith (*TMS* III.3.4) seems to hold out hope for the 'impartial spectator' – a key part of the sympathy procedure discussed below – in *extending* the scope of sympathy:

> To prevent, therefore, this paltry misfortune to himself, would a man of humanity be willing to sacrifice the lives of a hundred millions of his brethren, provided he had never seen them? Human nature startles with horror at the thought, and the world, in its greatest depravity and corruption, never produced such a villain as could be capable of entertaining it. But what makes this difference? When our passive feelings are almost always so sordid and so selfish, how comes it that our active principles should often be so generous and so noble? When we are always so much more deeply affected by whatever concerns ourselves, than by whatever concerns other men; what is it which prompts the generous, upon all occasions, and the mean upon many, to sacrifice their own interests to the greater interests of others? . . . It is reason, principle, conscience, the inhabitant of the breast, the man within, the great judge and arbiter of our conduct. It is he who, whenever we are about to act so as to affect the happiness of others, calls to us, with a voice capable of astonishing the most presumptuous of our passions, that we are but one of the multitude, in no respect better than any other in it; and that when we prefer ourselves so shamefully and so blindly to others, we become the proper objects of resentment, abhorrence, and execration. It is from him only that we learn the real littleness of ourselves, and of whatever relates to ourselves, and the natural misrepresentations of self-love can be corrected only by the eye of this impartial spectator.

On first glance, there appears to be no reason why sympathy is always limited to within a particular community for Smith: it could potentially be global in reach. Yet such a suggestion contradicts Russell Nieli's (1986: 622) 'spheres of intimacy' argument, which shows, through reference to Smith's own texts, that the 'outermost circle with which a person is connected, according to Smith, is the sphere of his nation-state'. The key part of the passage Nieli refers to is when he writes:

> The state or sovereignty in which we have been born and educated, and under the protection of which we continue to live, is in ordinary cases, the greatest society upon whose happiness or misery, our good or bad conduct can have much influence.
>
> (*TMS* VI.ii.2.1)

For Nieli (1986: 623), Smith's position is that it is 'useless' for someone to be concerned with others outside the nation-state as 'they are both physically and emotionally at a great distance from one's own life . . . and one cannot naturally sympathize with such people to the same degree that one can with people within one's own sphere of action'. Nieli (1986: 623) rightly recognises that Smith was writing 'at a time when communications and transportation were considerably different from what they are today' – and it is indeed important not to read him out of context. However, the real crux of the issue appears not to be national borders or identities as such, but the ability to have, and comprehend having, an 'influence' upon the lives of others.

The key restriction, then, is always *knowing* about others' actions, circumstance or suffering: people are simply more likely to share sympathetic moments with those with whom they have more frequent and meaningful interaction. Yet arguably this does not necessarily exclude an expansion of knowing others because in Smith, as in Hume, 'distance is overcome by a deliberate act of imagination' (Boltanski 2004: 38). Indeed, Boltanski (2004: 49) claims that it is this very 'possibility of accounting for a sympathy which can overcome the obstacle of distance' that leads Smith to use his Chinese earthquake example.

Furthermore, according to Boltanski (2004: 37), the imaginative act on behalf of what he frequently referred to interchangeably as a 'bystander' and 'spectator' suggests that:

> Smith did not seek to emphasise the tension between a necessarily local face to face encounter, as in the figure of compassion, and the conveyance over distance of a representation of suffering that is required by a general politics of pity, as if the second figure could be directly derived, smoothly and uninterruptedly, by extension of the first.

Particularly relevant here is the idea that individual behaviour and social processes are understood to be governed by meanings and values that are generated and observed by people as part of a longing for what Smith terms 'mutual sympathy'. In his section 'Of the Pleasure of Mutual Sympathy', Smith (*TMS*

I.i.2.1) writes about this in terms of the potential pleasure to be derived from 'fellowfeeling', the tendency in people to feel pleased when they come to share a particular judgement. In a sense, then, mutual sympathy refers to 'the metaphor through which Smith expresses his fundamental belief that our feelings, thoughts and behaviour are related to an intersubjectively based framework of rules and values' (Peil 1999: 88). In his own words, Smith (*TMS* II.ii.2.1) is clear about the process through which rules and values are socially constructed among individuals in society:

> Though it may be true, therefore, that every individual, in his own breast, naturally prefers himself to all mankind, yet he dares not look mankind in the face, and avow that he acts according to this principle. He feels that in this preference they can never go along with him, and that how natural soever it may be to him, it must always appear excessive and extravagant to them. When he views himself in the light in which he is conscious that others will view him, he sees that to them he is but one of the multitude in no respect better than any other in it. If he would act so as that the impartial spectator may enter into the principles of his conduct, which is what of all things he has the greatest desire to do, he must, upon this, as upon all other occasions, humble the arrogance of his self-love, and bring it down to something which other men can go along with.

For Smith, then, '[s]ympathy forms the foundation of moral judgement by devising criteria of acceptable action after repeated similar observations and after determination of community judgement' (Weinstein 2006: 86). In this sense, Smith's sympathy is very much 'dependent on context' while being both 'contextual and perspectival': it is a 'constant balancing act between self-knowledge and knowledge of others' (Weinstein 2006: 86).

It is possible to suggest that for Smith, given the way in which he understands sympathy to operate as part of a process by which individuals judge their own behaviour and that of others, the rules and values that govern any particular society are subject to contestation and subject to change over time. If a process of socialisation is taken seriously in this way, agency is ultimately understood to be changeable according to specific historical situation: 'man is not an invariant element of nature, a stylised "agent" with a predetermined and constant behaviour' (Vaggi 2004: 31). Along these lines, Peil (1999: 63 emphasis in original) suggests that Smith's understanding of sympathy allows for ethico-political concepts such as moral behaviour or social justice to have a meaning and content that 'changes with the *ages and periods of society*'. This is also emphasised by Vivienne Brown (1994: 37) who suggests that for Smith moral discourse is very much part of 'social discourse' because 'it is learnt as part of social life and it partakes of the same motivations and forms of persuasion that constitute the socialised communication of everyday life'. Again, this is in stark contrast to the economistic idea of behaviour and action as governed by certain fundamental causal laws. Sympathy illustrates how ethics and politics might come to be interactively formed between the individual and the broader social system; yet, rather than being fixed, this interaction is an on-going process of generating a matrix of judgement and standards still ultimately negotiated at the individual level.

Sympathy as procedure

One insightful way to think about Smith's sympathy along these lines, I suggest, is to view it as involving a 'processual' conceptualisation of the ethico-political individual rather than an understanding of the individual that outlines transcendental or ahistorical standards and laws of behaviour. This is because, as Teichgraeber (1986: 131) points out, Smith views moral judgements as essentially 'comparisons between, on the one hand, particular feelings of people whose conduct we observe, and, on the other, our own sympathetic responses as spectators of their conduct'. This is related to how he frequently speaks of the sympathetic process of entering into a position of an 'impartial spectator' in order to be able to form an opinion on the situation of others. Smith (*TMS* I.i.5.4) writes:

> The insolence and brutality of anger, in the same manner, when we indulge its fury without check or restraint, is, of all objects, the most detestable. But we admire that noble and generous resentment which governs its pursuit of the greatest injuries, not by the rage which they are apt to excite in the breast of the sufferer, but by the indignation which they naturally call forth in that of the impartial spectator; which allows no word, no gesture, to escape it beyond what this more equitable sentiment would dictate; which never, even in thought, attempts any greater vengeance, nor desires to inflict any greater punishment, than what every indifferent person would rejoice to see executed.

For Smith (*TMS* III.3.1), then, the procedural mechanism for making these judgements comes through a sympathy procedure; the interaction between the individual and broader social systems as interpersonal ethics come to be negotiated:

> But though the approbation of his own conscience can scarce, upon some extraordinary occasions, content the weakness of man; though the testimony of the supposed impartial spectator, of the great inmate of the breast, cannot always alone support him; yet the influence and authority of this principle is, upon all occasions, very great; and it is only by consulting this judge within, that we can ever see what relates to ourselves in its proper shape and dimensions; or that we can ever make any proper comparison between our own interests and those of other people.

It is possible to take Smith's sympathy in various directions. Interestingly, Amartya Sen (2009: 70) invokes Smith's reasoning here involving the impartial spectator because he claims it allows for 'incompleteness in social assessment' while 'still providing guidance in important problems of social justice'. This is part of Sen's (2009: 70) suggestion that in contemporary questions of justice it is more important to find ways of 'dealing with comparative assessment' rather than identifying 'transcendental solutions'. There is certainly some merit in interpreting Smith's sympathy as part of an active process of comparison. Indeed, following Brown (1994: 25 emphasis added), it is possible to claim that for Smith there is an emphasis on 'seeing, observing, [and] watching from appropriate viewpoints' as these all 'constitute the essence of *an active process of moral judgment* in which the moral agent is absorbed'. The active mental process that Smith (*TMS* III.3.3) describes is as follows:

> Before we can make any proper comparison of those opposite interests, we must change our position. We must view them, neither from our own place nor yet from his, neither with our own eyes nor yet with his, but from the place and with the eyes of a third person, who has no particular connexion with either, and who judges with impartiality between us.

For Smith this active process in which individuals in society take part is one in which imagination plays a central role. Indeed it has been suggested that the 'capacity of imagining oneself in the position of someone else, changing places and personhood, constitutes the main pillar of Smith's moral philosophy' (Montes 2004: 51). Smith (*TMS* I.i.1.4) writes:

> In every passion of which the mind of man is susceptible, the emotions of the by-stander always correspond to what, by bringing the case home to himself, he imagines should be the sentiments of the sufferer.

Thus Smith (*TMS* I.i.4.6) is very clear that sympathy is 'founded' on an 'imaginary change of situation', a theme to which I return below. As D.D. Raphael (2007: 13) has it:

> An explicit exercise of the imagination is certainly part of Smith's account of moral judgement. In that context imagining oneself in someone else's place is more pervasive than the actual experience of sympathy.

Indeed Raphael (2007: 15 emphasis in original) further suggests that for Smith imagination plays 'an elaborate double role':

> [W]e have to imagine what spectators would feel if they imagined themselves in our situation; and, while sympathy, or the lack of it, comes into the picture in characterizing the feeling of the spectators, that feeling is an *imagined* feeling; and indeed, in the end, spectators in the real world are replaced by an *imagined* impartial spectator conjured up 'in the breast'.

One consequence that might stem from this understanding of sympathy involving a process of imagining situation and circumstance is that the matrix of judgement and standards of ethics that are produced at the individual level contain within them a certain level of continuous contestability. In fact, Smith (*TMS* I.i.4.7) makes clear that there is always likely to be a level of variation in what might be thought of as the 'outcome' of the sympathetic process:

> What they [the spectator] feel, will, indeed, always be, in some respects, different from what he [the person principally concerned] feels, and compassion can never be exactly the same with original sorrow; because the secret consciousness that the change of situations, from which the sympathetic sentiment arises, is but imaginary, not only lowers it in degree, but, in some measure, varies it in kind, and gives it a quite different modification. These two sentiments, however, may, it is evident, have such a correspondence with one another, as is sufficient for the harmony of society. Though they will never be unisons, they may be concords, and this is all that is wanted or required.

To understand certain norms, values, passions and so on, as the outcome of a sympathy procedure is to accept the possibility of many potential variations in human behaviour (Vaggi 2004: 30). Charles Griswold's (1999: 165) point that Smith was 'consciously nonfoundationalist' in his approach to moral sentiments is illuminating here: Smith provides what is a situational account of the formation of ethical judgement. Another insightful way of expressing this is the notion that Smith held 'an essential attachment to *conventionalist* ontology: individuals discover their sense of who they are and of who they should aim to be through being called to pass judgement on the propriety of other people's conduct' (Watson 2013: 19 emphasis added).

Concluding remarks

In summary, it is possible to suggest that Smith's understanding of sympathy as constituting an active process of both conceptualising and assessing individual behaviour, action, and suffering contains within it a certain level of contestability. It relates to *other people's* opinion; to the social construction of rules and values *in society*; and is part of an *active process* of judgement and comparison. Thus, Smith's conception of sympathy allows for an understanding of the individual as a site at which ethico-political questions come to be resolved, at least temporarily, as part of the interactive generation of a matrix of judgement and standards of ethics.

In this chapter, I have constructed an account of Smith's sympathy that remains attentive to his intentions in writing and his socio-linguistic context. I will further develop this in the next chapter in relation to present-day understandings of the individual. I conclude by reiterating the point that it provides a promising way of conceiving market-oriented behaviour in a distinctly different way to economistic understandings. It also offers a platform for critiques of those understandings. A sympathetic sensibility draws attention to the ethical constitution of individual market-oriented behaviour in ways that many perspectives cannot grasp, often because of the lasting hold over the ethical imagination of Mandeville's 'interest doctrine', which Smith showed to be redundant.

One potential danger here is that by focusing principally on an account of Smith's sympathy, I may inadvertently follow some Smith studies scholars (e.g. Macfie 1967; Raphael and Macfie 1982) who appear to uncritically reproduce Skinner's mythologies of doctrine and coherence (Chapter 1) by suggesting that his concept of sympathy holds the 'real' essence of the entirety of his work, to the expense of certain aspects of *WN*, for example. However, my claim is more modest. Rather than attempting to provide a doctrinal account of his entire oeuvre, or a definitive 'solution' to the Adam Smith Problem, I merely wish to present an account of his engagement with questions about individual moral agency at this stage and on this subject, when suitably historicised in its socio-linguistic context, the sympathy procedure is clearly fundamental. The account presented here will be used in the following chapter as the basis on which to present a dialogic conversation between Smith's texts and the 'economistic liberalism' of governance today.

3 Sympathy and economism in Anglo-American finance

This chapter stages an encounter between Smith's sympathetic political economy and contemporary economistic liberalism. In a further attempt to sustain an historicised engagement the chapter is organised around the themes Smith uses at the beginning of *TMS*, which is the most important point at which the concept of sympathy is set out (Otteson 2002: 13). The chapters of *TMS* in question are entitled 'Of Sympathy', 'Of the Pleasure of Mutual Sympathy' and 'Of the Manner In Which We Judge of the Propriety Or Impropriety of the Affections of Other Men, By Their Concord Or Dissonance With Our Own'. Somewhat abbreviated here the themes (1) sympathy, (2) mutual sympathy and (3) the sympathy procedure are juxtaposed with three significant aspects of finance implicated in the GFC. In turn, for reasons expanded upon below, these are questions about the place of (1) asset-based welfare, (2) credit risk management and (3) personal indebtedness in Anglo-American societies. To introduce these issues at a conceptual level I critically engage political economy literature, broadly defined, including from IPE, economics, sociology and social theory.

In the first section I focus directly on what sympathy implies for conceptualising the individual under contemporary economic governance. By 'the individual', I refer to the individual subject or agent, understood in broad terms as both a cultural product of a particular society and as an analytical subject of a perspective of thought. A sympathetic political economy, as an approach to understanding market-oriented behaviour, gives a complex account of how ethico-political conventions come to be interactively formed at the level of the individual. By contrast, the individual of economistic liberalism tends to take the ideal of instrumental rationality par excellence: *homo economicus*. In the context of the GFC, I use a discussion of programmes of asset-based welfare to explore this difference and indicate the potential crisis of ethical imagination at the heart of economistic liberalism to be investigated in later chapters.

In the second section I build on this account to juxtapose the notion of *mutual* sympathy with economistic liberalism to show how the latter tends to address political economy questions by *individualising* them at the expense of contestable interpersonal ethics. I use a discussion of credit risk management, broadly understood, to illustrate this claim. In the final section, I focus on the continual contestability of the very content of sympathy in the sympathy procedure. I suggest that Smith's sympathy constitutes an active *process* of both conceptualising and assessing ethico-political dilemmas that contains within it a certain level of ongoing contestability. By contrast, economistic liberalism ultimately *depoliticises* political economy questions, or at least attempts to, by denying contestable ethics at the individual level. In the context of the GFC, I use a discussion of personal indebtedness to illustrate this claim and again indicate the potential crisis of ethics at the heart of economistic liberalism to be expanded upon in Chapters 4 and 5.

I do not expect to find straightforward 'answers' in the work of Smith. As has been stressed, his political economy is 'of another time' in the sense that it is simply not possible to make a direct translation of Smith's ideas to contemporary questions. Rather, his concept of sympathy – appropriately historicised and celebrated as 'of another time' – can be used to reflect on how to approach certain contemporary issues. In short, it provides an alternative platform from which to understand the way economistic liberalism works to constitute the individual of the market form and produce standards of market-oriented behaviour. Given that the issues dealt with here relate to how individual behaviour is cultivated in society, they are areas of investigation at least similar in intent to the type of inquiry with which Smith was concerned when he explored the cultivation of moral behaviour in eighteenth-century commercial society.

The conceptual argument, to be interrogated further in the next two chapters, is that in the context of the GFC, the consequences of a crisis of ethical imagination are visible when state programmes promoting asset-based welfare go unquestioned, when risk management is normalised to the everyday, and when creditor-debtor relations are depoliticised. All three of these developments in Anglo-American finance shed light on the crisis of ethics in economistic liberalism. Smith's sympathetic political economy, at the very least, provides a platform for attempts to understand this crisis.

Sympathy and the economism of asset-based welfare

> How selfish soever man may be supposed, there are evidently some principles in his nature, which interest him in the fortune of others, and render their happiness necessary to him, though he derives nothing from it except the pleasure of seeing it.
>
> (*TMS* I.i.1.1)

Alongside a gibe at the interest doctrine of Mandeville, out of which arguably economistic liberalism finds its origin, in the opening to *TMS* Smith presents the essence of his concept of sympathy. The capacity for imagination is central to his account of how moral sentiments are formed:

> As we have no immediate experience of what other men feel, we can form no idea of the manner in which they are affected, but by conceiving what we ourselves should feel in the like situation.
>
> (*TMS* I.i.1.2)

On this premise, Smith introduces his account that subtly shifts the meaning of sympathy away from existing use:

> Pity and compassion are words appropriated to signify our fellow-feeling with the sorrow of others. Sympathy, though its meaning was, perhaps, originally the same, may now, however, without much impropriety, be made use of to denote our fellow-feeling with any passion whatever.
>
> (*TMS* I.i.1.5)

This is Smith's introduction to the concept of sympathy that, building on the previous chapter, I suggest provides a compelling account of how ethico-political conventions might come to be interactively formed and contested at the individual level.

How does this provide a frame of reference with which to engage economistic liberalism? As the foreword to *The Stiglitz Report: Reforming the International Monetary and Financial Systems in the Wake of the Global Crisis* (UN 2010) rightly attests, many of the classical political economists did not assume away the contestability of the individual market agent. For them, people are not the 'socially atomistic construct' who figures in the economistic approaches that populate much of academic economics. Rather, they supposed, market agency cannot be distinguished from the broader ethico-political roles that people perform and the larger ethico-political institutions prevalent in the social world. The *Stiglitz Report* (UN 2010: xxviii) is correct to emphasise this idea because it is important in relation to understanding the crisis:

> As the greatest economic philosophers – whose number surely includes Aquinas, Smith, Marx, and Keynes – have all recognized, homo economicus, the acquisitive, emotionally cardboard, and socially atomistic construct of academic economics is a reductio ad absurdum. They did not merely assume that the ethical vocation of human beings should inform their economic decisions and institutions; they insisted on it, and in ways that today are far out of fashion but are also therefore far more necessary today. It is difficult to read this Report and not come to the conclusion that the Commission members share this perspective.

In a sense, this aspect of the *Stiglitz Report* is indicative of the way in which there is at least a questioning of *homo economicus* from within some areas of the academic economics profession, particularly from more 'heterodox' economists. An example is the work of Paul Ormerod (1994: 35), who suggests that a great merit of a socially-situated approach is that by emphasising 'the fundamental interdependence and interconnectedness of human actions' it provides a 'sharp contrast to the individualistic behavioural model of orthodox economics'.

In recent years, related to this sense of disgruntlement from within the economics profession, there has been significant growth in the field of behavioural economics and the related area of behavioural finance, which also provides a sharp critique of *homo economicus* (Akerlof and Shiller 2009). Self-styled behavioural economists deliberately set out to provide accounts of the social world that take seriously the role of such things as sentiment, emotion and affect in their analysis. In his book on the GFC, *The Subprime Solution*, Robert Shiller (2008: 118–119) claims that behavioural advances in the 'human sciences' mean that there is now 'a much better grasp of how and why people make economic errors, and of how we can restructure institutions to help avoid these errors'.

However, while in general potentially a productive development for economics, and in many ways not necessarily a homogeneous movement, the behavioural turn is actually something of a red herring. For a start, the notion of taking sentiments and emotion seriously is extremely useful, but to treat them as 'factors' among competing influences on market agency does not get to the crux of the issue of the ethico-political constitution of standards of market-oriented behaviour. Smith's sympathy concept certainly allows for sentiments, emotion and affect to run a little deeper into the very constitution of the individual than behavioural analysis seems to allow.

Furthermore, notice how Shiller talks about grasping how and why people make economic 'errors' and how institutions might 'help' correct for them. This is a worldview that is trapped by its other: how to explain why people *do not* conform to *homo economicus* in a world in which ethico-political ends are already defined. It then becomes possible to 'help' people act more rationally, for their own good. Putting aside the inherent paternalism of such an approach, there might be reasons why Shiller does not talk of how advances in understandings of deliberative politics or ethics might be brought into economics. Trapped by the need to confront instrumental rationality, behavioural economics does not allow for such a degree of ethico-political contestation. In a sense, then, such a perspective is just as wedded to assumptions of instrumental rationality as the economistic liberalism that the *Stiglitz Report* criticises: contestable ethics at the individual level are ignored, denied or assumed away.

However, this is not to suggest that the issues with which behavioural economics and especially behavioural finance engage are not significant. Particularly in light of the bursting of the subprime housing bubble at the onset of the GFC, much attention has been given to such ideas as 'irrational exuberance' and 'animal spirits'. The ways in which people observe and base their actions on the actions of others is rightly seen as central to market-oriented behaviour, an insight popularised by John Maynard Keynes. Yet, Smith's sympathetic political economy provides an account of the formation of intersubjective understandings of market-oriented behaviour that does not divorce it from broader ethico-political questions, as economistic approaches tend to do.

The real crux of the issue here is sympathy as an imaginative act. How might norms of appropriate standards of ethico-political behaviour come to be formed, learned and reproduced? To return to Smith's primary assumptions:

> Whatever is the passion which arises from any object in the person principally concerned, an analogous emotion springs up, at the thought of his situation,

> in the breast of every *attentive spectator*. Our joy for the deliverance of those heroes of tragedy or romance who interest us, is as sincere as our grief for their distress, and our fellow-feeling with their misery is not more real than that with their happiness.
>
> (*TMS* I.i.1.4 emphasis added)

Some Smith scholars have called this a 'spectator theory' of morality (Haakonssen 2003: 217; Raphael 2007: 31), yet the most important notion introduced by this 'attentive spectator' is the capacity to imagine and mentally reconstruct the situation of another person in order to engage with questions of interpersonal ethics (Fleischacker and Brown 2010: 5).

Crucially this spectator theory, of which sympathy is a central part, is not just used by Smith in his moral philosophy, but in his political economy as well (Lamb 1974). As has been stressed in Chapter 1, the latter is actually part of the former for Smith; but even so, the idea of constructing and assessing standards of appropriate behaviour can be found at significant points in *WN* as well as *TMS*. To be sure, I am not making the claim that sympathy provides a 'solution' to the Adam Smith Problem, but merely that sympathy-type dynamics have a role to play in *WN* that should not be overlooked (Macfie 1967: 75). For instance, a concern for others' judgment can be found in a discussion of trust. Here Smith (*WN* I.x.b.20) claims that it is the opinion of others that determines whether or not someone is trustworthy in their market-oriented behaviour. He suggests that it is not the 'nature of his trade' but other peoples' 'opinion of his fortune, probity and prudence' that determines their interactions (*WN* I.x.b.20). Likewise, in a discussion of the legitimate gains to be had from various forms of employment, Smith (*WN* I.x.b.25) suggests that people are sometimes offered better pay because they are considered to be engaging in jobs that come attached with a certain degree of 'discredit' in the eyes of the public at large. He goes on to say that it is 'publick opinion' or 'prejudice' that will often alter the amount people are justly viewed as deserving for employing their talents (*WN* I.x.b.25).

Some scholars suggest that *WN* 'presupposes the *framework* of justice' set out in *TMS* (O'Brien 2004: 37 emphasis in original), but I would take a more thoroughgoing stance and point to the centrality of sympathy as an account of the process through which institutions and norms of interpersonal ethics are internalised at the individual level throughout Smith's oeuvre (Teichgraeber 1986: 47). From such as perspective, to follow a sympathetic political economy is to be able to recognise that sympathy dynamics are potentially in operation across a range of social circumstances, not least in the performance of market-oriented behaviour. This leads to a position which takes the starting point of political economy as the recognition that the 'conditions under which market institutions will prove operable are not economic conditions at all, but relate to the constitution of the individual as a moral being' (Watson 2005b: 144).

What type of political economy does this produce? In contrast to economistic liberalism, it is a question of starting from the position of contestable ethics at the individual level. For Smith, as imaginative sympathy is always potentially incomplete and provisional, so too is the construction of standards of market-oriented behaviour. Crucially, he writes, sympathy 'does not hold universally, or with regard to every passion' (*TMS* I.i.1.7). Much depends on a process of negotiation over appropriate standards of action at that very moment of sympathy. To be sure, for Smith, to exercise a capacity for sympathy is to imagine both intent and circumstance as part of a balancing act that is often *imprecise* (Montes 2004: 48):

> Even our sympathy with the grief or joy of another, before we are informed of the cause of either, is always extremely imperfect. General lamentations, which express nothing but the anguish of the sufferer, create rather a curiosity to inquire into his situation, along with some disposition to sympathize with him, than any actual sympathy that is very sensible. Sympathy, therefore, does not arise so much from the view of the passion, as from that of the situation which excites it. We sometimes feel for another, a passion of which he himself seems to be altogether incapable; because, when we put ourselves in his case, that passion arises in our breast from the imagination, though it does not in his from the reality.
>
> (*TMS* I.i.1.9–10)

Drawing these points together, the first step in the argument of this chapter is that to utilise a sympathetic political economy it is necessary to confront contestable ethics at the level of the individual. From such a perspective, political economy and in turn IPE might become 'the study of individual action within the context of institutionalized economic norms' with the important recognition that '[s]ome individuals may internalize those norms to the point at which they are subject to routine reproduction within their conduct, while others will attempt to operate outside them having first accepted the legitimacy of alternative bases of behaviour' (Watson 2005a: 5). The crucial point is that, *contra* assumptions of instrumental rationality, market-oriented behaviour is understood to be both the outcome of and inherently involved with contestable interpersonal ethics. In the context of the GFC as a problem of contemporary economic governance, I use a discussion of recent government programmes of asset-based welfare to illustrate the difference between a sympathetic political economy, which allows for contestable interpersonal ethics, and economistic liberalism, which does not. In the final analysis, the engagement indicates a crisis of ethical imagination at the heart of contemporary economic governance.

Asset-based welfare as a feature of economic governance

The 'financialisation' of Anglo-American economy and society is central to understanding the shift towards programmes of asset-based welfare over the last 30 years or so. Shaun French *et al.* (2011: 2) provide an insightful account of the processes involved. On the one hand, they point to how the term financialisation is used, in basic terms, as a descriptor of a 'transformation in economy and society, whereby the financial sector and financial markets come to occupy a dominant or quasi-dominant position'. This first form mobilises the epochal idea of emergent 'finance-led economic systems' in countries such as the United States and the United Kingdom. On the other hand, French *et al.* (2011: 2) point to how financialisation is also used in a 'narrower sense to describe the processes and effects of the growing power of financial values and technologies on corporations, individuals and households'. Clearly related, this second form emphasises how discourses, interests and expectations come to be realigned by the increasing influence of financial values. As Randy Martin (2002: 12) puts it, financialisation is about asking people 'to accept risks into their homes' and, even though they may not have significant capital, asking them 'to think like capitalists'.

For my discussion of the character of the economistic liberalism in the context of the GFC, it is this second sense in which financialisation is important because it captures something of 'the growing reliance, directly or indirectly, on capital markets, securitized products and contracts, and institutions allied to a transaction-driven mode of financial activity' (French *et al.* 2011: 10). Another term used for this second form is 'coupon pool capitalism', which exists 'where the financial markets are no longer simple intermediaries between household savers and investing firms but act dynamically to shape the behaviour of both firms and households' (Froud *et al.* 2002: 120).

An important aspect of financialisation processes is state restructuring towards a greater reliance on asset-based systems of welfare (Crouch 2009). Such systems involve the use of policy mechanisms to reconfigure notions of personal financial responsibility and a wider restructuring of the welfare state, shifting onus for basic welfare provision from the collective to the individual. As Alan Finlayson (2009: 411) puts it, asset-based welfare policies mark a shift not only in the knowledge and skills deemed necessary to successfully partake in individual savings and investment practices, but also alterations in 'a certain kind of ethos or orientation towards finance and towards the self'. The individualisation of responsibility for welfare is not simply an 'ideological shift', but something more profound: it relates to a reconfigured *ethos* towards finance and the *self*.

The restructuring of the UK and other Western states along asset-based welfare model lines is intimately related to how economistic liberalism comes to inform particular governance attempts to promote market-oriented behaviour. This is because the shift from the collective to the individual relies on certain notions of personal financial responsibility that are deeply ingrained with assumptions about autonomous and instrumentally rational behaviour. In other words, such attempts at reconfiguration of ethos are based on dominant ideas about how people *ought* to behave and see themselves in relation to wider society. Watson (2009a: 199) has shown how the move towards an asset-based system of welfare in the UK assumes 'autonomous selves' based on a particular construction of 'duty' in which the individual is required to internalise nothing more than 'a technical understanding of norms of justice laid down by the broader body of law'. Essentially, then, contestable interpersonal ethics are denied by the production of the model citizen of asset-based welfare. The autonomous selves of such a system are not expected to mentally reconstruct the situation of others through an imaginative sympathetic act, they merely pursue their own ostensive financial gain through investment in housing, for example, as an asset to bring themselves personal financial security. Presumably there simply are none of Smith's 'attentive' spectators in such a financial*ised* society.

In this regard the performance of what has been called financial 'subject positions' is central to financialisation processes (Hall 2011). In Paul Langley's (2006: 922) terms, financial subjects refer to those people 'who, self-consciously and responsibly, further their own security and freedom through the market in general and through the financial markets in particular'. Notably the subprime era seemingly involved the production of ever greater numbers of financial subjects given the spread of such products as interest-only adjustable-rate mortgages that 'enabled the inclusion of borrowers as agents within the mortgage and housing markets' (Langley 2008a: 479). In the contingent context of a rising property market, this 'inclusion' seemed all the more necessary given that gaining 'a foot on the property ladder' was part of the widespread performance of finance (Langley 2008a: 479). Anglo-American governments were quite happy to allow and even promote asset price inflation in housing as it satisfied an attendant homeowner ideology (Hay 2009; Ronald 2008).

Arguably, then, particular character traits are legitimised and cultivated to the exclusion of others in the promotion of asset-based welfare, especially owning one's home as a primary financial asset. State restructuring along these lines involves reconfiguring notions of responsibility more firmly towards 'autonomous' individual selves who act 'rationally' in the face of the demands of model financial citizenship. In this regard, whether in the area of retirement savings, personal investment, or homeownership, what unites the appropriate character traits of a 'good' financial citizen is an economistic emphasis on displaying instrumental rationality. Whereas Smith's sympathetic political economy provides an account of how market-oriented behaviour is made possible that does not assume away contestable ethics and politics, this outlook almost welcomes *homo economicus* as a legitimate blueprint for behaviour. In a sense, then, market-oriented behaviour under asset-based systems of welfare is predefined and absolute: it is presumed that there can be no ethico-political contestation through the capacity to perform a sympathetic imaginative act.

However, this aspect of financialisation was seemingly the most threatened by the GFC (Aalbers 2008). After all it was the US subprime mortgage sector in which the crisis originated, a site of finance deeply intertwined with the promotion of homeownership (Nesvetailova 2010: 86). Therefore, in certain respects, the GFC can be thought of as bringing asset-based welfare and the financial individual at least potentially into doubt. In Finlayson's (2009: 416) terms, the subprime crisis 'deals a blow' to the whole ethos that the UK government sought to instil in the nation. How could excesses occur if people were acting as good financial citizens? Were people not acting responsibly?

Interestingly the behavioural finance literature (e.g. Akerlof and Shiller 2009) that has blossomed in response to the crisis reaffirms an economistic mode of reasoning: people need to be better financial subjects, they need to act *more* like good economistic individuals, understand risks better, not take on such unsustainable levels of debt, and so on. Notably, the basic point is that financialisation is essentially a 'good' thing, so rather than question it the task is to make it more efficient. As Shiller (2008: 119–120 emphasis in original) claims: 'We have a comparable opportunity today with the advent of behavioral economics and behavioral finance, which have the potential to facilitate exciting advances in *financial* engineering'. There is thus continued faith in the 'improvement' of individual behaviour to make it conform to economistic lines: *Nudge* (Thaler and Sunstein 2008), after all, is about 'nudging' people in the 'right' direction.

Read through the lens of a sympathetic political economy, the major flaw of the economistic accounts that legitimate financialisation tendencies, and in the behavioural response to the GFC, is that they attempt to exclude contestable interpersonal ethics. In the process of cultivating autonomous individuals through asset-based systems of welfare, '[w]hat gets lost . . . are the multiple projections of self and other which for Smith worked together in an iterative process that produced the ability to exercise real fellow-feeling' (Watson 2009a: 208). Certainly there is a paternalistic aspect to such systems given that they are 'about being told what to do and following that advice accordingly, not learning what to do through the agential self-actuation of the relational self' (Watson 2009a: 205). Put simply, asset-based systems of welfare tend to promote a conception of model citizenship that appears to deny or simply ignore the capacity people have to negotiate interpersonal ethics through engaging in imaginative sympathetic acts.

However, even though the economistic ethos of asset-based welfare systems can be understood in this way, it does not mean that market-oriented behaviour as it is actually experienced is always completely and successfully constituted in financialised terms. Indeed performances of the financial subject are best understood not as complete or final, but as one among many possible performances of finance. They are always revisable and open to contestation and subversion through political action. As Rob Aitken (2007: 13) argues, a focus on 'the ways in which "finance" is "performed" can help facilitate a certain kind of critique by provoking analyses that conceive of capital as a historically specific and politically malleable set of practices; a set of practices in which "we," as everyday actors, are deeply implicated'. This theme is one to which I return in Chapter 6 because it picks up on the idea of ongoing contestable ethics at the individual level, as a sympathetic political economy more adequately recognises than economistic liberalism.

Overall, asset-based systems of welfare represent an aspect of financialisation that can be read as an attempt to exclude interpersonal ethics from market-oriented behaviour by inducing an economistic and autonomous individual detached from the rest of society. That the model financial citizen is made up by many of the character traits of *homo economicus* is no coincidence because, as I explore in the following chapter, it is economistic perspectives, behavioural or otherwise, that largely provide the blueprint for regulatory forms of economic governance. In a sense, then, the shift to asset-based welfare in Anglo-America embodies the ethos of economistic liberalism. Yet in the context of the GFC, Smith's sympathetic political economy indicates how this economism is ultimately flawed. To take Smith's ideas about imaginative sympathetic acts seriously is to recognise that questions of interpersonal ethics are not predetermined as the economistic ethos of asset-based welfare appears to presume. In Chapters 5 and 6, I return to the theme of asset-based welfare at the levels of regulatory and everyday finance respectively, in order to further explore this potential crisis of ethical imagination at the heart of economistic liberalism.

Mutual sympathy and the individualisation of risk

I now turn to Smith's notion of mutual sympathy to explore more precisely the mechanism through which he accounts for the formation of interpersonal ethics. On one simplified level, mutual sympathy points to the importance of shared norms and understandings of appropriate behaviour, which are formed and experienced in society (Macfie 1967: 83; Skinner 1996: 59). Smith (*TMS* I.i.2.1) explains the process by assuming that people find pleasure in experiencing fellow-feeling:

> whatever may be the cause of sympathy . . . nothing pleases us more than to observe in other men a fellow-feeling with all the emotions of our own breast; nor are we ever so much shocked as by the appearance of the contrary.

This account actually forms part of another attack by Smith (*TMS* I.i.2.1) on the interest doctrine, in which he claims that the derivation of pleasure through fellow-feeling is nothing to do with 'self-interested' considerations.

For Smith (*TMS* I.i.2.2) people derive gratification from a more specific 'correspondence of the sentiments of others with our own', as opposed to an expectation of assistance to suit their self-interest. This possible process of constructing interpersonal ethics through an essential *sociality* tends to be denied in economistic approaches. In many respects economic sociology has come to represent a direct critique of mainstream economics, especially its foundations built on a narrow utilitarian conception of instrumentally rational behaviour (Hirsch *et al.* 1990). From many perspectives in economic sociology, economics can only ever offer a partial account of 'the economy' because it is unable to explain the interactive relationship between, and mutually constituted nature of, economy and society (Swedberg *et al.* 1990). Indeed it is commonly said that a defining feature of economic sociology, found in the work of Max Weber and Emile Durkheim for instance, is a rejection of the economistic standpoint on society that views interaction as founded purely on competing economic interests and the struggle for economic wants (Holton 1992: 181). Incidentally, however, in the process of providing a critique of narrow utilitarian conceptions of economic behaviour, economic sociology tends to construct the work of Smith as its 'other': as the archetypal and foundational work of a scholar of the mainstream economics paradigm (e.g. Block 1990; Holton 1992). In this sense, it is guilty of following some of the economistic historiography of Smith that is found in IPE and political economy more broadly.

Nevertheless, the way in which economic sociology provides a critique of economistic liberalism by insisting on a more socially oriented account of individual behaviour in many ways parallels Smith's emphasis on people's capacity for mutual sympathy taking place *within* society. After all, for Smith, such a capacity develops in society as people come into social contact with the moral standards that are embodied in social institutions (Macfie 1967: 95). On his account, experience of life in society both enables and potentially improves the capacity for imaginative sympathy. In Smith's own terms, he later refers to society as something of a 'mirror' that allows the individual to view 'the propriety and impropriety of his own passions; the beauty and deformity of his own mind' (*TMS* III.i.3). In *WN* as well, he alludes to how 'observation' and 'censure' by others in society acts as an important conditioning influence on conduct (*WN* II.iii.40).

What it means to live in a particular kind of society was a foundational issue for Smith, just as it was for many sociologically inspired scholars who came after him. Karl Polanyi (2001), for instance, was interested in how the increasing control of the economic system by the market had huge consequences for society as a whole. The danger, he insisted, was that in such a society '[i]nstead of economy being embedded in social relations, social relations are embedded in the economic system' (Polanyi 2001: 57). Smith did not have the same terminology available to him, but there is certainly a degree of similarity between his sociological account of market-oriented behaviour and Polanyi's (2001: 71) concern for how the shift towards self-regulating markets 'represented a complete transformation in the structure of society'. Polanyi provided an astute institutional critique of 'the market' and like Smith he would not have conceived of market-oriented behaviour as anything other than very specific to particular historical and cultural determinants.

Georg Simmel offers a different approach in his classic study of *How is Society Possible?* that also emulates some of Smith's sociological concern for the place of the individual in relation to society. Simmel (1910: 376–377) emphasises the fact that 'knowing about the other as the associated' is part of what constitutes society in the minds of individuals. Notably, he also argues that rather than 'in the abstract . . . this recognizing of the whole complex as a society usually occurs with reference to particular concrete content' (Simmel 1910: 376–377). This again appears to echo Smith's socially situated account of how individual behaviour is made possible and moral standards are developed. It also relates to Smith's arguments about how it is the consideration of specific situations that allows for sympathy to be developed. Interestingly in this regard, Smith (*TMS* I.i.4.9) suggests that 'the effect of sympathy is instantaneous' between people who know each other's circumstances well, while there is expected to be 'less sympathy' between common acquaintances, and 'still less sympathy' between an 'assembly of strangers'. Yet, even among strangers, the presence of other people allows for the sympathy procedure to operate through imagining appropriate behaviour in any particular circumstance (*TMS* I.i.4.9).

An important point at this stage is that Smith's sympathy is not just about a straightforward notion of people being sociable or feeling compassion for those less well off. In fact, Thomas Wilson (1976: 94) makes the argument that rather than 'opposite poles', sympathy can be the 'basis for individualism'. Smith's position in this regard is quite clearly expressed:

> Every man, as the Stoics used to say, is first and principally recommended to his own care; and every man is certainly, in every respect, fitter and abler to take care of himself than of any other person. Every man feels his own pleasures and his own pains more sensibly than those of other people. The former are the original sensations; the latter the reflected or sympathetic images of those sensations. The former may be said to be the substance; the latter the shadow.
>
> (*TMS* VI.ii.1.1)

In a sense, then, sympathy is about deliberation, contestation and specific moments of mutual sympathy. For Smith the person principally concerned, 'the sufferer' in other words, is aware that an 'imaginary change of situation' does not allow for a complete appreciation of their suffering to the same 'degree of passion' (*TMS* I.i.4.7). Yet, because the sufferer desires 'a more complete sympathy', that is they want the observer to understand and in some sense share their suffering, they may attempt to moderate or 'flatten' their emotions by 'lowering [their] passion to that pitch . . . spectators are capable of going along with' (*TMS* I.i.4.7). This related point about understanding how moments of mutual sympathy are arrived at again indicates how sympathy is very much a question of 'balance' or a process of negotiating appropriate forms of sentiment and behaviour (Weinstein 2006: 86).

Rather than as an other-directed ontology, or the more obvious point that individuals form understandings of appropriate behaviour by living in society, sympathy might be thought of in terms of 'the society in the individual'. Clearly, though, Smith is not merely referring to a respect for public opinion (Wilson 1976: 74). More fundamentally, as referred to in the previous chapter, the individual and society in some sense presuppose each other in a sympathetic political economy (Peil 1999: 58). What is more, individual selfhood *and* social processes are understood to be governed by meanings and values that are generated and observed by people as part of a presumed *longing* for mutual sympathy:

> As the person who is principally interested in any event is pleased with our sympathy, and hurt by the want of it, so we, too, seem to be pleased when we are able to sympathize with him, and to be hurt when we are unable to do so. We run not only to congratulate the successful, but to condole with the afflicted; and the pleasure which we find in the conversation of one whom in all the passions of his heart we can entirely sympathize with, seems to do more than compensate the painfulness of that sorrow with which the view of his situation affects us.
>
> (*TMS* I.i.2.6)

Mutual sympathy is here a metaphor for an 'intersubjectively based framework of rules and values' (Peil 1999: 88). To be sure, again, sympathy works in a similar way in *WN* as well by giving people a capacity to think in terms outside of the self (Lamb 1974: 678–679). For instance, in Smith's discussion of basic standards of living in a society:

> Servants, labourers and workmen of different kinds, make up the far greater part of every great political society. But what improves the circumstances of the greater part can never be regarded as an inconveniency to the whole. No society can surely be flourishing and happy, of which the far greater part of the members are poor and miserable. It is but equity, besides, that they who feed, cloath and lodge the whole body of the people, should have such a share of the produce of their own labour as to be themselves tolerably well fed, cloathed and lodged.
>
> (*WN* I.viii.36)

Likewise, Smith discusses the way in which someone in the public eye must be attentive to society's mores and values (*WN* V.i.g.12). They must regulate their 'conduct', he suggests, because their position depends on a degree of 'respect' and the 'the general consent' of society (*WN* V.i.g.12). Indeed, it is possible to suggest that for Smith, '[s]ympathy forms the foundation of moral judgement by devising criteria of acceptable action after repeated similar observations and after determination of community judgement' (Weinstein 2006: 86). In this sense, Smith's sympathy is very much 'dependent on context' while being both 'contextual and perspectival' – it is a 'constant balancing act between self-knowledge and knowledge of others' (Weinstein 2006: 86).

Drawing these points together, the concept of mutual sympathy presents a very different picture of interpersonal ethics compared to economistic liberalism. As sociologists point out well, the latter tends to build from the assumption of narrow utilitarian understandings of instrumental rationality, which ultimately means that political economy problems are solved by individualising them and denying society. From a sympathetic political economy perspective, though, the most pressing problem with this is that the denial of society serves to erroneously deny contestable interpersonal ethics. In the context of the GFC, a consideration of how notions of 'credit risk', broadly understood, come to be constructed and legitimised in society presents a telling example of how the notion of sympathy sheds light on the potential crisis of ethical imagination at the heart of economistic perspectives.

Credit risk as a feature of economic governance

There is no single thing called 'risk'. In the realm of financial practice, credit, liquidity and market risk are conceptually distinct. Risk usually appears as a concept that attempts to define the unknown in terms of a probabilistic calculation (Best 2010). Yet the characteristic of different levels of risk does not really refer to features inherent in a financial asset itself because much depends on *who* is holding that asset and their capacity to 'manage' or 'cope' with it (Warwick Commission 2009: 16). In this sense, risk itself depends on the behaviour of holders of risk, which is arguably an inherently interpersonal matter. Tony Porter (2005: 185) notes that political conflict can be associated with financial risk practices because of the way in which they transform 'earlier patterns of mutual obligation into a cold statistical socialization of risks'. The individualisation of responsibility that comes with moves towards risk playing a greater role in society is at once liberating for some and presents to other people 'a terrible burden of dealing with hardships alone, without the help of others' (Porter 2005: 185).

How financial risk is understood, managed and coped with has to be negotiated in society and thus might be thought of as subject to ethico-political contestation. As Ulrich Beck (1992: 23) insists, the inescapability of interpretation makes risk more broadly infinitely malleable and 'open to social definition and construction'. According to this socio-cultural understanding of risk, it is 'manufactured, not only through the application of technologies, but also in the making of sense and by the technological sensibility of a potential harm, danger or threat' (Adam and van Loon 2000: 2). While the application of particular forms of expertise and knowledge, often sophisticated mathematical modelling, may furnish certain risk management practices with legitimacy, it is important to pay close attention to the contested nature of *who* is defining *what* as risk and how. In other words, according to work in the socio-cultural study of risk at least, 'disembodied information [is] a farce'; rather, 'knowledge is principally embodied, contextual and positional' and 'taking up a position and to be positioned is inevitably a question of ethics' (Adam and van Loon 2000: 4). This idea also relates to sociological approaches to financial categories such as money more broadly that refuse to ignore the social relations between users that actually bring them into existence (Dodd 2014).

Crucially, Smith's notion of mutual sympathy draws attention to the contestable place of risk in society. A sensibility to mutual sympathy provides an account of the mechanism through which ethico-political norms of and attitudes towards constructions such as risk are negotiated in society. It echoes recent moves in the cultural political economy perspective developed by Jacqueline Best and Matthew Patterson in which risk management is understood as a 'symbolic practice' (Best 2009: 462). For instance, practices such as bond rating carry with them specific meanings that serve to reproduce underlying ideas about what credit rating involves and how it is culturally legitimate (Best 2009: 462). It can then be shown that it is only a very *specific* historical conjuncture that 'translates' seemingly ordinary objects 'like houses and individuals' economic histories . . . into standardized measurements and exchangeable assets' (Best 2009: 464).

However, by contrast, in the subprime era economistic approaches to understanding risk, particularly credit risk, appear to deny this negotiated aspect by relying upon ostensibly disembodied, objective and 'scientistic' representations (Power 2007). Credit risk has increasingly become something that can be seemingly successfully managed using securitisation and scientistic risk management techniques (Wainwright 2009). These 'calculative and scientific' aspects of risk management in turn played an important role in making such practices as sub-prime lending appear to be a 'legitimate part of the contemporary financial markets' (Langley 2008a: 472). Indeed the process of sorting borrowers into 'risk cohorts' through credit scoring calculations essentially depoliticised the issue of charging high rates of interest and made them 'very difficult to question' (Langley 2008a: 475).

In a sense, then, recent theories of – and faith in – techniques of credit risk management are based on an approach that at least *attempts* to depoliticise risk by propagating a 'science' of risk management. Certainly, in the main, this was the widespread approach to risk that developed in the boom period in the run-up to the GFC. Banks, financial institutions and credit rating agencies believed that existing levels of expertise and knowledge had translated the fundamental ambivalence and indeterminacy of risk into statements of certainty and quantifiable probabilities. This led to new levels of 'financial engineering' to manufacture products such as mortgage-backed securities, which of course became a multitrillion-dollar market on Wall Street (Williams 2010: 91).

In important ways, credit risk management practices were thus central to the GFC. One of the key factors was the 'progressive underestimation, or misunderstanding, of risk by financial agents' (Nesvetailova 2010: 18). This of course relates to the well-known story of the place of US subprime lending in the GFC (Lanchester 2010). In his book on the fall of Lehman Brothers, Mark Williams (2010: 102) explains how despite being widely known to be one of the riskiest forms of consumer loans, 'securitization, government financial support, and a seal of approval from the credit rating agencies had magically legitimized investment in subprime mortgages'. For him, effective risk management was absent from the operations of major investment banks because of their obsession with product innovation and intense profit seeking. 'In this atmosphere', Williams (2010: 102) writes, 'credit risk was allowed to grow and go little noticed'.

For a sympathetic political economy, which recognises the place of societal construction and contestation of interpersonal ethics, the important point is that the 'atmosphere' to which Williams refers is fundamentally ethical and political in nature. The creation and management of credit risk are endeavours that cannot be premised on a society of autonomous individuals because they relate to something that is a social construction and has to be negotiated within society. On this view, the political context of US subprime lending matters. For instance, housing-related risk was 'desocialized' as the activities of mortgage securitisation that begun at the government-sponsored enterprises expanded rapidly as part of a neoliberal deregulation of housing (Schwartz 2009: 201). The entry of the large investment banks into the market for instruments such as CDOs from the 1990s onwards marked a significant transfer of the responsibility for handling risk to be passed from the banks themselves to market-pricing dynamics (Dodd 2014: 123). Essentially, securitisation practices involved the transfer of risk to *others*: either to often ill-informed counterparties willing to buy or, once deemed 'toxic', to society through government steps to socialise the debt as the crisis hit (Dodd 2014: 124).

The politics of credit risk management are thus central to an understanding of the GFC. Whereas an economistic approach to risk management might make claims to scientistic and objective status, a socio-cultural or mutual sympathy perspective recognises that risk is *created* and *negotiable* as well as managed. Read through the lens of Smith's sympathetic political economy, the major flaw contained within an economistic understanding of credit risk is that it attempts to exclude contestable interpersonal ethics. It makes very little sense to deny society, especially in this instance, because what counts as acceptable risk-taking as a societal norm is crucial to understanding how people view themselves, others and how they act accordingly. So, for instance, the dream of homeownership has to exist as a cultural product in society in order for governments to legitimately promote or allow for schemes to increase homeownership, such as through the deregulation of the housing finance sector (Smith 2008).

Widespread practices of credit risk management in the run-up to the GFC appear to be based on scientistic understandings of risk, which tend to deny the constructed and contestable place of risk in society. The crisis itself, by placing such practices as subprime lending under close scrutiny, can be read as a moment in which risk is *re-politicised*, or at least recognised as a negotiated social construct. What a sympathetic political economy adds to this conversation is an account of how moments of mutual sympathy represent the negotiation of ethico-political standards and how norms might come to be formed and contested in society. In a sense then, rather than attempting to negate or eliminate all practices of risk management, a sympathy perspective might merely involve re-politicising the place of risk in society. Subprime lending may not be problematic in and of itself, but if homeownership is to be promoted by programmes of government, then it must be recognised as open to ethico-political contestation, which could easily be just as harmful as beneficial to the individuals principally concerned. In Chapters 5 and 6, I return to the theme of credit risk management at the levels of regulatory and everyday finance respectively, in order to further substantiate this claim about the potential crisis of ethical imagination at the heart of economistic liberalism.

The sympathy procedure and the depoliticisation of debt

In this final section, I show how sympathy understood as a 'procedure' draws attention to continually *negotiable* and always *provisional* contestable interpersonal ethics. Smith introduces the section on 'the manner in which we judge' by giving a psychological account of the process through which people come to approve or disapprove:

> When the original passions of the person principally concerned are in perfect concord with the sympathetic emotions of the spectator, they necessarily appear to this last just and proper, and suitable to their objects; and, on the contrary, when, upon bringing the case home to himself, he finds that they do not coincide with what he feels, they necessarily appear to him unjust and improper, and unsuitable to the causes which excite them.
>
> (*TMS* I.i.3.1)

For Smith the sympathy procedure involves a very active mental process of ethico-political judgement (Bagolini 1975: 104), not unlike the formation of opinions on a given subject:

> To approve of another man's opinions is to adopt those opinions, and to adopt them is to approve of them . . . To approve or disapprove, therefore, of the opinions of others is acknowledged, by every body, to mean no more than to observe their agreement or disagreement with our own. But this is equally the case with regard to our approbation or disapprobation of the sentiments or passions of others.
>
> (*TMS* I.i.3.2)

Essentially Smith presents an account of the interactive formation of ethical standards through people's capacity to perform imaginative acts. This idea has been central to the work of Luc Boltanski (2004) who develops a spectatorial theory of morality to argue that spectators of suffering can actively involve themselves in the circumstances of others in order to derive morally acceptable responses to the sight of suffering. Boltanski (2004: 35) appeals directly to Smith's spectator theory, correctly suggesting that it is a form of moral theory which also appears as an 'empirical social psychology and a political philosophy'. In essence, this captures why Smith's sympathy concept is the foundation of what I term an 'ethico-political' theory. On Boltanski's (2004: 37) reading, Smith plays down the tension between how sympathy might operate in a 'face to face encounter', on the one hand, and a 'general politics of pity' based on 'a conveyance over distance of a representation of suffering', on the other. Boltanski (2004: 38) helpfully stresses that in Smith's work this is because 'distance is overcome by a deliberate act of imagination'.

Zygmunt Bauman (2005) picks up a similar line of thinking in his writing on consumerism and the new poor. 'Distant people in distant places' may experience extreme suffering, even as they labour to produce luxury goods for others, but their suffering 'does not evoke an ethical response and does not prompt a willingness to act as intense as those triggered by the sights of human distress nearby' (Bauman 2005: 94). Their suffering may 'stay invisible and escape attention' for some time but mutual dependence means that left unattended the 'global' will 'sooner or later rebound on the domestic scene' (Bauman 2005: 94). In essence Bauman's account, akin to Boltanski's, draws on the central point that imaginative acts, along with the centrality of the *visibility* of suffering, are needed to overcome the issues involved in grappling with distance and ethical responsibility.

For Smith it is exactly through this process of imaginative reconstruction and learning from 'our preceding experience of what our sentiments would commonly correspond with' that ethical standards are negotiated (*TMS* I.i.3.4). It involves an imaginative internalisation of another's position so that judgement can be made in light of existing understanding (Teichgraeber 1986: 131):

> When we judge in this manner of any affection . . . it is scarce possible that we should make use of any other rule or canon but the correspondent affection

> in ourselves. If, upon bringing the case home to our own breast, we find that the sentiments which it gives occasion to, coincide and tally with our own, we necessarily approve of them as proportioned and suitable to their objects; if otherwise, we necessarily disapprove of them, as extravagant and out of proportion. Every faculty in one man is the measure by which he judges of the like faculty in another. I judge of your sight by my sight, of your ear by my ear, of your reason by my reason, of your resentment by my resentment, of your love by my love. I neither have, nor can have, any other way of judging about them.
>
> (*TMS* I.i.3.9–10)

Later in *TMS*, the 'impartial spectator' construction becomes central to this account of how an individual might negotiate and construct their *own* ethico-political stance (Raphael 1975). In Smith's terms, '[w]e endeavour to examine our own conduct as we imagine any other fair and impartial spectator would examine it' (*TMS* III.1.2). Crucially, it is here that he sets out the role of 'self-tutoring' the imagination in his moral system:

> We begin, upon this account, to examine our own passions and conduct, and to consider how these must appear to them, by considering how they would appear to us if in their situation. We suppose ourselves the spectators of our own behaviour, and endeavour to imagine what effect it would, in this light, produce upon us. This is the only looking-glass by which we can, in some measure, with the eyes of other people, scrutinize the propriety of our own conduct.
>
> (*TMS* III.1.5)

The self-tutoring element of the imagination is important to Smith because of how he believes in a progressive element to learning standards of appropriate behaviour. As D. D. Raphael (2007: 34–35) puts it, for Smith, 'conscience' is an 'effect of judgements' made on a number of levels. A person always judges others, knowing that others are judging them. In turn this leads to a process of learning whereby interactively formed judgements of oneself are developed through imagining whether or not an impartial spectator would approve. In other words, one must learn how to be a spectator of others before being able to develop the capacities of an impartial spectator.

Raphael (2007: 36) makes the further point that conscience for Smith is not purely 'a reflection of actual social attitudes' because the impartial spectator, 'the man within', may judge *differently* from the actual spectator, 'the man without', and so the 'voice of conscience reflects what I imagine that I, with all my knowledge of the situation, would feel if I were a spectator instead of an agent'. This leads to his argument that Smith's impartial spectator 'is disinterested, but neither omniscient nor omnipercipient, and . . . certainly not dispassionate' (Raphael 2007: 44). In many ways this parallels Stephen McKenna's (2006: 139) suggestion that the impartial spectator concept is 'less a metaphysics of conscience or a moral epistemology than it is a description of a kind of perpetually situated practice'.

Returning to the beginning of *TMS*, this theme is related to how Smith understands the imaginative internalisation of another's position to be always in a sense incomplete and open to negotiation:

> After all this, however, the emotions of the spectator will still be very apt to fall short of the violence of what is felt by the sufferer. Mankind, though naturally sympathetic, never conceive, for what has befallen another, that degree of passion which naturally animates the person principally concerned. That imaginary change of situation, upon which their sympathy is founded, is but momentary. The thought of their own safety, the thought that they themselves are not really the sufferers, continually intrudes itself upon them; and though it does not hinder them from conceiving a passion somewhat analogous to what is felt by the sufferer, hinders them from conceiving any thing that approaches to the same degree of violence.
>
> (*TMS* I.i.4.7)

In other words, as Andrew Skinner (1996: 60) explains, 'accuracy of judgement' will always be 'a function of the information available' such that the correspondence of feeling 'can never be complete'. Nevertheless, despite being incomplete, Smith still thinks that the imaginative act is successful enough to allow interpersonal ethics to be formed in society (*TMS* I.i.4.7). Again, this is echoed in Simmel's (1910: 378) work, who claims that the 'picture which one man gets of another from personal contact is determined by certain distortions which are not simple deceptions from incomplete experience, defective vision, sympathetic or antipathetic prejudice'. On his terms, everyone has a certain 'individuality-nucleus which cannot be subjectively reproduced by another whose deepest individuality is essentially different' (Simmel 1910: 378). Yet, society is still constituted through such interactions because as an 'object' it is made up of these imperfect interpersonal constructions (Simmel 1910: 378).

To summarise, Smith's account of the sympathy procedure contains a number of important aspects. First, 'the manner in which we judge' is an *active* mental procedure. 'Situation, impartiality, and information' are elements that integrate to form the 'moral-evaluative process' of the sympathetic act (Bagolini 1975: 105). Second, as a process of negotiating standards of interpersonal ethics, it involves an imaginative *internalisation* of another's situation so that it might be judged against existing understanding (Montes 2004: 51). Third, this imaginative internalisation of another's position is *always incomplete*, yet it is *sufficient* for the formation of standards of interpersonal ethics (*TMS* I.i.4.7). These aspects of the sympathy procedure might be thought of as pointing towards constantly contestable interpersonal ethics at the individual level. On this account, there is no 'single encompassing description of human behaviour' (Vaggi 2004: 31). Put another way, as Alec Macfie (1967: 57) suggests, Smith's social rules reflect 'the constant criticism of the "impartial spectator" and the constant pressure of "propriety"'.

Therefore as opposed to a static or predetermined standard of model individual behaviour alluded to above in economistic accounts, a sympathetic political economy might provide understandings of market-oriented behaviour that allow for interpersonal ethics to be formed and negotiated in particular ways at specific moments in time and space. In a sense then, for Smith, standards of appropriate behaviour develop over time as societies change and as such are specific to them. This is the case at least in the sense that the content of notions of impartiality and interpretations of 'fair play' depend on the socio-historical situation of the individual concerned (Macfie 1967: 83–84). At certain times, particular configurations of appropriate standards of ethico-political behaviour will be formed and legitimated by feelings of mutual sympathy, but this does not rule out indeterminable contestation over appropriate ethico-political standards. This picks up on McKenna's (2006: 139) important reading of Smith that emphasises how moral development for Smith is 'an unintended consequence of rhetorical practice'. The ways people communicate can never directly impart intentions and sentiments in perfect form, which means that language has to be adapted to 'speaker, audience, subject, and context to do this' (McKenna's 2006: 139). On McKenna's reading, 'Smith thus rejects the either/or fallacy of a choice between foundational knowledge (or transcendent criteria) on the one hand or pure contingency of value on the other as a basis for morality'.

Given its allowance for historical, spatial and cultural specificity, Smith's sympathy concept might be viewed as an imprecise or even confused account of interpersonal ethics for political economy. In light of more rigid assumptions of instrumental rationality, or especially in light of recent trends in contemporary political theory, to insist on contestable interpersonal ethics might appear ineffectual. However, more plausibly, Smith's sympathy might instead be celebrated as *re-politicising* political economy by fundamentally opening up contestable interpersonal ethics at the site of the individual. In this view, the 'individual is not a purely passive actor' because market-oriented behaviour is understood to evolve from the 'existing social and institutional framework' and is *not* viewed as fundamental to some construction of human nature (Vaggi 2004: 36). Rather than deny or assume away ethico-political contestation, the sympathy procedure invites political economy to grapple with the *constitution* of market-oriented behaviour as a foundational issue.

In important ways, then, Smith's sympathy procedure necessitates a re-examination of primary questions of political economy. If the formation and reproduction of market-oriented behaviour is open to historical circumstance and prevailing custom then, most forcefully, this opens the door for ethico-political contestation over the character of that market-oriented behaviour. To give just one example of how this might be understood, in *WN* Smith himself gives an account of how the problematic distinction between needs and wants is ultimately only resolvable based on circumstance and custom:

> By necessaries I understand, not only the commodities which are indispensably necessary for the support of life, but whatever the custom of the country

> renders it indecent for creditable people, even of the lowest order, to be without. A linen shirt, for example, is, strictly speaking, not a necessary of life. The Greeks and Romans lived, I suppose, very comfortably, though they had no linen. But in the present times, through the greater part of Europe, a creditable day-labourer would be ashamed to appear in publick without a linen shirt, the want of which would be supposed to denote that disgraceful degree of poverty, which, it is presumed, no body can well fall into without extreme bad conduct. Custom, in the same manner, has rendered leather shoes a necessary of life in England . . . Under necessaries therefore, I comprehend, not only those things which nature, but those things which the established rules of decency have rendered necessary to the lowest rank of people. All other things, I call luxuries; without meaning by this appellation, to throw the smallest degree of reproach upon the temperate use of them. Beer and ale, for example, in Great Britain, and wine, even in the wine countries, I call luxuries. A man of any rank may, without any reproach, abstain totally from tasting such liquors. Nature does not render them necessary for the support of life; and custom no where renders it indecent to live without them.
>
> (*WN* V.ii.k.3)

Overall, without dwelling on the contemporary relevance of this particular discussion more applicable to Smith's time, it is possible to see how a sympathetic political economy that takes seriously the ongoing contestation of interpersonal ethics begins to open up extremely important questions for political economy that are otherwise closed down in economistic approaches. To take seriously the idea that the ethico-political constitution of market-oriented behaviour can be understood as open, reflexive, and yet to be decided, might serve to re-politicise problems of economic governance. In the context of the GFC, I now use a discussion of personal indebtedness to illustrate this claim and indicate the potential crisis of ethical imagination at the heart of economistic liberalism.

Personal debt as a feature of economic governance

Closely related to the issues of financialisation in general, and asset-based welfare and credit risk management in particular, are questions of how to understand and cope with debt. As indicated above, financialisation is recognised as a pervasive social process that extends well beyond a series of relations that merely link individuals directly to capital markets. Johnna Montgomerie (2009: 10) suggests that more deeply in the run-up to the GFC there was 'a consensus among policy makers that debt was a virtue, rather than a vice, for the economy as rational individuals, guided by their own preferences, responded to economic stimuli and in doing so created wealth and economic expansion'. She further argues that financialisation is 'unique' in a sense because it 'incorporated ongoing processes of socioeconomic transformation through households' use of unsecured debt' (Montgomerie 2009: 15). In many ways, then, *personal* debt plays a significant role in the constitution of market-oriented behaviour more broadly.

In the subprime era, arguably financialisation facilitated and even promoted the expansion of personal indebtedness. Based on the explicit assumption that acquiring debt allowed households to benefit from rising asset prices in stock and property markets, practices of financialisation went largely unquestioned in economistic approaches to governance. For instance, subprime mortgages 'made sense only in an economic environment in which housing prices kept going up, enabling their mortgagers to refinance into a conforming mortgage at lower interest rates' (Schwartz 2009: 225). The problem, as Montgomerie (2009) alludes to, is that the prevailing view of debt as entirely virtuous if it facilitates access and even contributes to the gains of economic expansion, was based on an economistic interpretation of instrumentally rational individuals responding appropriately to external economic stimuli. In such a scenario, ethico-political questions related to such things as excess, sustainability, or suffering do not really enter the picture because people are assumed to be acting perfectly properly, with both creditors and debtors alike proceeding as good financial citizens helping to contribute to economic expansion. Within such a framework, the sort of constant contestation over interpersonal ethics that a sympathetic political might insist on is ignored.

Relatedly, Montgomerie (2006: 112) argues that the 'precipitous rise in Anglo-American household indebtedness in the mid-1990s was an inadvertent outcome of the concomitant process of wage stagnation and financial services liberalization'. Households became more dependent on debt because of political strategies to pursue 'non-inflationary growth policy', which involved significant government commitments to price stability rather than full employment, and the 'structural transformation of labour and financial services markets' (Montgomerie 2006: 112). In the context of the ostensible financialisation of society, such arguments draw attention to the structurally unequal nature of creditor-debtor relations that might be entirely overlooked by economistic perspectives. In contrast to an understanding of behaviour as instrumentally rational, which is unable to even engage with ethico-political contestation about the appropriate place of personal debt in society, a sympathetic political economy perspective at the very least problematises creditor-debtor relations by recognising them as part of contestable interpersonal ethics.

Interestingly, in her book *Payback*, Margaret Atwood (2008: 2) has written about debt as 'an imaginative construct' that in many ways parallels how a sympathy perspective might recognise the complex nature and ongoing contestability of creditor-debtor relations. Smith's sympathy procedure, after all, is about the imaginative internalisation of another's position in order to negotiate standards of interpersonal ethics (Teichgraeber 1986: 131). As part of this process, ideas about the role of debt in society thus might be problematised and recognised as inherently political, rather than assumed away as *normal*. Atwood (2008: 50–51 emphasis in original) writes:

> Borrowing and lending would seem to exist in a shadowland – neither 'taking' nor 'trading' – changing their natures depending on the final outcome. They're like those riddles in fairy tales: *Come to me neither naked nor clothed, neither*

> *on the road not off it, neither walking nor riding*. A borrowed object or sum is neither taken nor is it traded. It exists in a shadowland between the two: if the interest exacted for a loan is of a loan-shark magnitude, the transaction verges on theft from the debtor; if the object or sum is never returned, it also verges on theft, this time from the creditor. Thus it's 'taking,' not 'trading.' But if the object is borrowed and then returned with a reasonable amount of interest, it's clearly trading. Hostage-taking is the same kind of shadowland transaction: part theft or taking, part trade.

Nigel Dodd's (2014) work similarly explores the ambiguous nature of debt through the lens of Simmel's foundational definition of money as a 'claim upon society'. On this reading, 'money is a form of *socialized debt*, a relationship between the *individual* and *society*' (Dodd 2014: 125 emphasis in original). It suggests that the 'debt' that money involves is always one based between the individual concerned and a wider society. As Dodd (2014: 89) explains, it is only very recently that debt has been considered 'narrowly as a financial relationship', as opposed to the broader role it played in society's 'religious, ethical, and moral belief systems' historically. A sympathetic sensibility produces a route to recognising the historically and culturally specific nature of such claims about debt by fundamentally reorienting political economy analysis.

In sum, a consideration of personal debt can be used to illustrate important differences between an economistic and a sympathetic approach to economic governance. The former tends to deny contestable interpersonal ethics, which means that issues such as personal debt are ostensibly depoliticised. The latter insists on the ongoing contestability of the constitution of market-oriented behaviour such that creditor-debtor relations are understood as inherently ethico-political. So while in the run up to the GFC financialisation and debt were largely seen as unproblematic in economistic approaches, a sympathy perspective at the very least problematises and re-politicises financialisation in general and creditor-debtor relations in particular.

Concluding remarks

In this chapter, I introduced an outline of a sympathetic political economy built up in three stages, each corresponding to three foundational features of contemporary economic governance. In the following two chapters, I use these sites as the central themes on which to engage questions about the GFC. In the first section, I made the basic point that whereas economistic liberalism tends to build from assumptions about instrumentally rational behaviour, such as in the model citizen of asset-based welfare systems, a sympathetic political economy conceives market-oriented behaviour to be both the outcome of and inherently involved with contestable interpersonal ethics at the individual level. In the second section, I argued that the concept of mutual sympathy presents a very different depiction of interpersonal ethics compared to economistic liberalism. The latter tends to build from the assumption of narrow utilitarian understandings of instrumental rationality, which ultimately means that political economy problems are solved by individualising them and denying society, as in many contemporary approaches to credit risk management. Finally, I suggested that a sympathetic political economy begins to open up important questions for political economy that are otherwise closed down in economistic approaches. I argued that to take full account of the idea that the ethico-political constitution of market-oriented behaviour is open, reflexive, and yet to be decided, might serve to re-politicise certain problems, such as the place of creditor-debtor relations in society.

This chapter can be read as a mobilisation of a Smithian sympathetic political economy in order to provide an illustrative conceptual critique of economistic liberalism. In some ways, at the conceptual level, what I have referred to as 'economistic liberalism' is essentially tied to, but is not a synonym for, mainstream academic economics and attendant approaches in political economy that tend to be categorised as part of the 'liberal tradition'. A critique of economistic liberalism of this sort in relation to the GFC is of significance for a number of reasons. For a start, it has been argued that 'the global meltdown . . . is a crisis of economics as a profession as much as it is the crisis of finance' (Nesvetailova 2010: 170). Indeed, even the University of Chicago professor and conservative author Richard Posner (2009: 260) has suggested that '[e]xcessive deregulation of the financial industry was a government failure abetted by the political and ideological commitments of mainstream economists'. Yet, moving beyond this, I make the case that the GFC provides an illustration of how there is a crisis of ethical imagination at the very heart of economistic liberalism as it comes to be embodied in contemporary governance. In the next two chapters, then, I demonstrate the potential of a sympathetic political economy by using it to analyse the issues of asset-based welfare, credit risk and personal debt in order to empirically substantiate this claim.

4 The regulatory governance of finance in crisis

> In the same year that America declared its independence, Adam Smith published his famous treatise, *The Wealth of Nations*, in which he argued that the pursuit of self-interest would lead to the general well-being of society. A hundred and seventy-five years later, Kenneth Arrow and Gerard Debreu, using the Walrasian model, explained what was required for Smith's insight to be correct.
>
> (Stiglitz 2010b: 241)

As Chairman of the United Nation's (2010) *The Stiglitz Report* and former senior vice president and chief economist at the World Bank, Joseph Stiglitz is an established leader in global financial governance. It is of particular significance how someone in Stiglitz's position interprets Smith because, as I have argued, the contest over historiographical issues often performs a significant role in the very construction of contemporary debates themselves. Plainly though, as the above quote reveals, Stiglitz appears to reproduce some basic mythologics of interpretation. Aside from the fact it is a 'misdescription' of meaning to claim that 'the pursuit of self-interest would lead to the general well-being of society', surely it is also to replicate a mythology of parochialism to suggest that later economists were able to prove that Smith was 'correct' through the use of a subsequent and distinctly different 'Walrasian model'? This problem of historical foreshortening is seemingly not discerned by economistic interpretations such as Stiglitz's, even though it is highly imprudent to even attempt to employ Smith's ideas without seeking to provide an historicised account. In this chapter, by contrast, I build on my historicised reading of sympathy in order to analyse economistic liberalism at the regulatory level of finance.

It is not my intention to provide a complete empirical survey of global financial governance during and in response to the GFC. Rather I use the same sites of finance as in the previous chapter, asset-based welfare, credit risk management and personal debt, as the central themes in regulatory governance on which to engage economistic liberalism in the context of the crisis. In the first section, I expand on the argument that asset-based systems of welfare represent a central aspect of financialisation tendencies that can be understood as an attempt to exclude interpersonal ethics from market-oriented behaviour by inducing an economistic and autonomous individual detached from the rest of society. I argue that instrumentally rational behaviour is promoted at the regulatory level when the politics of asset-based welfare are left unquestioned and the consequences of this are revealed in the contradictory attempts to assign responsibility for the crisis.

In the second section, I develop the suggestion that widespread practices of credit risk management in the run-up to and during the GFC appear to be based on scientistic understandings of risk, which tend to contradict the constructed and contestable place of risk in society. I argue that risk management is essentially normalised in society and the consequences of this are revealed in the flawed scientistic approaches to understanding the crisis. Finally, in the third section, I make the argument that by attempting to deny contestable interpersonal ethics, economistic liberalism tends to depoliticise creditor-debtor relations whereas a sympathetic political economy would insist that, as with all formations of market-oriented behaviour, they are inherently ethico-political and continually contestable. I argue that debt is essentially depoliticised and the consequences of this are revealed in how taking on personal debt to maintain standards of living is understood as appropriate behaviour before and in response to the crisis.

This chapter takes its cue from the suggestion that the GFC is not merely a moment of instability in an otherwise well-ordered and successful political settlement for finance, but is more of a signifier moment drawing attention to the deeper changes and potential contradictions related to financialisation (Brassett *et al.* 2010). One such site of contradiction is the construction of financial market agency that is contained within regulatory accounts of and responses to the crisis. As Andrew Gamble (2010: 6) suggests, 'over-borrowing and under-saving both in the public and private sectors' are widely viewed as having played central roles in causing the crisis. Yet at the very same time, he continues, national economies such as the United States and the United Kingdom have become 'increasingly reliant on policies that promote financialisation and on the provision of cheap credit' (Gamble 2010: 7). As such Gamble (2010: 7) rightly argues that it is difficult to achieve re-regulation and reform in light of the crisis because it would be regarded as threatening the key drivers of growth in the last 30 years or so.

Put another way, the GFC presents a curious conundrum at the regulatory level. On the one hand, over-borrowing and under-regulated markets come up for potential blame for the crisis, in part the problematic activation of *overly*-financialised individuals. On the other hand, re-regulating national economies in response to the crisis might involve challenging some of the very fundamental tenets of financialisation, which is problematic in a context in which basic ways of life, in Anglo-America especially, are increasingly understood and constituted in financial terms.

A sympathetic political economy demonstrates some of the problems of continuing to treat financial market agency in economistic terms. At the three sites of finance explored at the regulatory level, the GFC is understood as a crisis based on the denial of contestable ethics within finance at the individual level. When asset-based welfare goes unquestioned, when risk management is normalised to the everyday and when debt relations are depoliticised, an economistic approach to financial market agency is reproduced, even though it is ultimately flawed on its own terms. By contrast, Smith's concept of sympathy, at the very least, problematises and opens up contestable ethico-political space at these important sites of finance intimately involved with the GFC.

The regulatory governance of asset-based welfare

A central feature of asset-based systems of welfare lay at the heart of the GFC: homes *as* a financial asset. As with many previous booms and busts, US house price gyrations are understood to have inflicted significant costs on the world economy (IMF 2011a: 112). The way in which declining US house prices led to the 'subprime crisis', through the ensuing 'credit crunch', to the full-blown world recession is part of the well-known story of the GFC. Certainly regulatory accounts often pick up on the pivotal place of homeownership, or more accurately *attempts* at homeownership, in the crisis. The Financial Crisis Inquiry Commission (FCIC) (2011: 6), appointed by the US government to investigate the causes of the crisis, notes how 'familiar market mechanisms were . . . transformed' as investors around the world sought to purchase securities built on US real estate: 'seemingly one of the safest bets in the world'. Similarly, the major report on the crisis produced by the US Senate Permanent Subcommittee on Investigations (PSI) (2011: 17), details how lenders began to make money 'not from holding onto the loans they originated and collecting mortgage payments over the years, but from the relatively short term fees associated with originating and selling the loans'.

However, as weak origination standards contributed to rising delinquencies in the US subprime market, the asset-backed security (ABS) collaterised debt obligation (CDO) market seized up when credit rating agencies announced widespread downgrades of subprime residential mortgage-backed securities (RMBS) in July 2007. Then the problems in credit markets spilled over into short-term money markets as banks around the world became concerned about the adequacy of their capital and the size of their balance sheets (BIS 2008a: 12; US Senate PSI 2011: 45). The securitisation of 'poorly underwritten' residential mortgages, particularly US subprime loans, eventually transmitted significant losses to the banking, securities, and insurance sectors globally (FSB 2011: 6). All this is widely known, but what a sympathetic political economy built on from the last chapter adds to the analysis is a much deeper questioning of the place of financialisation and asset-based welfare provision in the crisis.

Financial responsibility and the character of 'subprime'

The FCIC (2011: xxiii) stresses that the crisis cannot be put down to the actions of 'a few bad actors'. Yet, at the same time, it also points out that 'the breadth of this crisis does not mean 'everyone is at fault' (FCIC 2011: xxiii). Who, then, bears responsibility for the GFC in important regulatory assessments? On the one hand, the FCIC (2011: 125 emphasis added) describes how lending standards 'collapsed' because of a 'significant failure of accountability and responsibility *throughout each level of the lending system*'. In this sense, the notion of 'subprime' refers to something much wider than a particular borrower group: it represents 'an unprecedented, broad-based erosion of credit standards' (Zandi 2009: 33).

Yet, on the other hand, the question of who is 'creditworthy' or not when it comes to acquiring a residential mortgage is one that figures right at the heart of the subprime crisis. In regulatory accounts of the crisis, there tends to be emphasis placed on the character of the subprime borrower. As is now well-known, they are understood to typically have one or more of the following characteristics: 'weak credit histories that include payment delinquencies and bankruptcies; reduced repayment capacity as measured by credit scores or debt-to-income ratios; or incomplete credit histories' (IMF 2007b: 7fn).

Given these characteristics, regulatory accounts tend to openly suggest that the extension of mortgage credit to those who were in some sense 'unworthy' was a major contributing factor to the undermining of an otherwise successful securitisation model. 'For years, securitization worked well' the US Senate PSI (2011: 18) reports. The Bank for International Settlements (BIS) (2008a: 12), the international organisation of central banks, points to the 'extremely weak' underwriting standards for subprime mortgages which contained 'multiple layers of risk' including 'less creditworthy borrowers, high cumulative loan-to-value ratios, and limited or no verification of the borrower's income'. This of course is part of the 'predatory lending' phenomenon widely recognised as a foundational feature of the subprime debacle (Nesvetailova 2010: 111; Stiglitz 2010b: 175; Zandi 2009: 97).

The FCIC (2011: xxiii) also notes the fundamental problem of weak origination standards: 'Many mortgage lenders set the bar so low that lenders simply took eager borrowers' qualifications on faith, often with a willful disregard for a borrower's ability to pay'. It reports how in the first half of 2005 nearly one-quarter of all mortgages made were interest-only loans, and that for the year as a whole, 68 percent of 'option ARM [adjustable-rate mortgage]' loans originated by Countrywide and Washington Mutual (both later bailed-out by the US government) had 'low' or no-documentation requirements (FCIC 2011: xxiii). Similarly, the IMF (2008a: 5fn) states that in early 2008, the increasing rate of US foreclosures appeared to be 'a function of fraud, speculation, over-extension by borrowers, and the effects of weak underwriting standards'. It suggests that 'highly-leveraged nonprime lending' was driven by a combination of low interest rates and rapidly rising house prices, which 'masked the plummeting lending standards, since the overstretched borrowers found it easy to refinance or sell the house at a profit' (IMF 2009b: 92).

The Financial Stability Board (FSB) (2011: 6), the Basel based international body concerned with the global financial system, also reports that the surge in mortgage lending and house price growth experienced in the United States – and the United Kingdom as well – involved more emphasis being placed on property valuations as opposed to assessments of a borrower's capacity to repay. These countries witnessed the development of new 'riskier products that made use of more relaxed product terms, liberal underwriting and increased lending to higher-risk borrowers' (FSB 2011: 6). In its response to the crisis, the FSB

(2011: 4) recommends more thorough verification processes regarding a borrower's ability to repay. Therefore it welcomes the additional requirements that the US Dodd-Frank Act 2010 imposes on lending, including the instruction that '[c]reditors are required to make a reasonable and good faith determination, based on verified and documented information, that the consumer has a reasonable ability to repay a residential mortgage loan' (FSB 2011: 15). The FSB (2011: 21–22) also champions the use of a loan-to-value cap on mortgage lending because '[m]eaningful initial down payment requirements help to validate borrower capacity as well as ensure necessary commitment to the obligation'. Furthermore, it suggests that future house price appreciation ought not to be considered in the evaluation of a borrower's ability to repay a mortgage loan (FSB 2011: 23).

What was the state's role in producing these weaker lending standards that now need to be improved? The FCIC (2011: xxvii) reports that successive US governments set 'aggressive homeownership goals with the desire to extend credit to families previously denied access to the financial markets'. However, it continues, 'the government failed to ensure that the philosophy of opportunity was being matched by the practical realities on the ground' because the Federal Reserve and other regulators did not rein in 'irresponsible lending' (FCIC 2011: xxvii). Therefore, the FCIC (2011: xxvii) suggests that 'the talk of opportunity was tragically at odds with the reality of a financial disaster in the making'.

In terms of government participation in the US housing market, tax breaks and subsidies are widely recognised to have promoted homeownership, which in turn are thought to have encouraged higher levels of household debt, a relaxation of lending standards, and upward pressure on property prices (FCIC 2011: 424; IMF 2011a: 130; 143; OECD 2009: 49; US Senate PSI 2011: 41). The government-sponsored enterprises, Fannie Mae and Freddie Mac, were a key part of this government promotion of homeownership as they played a central role in providing liquidity to the mortgage market and leading the securitisation process (IMF 2008b: 34). The Community Reinvestment Act 1979 is also singled out because it encouraged lending in low-income neighbourhoods, which in turn 'promoted the purchase of more and bigger homes than would otherwise have been possible, exacerbating leverage and the severity of boom-and-bust dynamics' (IMF 2011a: 130).

Perhaps because of an understanding of the supposed *perfectibility* of the securitisation model, a great number of the regulatory accounts refer to the distorted 'incentives' that led lenders to extend mortgages to those who ought not to have had access. Specifically the suggestion is frequently made that the source of these perverse incentives was strong investor demand. For instance, the BIS (2008a: 7) suggests that origination standards in newly securitised asset classes were 'driven by the requirements of investors as much as by the credit views of the firms that originate the credits': demand from investors for ABS CDO tranches therefore in some ways 'drove' the growth in the US subprime market. Of course, investors could profit not only from the success of such products but also from their failure (US Senate PSI 2011: 318). As such, lenders 'had weak incentives to maintain underwriting standards given the strong investor demand for subprime risk' (BIS

2008a: 12; BIS 2005: 55). The Financial Stability Forum (FSF) (2008: 8), the predecessor of the FSB, concurs that high investor demand for securitised products 'weakened the incentives of underwriters and sponsors to maintain adequate underwriting standards'. It notes that lax loan underwriting included unverified borrower information and clear indications of fraud (FSF 2008: 36). As the US Senate PSI (2011: 19) report puts it, 'Subprime loans provided new fuel for the securitization engines on Wall Street'.

Reading across the basic regulatory account of the GFC, it is possible to discern a notable level of agreement over the fundamental *problem* of the character of the subprime. Specifically, the subprime borrower displays the character traits that are potentially threatening to the securitisation model if credit is extended to them on too lenient terms. In the build up to the GFC, 'they' were extended access to homeownership based on the promise of asset-based welfare with ultimately disastrous consequences. As former Federal Reserve Chairman Ben Bernanke lamented to the FCIC (2011: 423), at one point 'both lenders and borrowers became convinced that house prices would only go up'. This led to house price rises becoming a 'self-fulfilling prophecy' because borrowers were granted loans on the 'expectation that accumulating home equity would soon allow refinancing into more sustainable mortgages' (Bernanke cited in FCIC 2011: 423).

Incidentally, a few years earlier, Bernanke himself gave a rather different account to this suggestion that borrowers were at fault for expecting house prices to continue on an upward trend. In May 2007, only a matter of months before the housing market nosedived, Bernanke (2007) attempted to reassure US homeowners that there were no dangers visible to existing prices and that potential homeowners should actually assume the continued one-way trajectory of prices:

> given the fundamental factors in place that should support the demand for housing, we believe the effect of the troubles in the subprime sector on the broader housing market will likely be limited, and we do not expect significant spillovers from the subprime market to the rest of the economy or to the financial system. The vast majority of mortgages, including even subprime mortgages, continue to perform well. Past gains in house prices have left most homeowners with significant amounts of home equity, and growth in jobs and incomes should help keep the financial obligations of most households manageable.

Thus while lenders, regulators and governments are identified as at least complicit in the subprime debacle, it is the subprime borrower who is ultimately subject to a large degree of 'blame', even though they were given clear indications before the crash that house prices would continue to rise by these very same people. The behaviour of the subprime borrower is therefore highlighted as at least one significant cause of the GFC. This is the case even though for the most part the idea of a subprime borrower did not really have a defined collective personality – at least not one that existed in much of the mainstream commentary coming from market watchers – until the collapse came. The FCIC (2011: 7) reports that '[m] any people chose poorly', sometimes living 'beyond their means' and chose non-traditional mortgages 'because that was the only way they could get a foothold' in areas with high property prices. Some of these choices are said to be the result of certain inadequacies on behalf of borrowers – for instance, if they did not understand the terms of their mortgage or did not appreciate the risks attached to declining house values (FCIC 2011: 424).

A paper in a US Federal Reserve discussion series corroborates this line of argument by pointing to the role of 'borrower confusion' and how 'a sizable number of adjustable-rate borrowers . . . do not know the terms of their contracts' (Bucks and Pence 2006: 2). Notably, the authors suggest that 'households with low income and less education are less likely to know their mortgage terms' (Bucks and Pence 2006: 3). The US Federal Reserve also expresses concern that many subprime borrowers 'may not fully understand the risks and consequences' of obtaining certain kinds of mortgages (Board of Governors 2007: 2). In all, the regulatory depiction of the flawed subprime borrower can be summed up by the Organisation for Economic Co-operation and Development's (OECD) (2009: 64 emphasis added) suggestion that:

> Financial risks have been increasingly transferred to individuals in recent decades. Not only do defined-contribution pension plans transfer longevity and investment risks to individuals, but the crisis has exposed an array of vulnerabilities where *poorly-prepared households endangered their own financial security* by purchasing inappropriate products.

Some years after the collapse of the subprime mortgage market, little meaningful debate appears to have been forthcoming about the place of homeownership and the instability of asset-based welfare provision in Anglo-America. The Fed eral Reserve reports that after declines each year between 2005 and 2011 home purchases grew significantly in 2012 and 2013, although there were substantial disparities across demographic groups (Bhutta and Ringo 2014: 3). Along with the US government (Executive Office of the President 2013: 28), it typically welcomes associated price rises because this is considered to play a role in 'strengthening household balance sheets by raising wealth and by increasing the ability of some homeowners to refinance their mortgages at lower rates' (Federal Reserve 2014: 147). Although this is only available to 'some', rising house prices are 'seen as potentially leading to a *virtuous cycle* that could help support household spending and financial market conditions over time' (Federal Reserve 2014: 147 emphasis added). This is held to be the case, even in the face of data that show that six in ten of those in their 60s and four in ten of those over 70 carry debt secured against their homes (Federal Reserve 2014: 82). This presents a huge problem, the Federal Reserve (2014: 82) admits, given that 'homes are the largest component of net worth of many older adult households, and this debt may signal a lack of resources to help fund retirement or other expenses'.

In the UK context, Bank of England research shows that households with high levels of mortgage debt made the largest adjustments in spending as a consequence of the crisis from 2007 onwards (Bunn and Rostom 2014: 307). While the Financial Policy Committee of the Bank of England recognises the stability concerns associated with mortgage debt, it makes very clear that its remit should *not* include playing any role in controlling house price inflation but merely to 'mitigate the risks that a cycle of rising house prices and overextension of credit can pose to financial and macroeconomic stability' (HM Treasury 2014: 16). This is the case even though house price indices were rising at around nine percent a year in 2014, with average gains in London even higher (HM Treasury 2014: 12). It also comes in the face of the fact that the Bank has seemingly long played a role in securing conditions conducive to such house price inflation (Hay 2009: 475).

Coupled with this the UK Financial Conduct Authority (FCA) (2014: 29), the financial regulatory body for consumers established in 2013, continues to stress that an individual's wealth is 'reliant on their ability to accumulate assets and the performance of these assets over time'. The issue for the FCA is not that continual expectations of welfare improvements based on asset price inflation are unsustainable on their own terms. Rather, it restricts its concern to the fact that '[w]here asset prices are showing signs of misalignment with their basic foundations consumers could be making *ill-judged decisions* about their current and future needs' (FCA 2014: 29 emphasis added). The FCA's (2014: 14) chief worry in this regard is about the 'poor affordability decisions' consumers might make on their mortgages based on price expectations of their home.

As such, broadly speaking, in the United States and the United Kingdom there is a perfect storm of a continued faith in asset-based system of welfare built around house price gains. On the one hand, financial regulators, and governments for that matter, have little desire to stem rises in house price inflation, effectively endorsing an asset-based model of welfare. While, on the other hand, blame is placed on individuals themselves both for making 'poor' decisions when expecting prices to rise and for any situations when they cannot realise the gains to be had from asset-price inflation.

Mobilising a sympathetic political economy, it is possible to note how this economistic treatment of responsibility for welfare is expressed in distinctly individualised terms. Rather than understanding market-oriented behaviour as constituted by contestation over interpersonal ethics, regulatory accounts tend to be deeply economistic in their outlook by reinforcing standards of instrumentally rational behaviour. The highly ethico-political contention that people should take complete personal responsibility for their own welfare and, in the contemporary parlance, economic 'security' is therefore left unquestioned. The notion that a debt relation is inherently unequal and therefore highly political is largely overlooked. By contrast, as explored in the previous chapter, Smith's conception of the sympathy procedure differs markedly from what is being suggested here in financialised terms. The crucial point is that by taking Smith's sympathy seriously, market-oriented behaviour is understood to be both the outcome of and inherently involved with contestable interpersonal ethics at the individual level, which throws into doubt this entire notion of unquestionable and 'normal' behaviour of a financialised society.

Financial education and the reinforcement of asset-based welfare

The potential crisis of ethical imagination is revealed more fully in the regulatory attempt to 'educate' people out of the subprime debacle. In response to the identified problem of subprime borrower 'confusion' and 'poor' decision-making, there is an emphasis in the regulatory agenda on 'educating' people to act more rationally in their financial affairs to help prevent future crises and to 'better equip individuals to deal with a more complex world' (OECD 2009: 64). Most explicitly, the OECD (2009: 65 emphasis added) suggests that it is 'important that [government] policies are accompanied by education that promotes *rational household decision making*, in order to avoid future crises'. Stressing the benefits of this 'education', it also notes how 'rational' behaviour serves to legitimate government and regulatory responses themselves: 'Effective financial education and awareness campaigns help individuals to understand financial risks and products and thus take decisions better adapted to their personal circumstances. They also help them understand the need for policy action and reform' (OECD 2009: 65). What is more, the OECD (2009: 65) claims: 'Informed (or financially literate) consumers also contribute to more efficient, transparent and competitive practices by financial institutions. Better educated citizens can also help in monitoring markets, and thus complement prudential supervision'.

This agenda revolves around the central notion of an active, responsible and well-informed financial consumer who is able, unlike the subprime borrower, to behave in an economically sound way that serves to sustain the asset-based model of welfare. The FCIC (2011: 90) explains how 'borrowers are the first defense against abusive lending', summoning up the idea of a well-informed financial individual able to act in a perfectly instrumentally rational way in order to make the market. 'By shopping around', the FCIC (2011: 90) continues, such individuals will ensure that a lender will offer them the most suitable type of loan; rather than produce a situation as occurred in the GFC in which 'many borrowers [did] not understand the most basic aspects of their mortgage'. In support of this argument, it reports that at least 38 percent of borrowers with ARMs in the subprime era did not understand how much their interest rates could reset at one time, and more than half underestimated how high their rates could rise (FCIC 2011: 90).

The Independent Commission on Banking (ICB), established to look into the 'structural' reform of the UK banking sector, also emphasises model financial consumer action. Its final report states:

> In banking markets as elsewhere, what matters is not competition in the abstract but competition to provide what customers want – effective competition. In markets that work well, suppliers compete vigorously with each other, and with the real threat of entry by other firms, to provide a choice of products to *well-informed customers*. Moreover, this happens without damaging side effects on others. Customers, though individually small, enjoy *the power of informed choice*.
>
> (ICB 2011b: 153 emphasis added)

Furthermore the identified need to educate citizens to act as better financial consumers relates to other areas of asset-based systems of welfare. For instance, the OECD (2009: 97) also notes the importance of strengthening 'financial education programs for pensions'. It continues:

> The rapid growth of defined contribution plans in many countries means that individuals face more of the risk in, and assume more of the responsibility for, assuring their own long-term financial well-being. They are likely to make better decisions, and contribute to better overall functioning of financial markets, if they are well educated and informed about issues relating to management of personal finances.
>
> (OECD 2009: 97)

An emphasis on 'financial education' arguably serves to reinforce shifts towards asset-based systems of welfare in financialised economies. This is important in light of a sympathetic political economy because it shows that such an economistic approach works to the exclusion of contestable individual ethics: there *is* such a thing as a 'good' financial consumer, and ethico-political contestation at the individual level is not needed to derive what it is.

A shift towards inducing those preferred 'character traits' of a model consumer can also be detected across a number of programmes of financial literacy education in recent years (Clarke 2015; Marron 2013). Principally, in this regard, a new emphasis on encouraging people to be 'resilient' in the face of economic hardship has entered the financial literacy lexicon. This serves to both naturalise the financial market relations to which the education refers and individualise responsibility for successes and failures in material gains based on participation in those financial market relations. The nebulous concept of resilience itself does a lot of the work in explaining how improvements in consumer 'capability' and 'empowerment' are supposed to bring individual gains for financialised consumers, yet both of these are arguably built on an 'empty promise' about what such education can deliver for everyday people (Clarke 2015: 259). Nevertheless, the framing of debates about financial literacy education in terms of resilience helps dilute serious challenge to regimes of asset-based welfare in light of the crisis.

Moreover, quite remarkably given the extent to which it recognises some of the possible consequences involved in light of the crisis, many other aspects of the regulatory agenda still tend to reinforce asset-based systems of welfare in an almost unquestioned manner. On the one hand, the regulatory account of the GFC acknowledges the huge problem of risk shouldered by the individual – seemingly at least in part outside an individual's own control – in asset-based systems of welfare. For instance, the IMF (2007a: 5) points out that: weaker mortgage collateral is partly associated with adverse employment and income trends; tighter credit conditions fall most heavily on 'more marginally creditworthy borrowers' (2007b: 5); the fall in property and asset prices was *the* primary reason why 2008 US household net worth fell for the first time since 2003 (2008b: 11); and the deteriorating economy and massive job losses resulting from the crisis substantially increased levels of household debt (2009a: 66). Indeed the FCIC (2011:

391) reports that of the $17 trillion lost from 2007 to the first quarter of 2009 in US household net wealth, about $5.6 trillion was the result of declining house prices and much of the remainder due to the decline in value of financial assets, a staggering amount given that US GDP in 2008 was $14.4 trillion.

However, on the other hand, regulatory agendas tend to hold an enduring belief in the promise of the processes of securitisation that support asset-based welfare. The extension of homeownership and other financial assets to those who might otherwise not have access to them, itself a promotion of financialisation, is still one of the major perceived benefits of securitisation. The *Stiglitz Report* (UN 2010: 65), for instance, suggests that government policy-making needs to continue to promote securitisation to provide for 'mortgages that help individuals manage the risks of home ownership better, student loans with lower transaction costs, banking the un-banked, or insuring the uninsured'.

In this manner, the US Federal Reserve (Board of Governors 2007: 11) points out that subprime lending is not necessarily predatory in nature and the IMF (2010b: 21) expresses concern that high unemployment, waning consumer confidence and tighter underwriting standards could have the undesirable impact of discouraging new entrants into the property market. In terms of pensions, the IMF (2009b: 74) also seems to suggest that the 'increasing transfer of portfolio risk to households through defined-contribution schemes' should be welcomed because it fosters 'an increase in savings in order to achieve a target minimum income in retirement'. On a similar note, the OECD (2009: 92) celebrates the fact that younger workers with defined contribution plans may 'suffer less damage' than older workers or retirees because they 'have many years to wait for recovery, and most of their contributions to the plans lie in the future'.

The UK Financial Services Authority (FSA), now the FCA, follows a similar line of thinking by expressing, at least in part, the continued promise of asset-based welfare. It suggests that, in both the United Kingdom and the United States, 'rapid growth in mortgage credit was seen as driving a *democratisation* of home ownership' (FSA 2009: 108 emphasis added). The FSA (2009: 14) points out that simple forms of securitised credit have existed for 'almost as long as modern banking'. It also recounts how since the creation of Fannie Mae in the 1930s, securitised credit has played a major role in US mortgage lending and this position steadily increased until the explosive growth in both scale and complexity in the mid-1990s (FSA 2009: 14). Even if not explicitly articulated, there is a definite sense that asset-based welfare, here in the case of homeownership, is an undisputable good.

Of course in important ways, the regulatory agenda does not enunciate straightforward and unanimous support for asset-based welfare. For instance, the IMF (2011a: 124) notes that there is some recognition of renewed interest in 'alternative mortgage products' such as shared equity models because they 'encourage better risk management'. Likewise it suggests that some countries 'might want to reconsider their policies' in regard to promoting homeownership by recognising that rental housing could be a 'better option for low-income households' and introducing a more level tax treatment of rental compared to owner-occupied housing to help reduce 'the current bias toward homeownership' (IMF 2011a: 143). Yet arguably, with these types of caveat aside, the regulatory agenda on the whole tends to reinforce existing understandings as to the appropriateness of asset-based welfare, particularly with regard to homeownership.

Overall, therefore, in the regulatory accounts of the GFC it is possible to identify a distinct sense in which asset-based systems of welfare continue to be promoted as an appropriate model for a financialised economy. Even in light of the recognised disastrous consequences of extending credit and the dream of homeownership to those who display the 'flawed' characteristics of the subprime borrower, the regulatory agenda still articulates a deep-seated support for asset-based welfare. Particularly in the area of financial 'education', this can be shown to contain entrenched assumptions about instrumentally rational behaviour. In fact, the governance of asset-based welfare certainly continues to endorse an economistic and autonomous individual detached from the rest of society who is responsible for securing their future wellbeing through financial markets and asset price inflation.

It also relates to what Colin Crouch (2009: 390) has labelled a regime of 'privatised Keynesianism', in which '[i]nstead of governments taking on debt to stimulate the economy, individuals [do] so'. Under such circumstances, mortgage and other forms of debt have to be made widely available to keep the policies associated with the removal of the state from welfare provisioning tenable (Montgomerie 2013; Watson 2010). In a sense, then, even in the wake of the crisis, people in Anglo-America especially are asked to have continued faith in financialisation and in the central place that asset-based welfare must have in those societies.

Advancing a sympathetic political economy, which by contrast might attempt to open up the contestable nature of financial market agency in this regard, the regulatory agenda here appears to close down contestation over interpersonal ethics by fostering an economistic conception of market-oriented behaviour. Even after a degree of responsibility is put at the doorstep of the 'irrational' subprime borrower and their problematic inclusion in such systems, asset-based welfare is left almost completely unquestioned. The notion that a borrower might be in a vulnerable position compared to a lender is entirely overlooked. As explored in the previous chapter, Smith's conception of sympathy gives a more complex account of how ethics and politics might come to be interactively formed at the level of the individual. For Smith (*TMS* I.i.1.9–10), after all, to exercise a capacity for sympathy, which is inherently involved in all market-oriented forms of behaviour, is to imagine both intent and circumstance as part of an often imprecise balancing act (Montes 2004). This provides a means of understanding market-based behaviour that avoids the economistic implications of regulatory accounts which here can be shown to close down contestation over interpersonal ethics.

The regulatory governance of risk

Probabilistic risk management is identified as key 'problem' of the crisis in many regulatory accounts. The IMF (2011a: 10) reports that:

> At the heart of the global financial crisis was an abrupt rediscovery of credit risk. Following a period of almost indiscriminate availability of cheap credit,

> lenders suddenly took a fresh look at borrowers' capacity to repay debt and found reasons for concern. Focused initially on problems in the U.S. subprime mortgage sector, the reassessment of credit risk broadened over time, affecting households, nonfinancial corporations, banks, and sovereigns across much of the industrialized world.

Even though the 'growth and prosperity of recent years gave ample illustration of the benefits of financial innovation', the IMF (2008a: xii) further notes that the GFC has 'also shown that there are costs': 'Credit risk transfer products – innovations that were meant to disperse risk broadly – were not always used to move risk to those best able to bear it'. Mark Zandi (2009: 2–3 emphasis in original) describes the condition at the heart of the crisis: 'At every point in the financial system, there was a belief that someone – *someone else* – would catch mistakes and preserve the integrity of the process'. However, despite this general recognition of crisis dynamics based on extant understandings of risk management (HM Treasury 2012: 5), in regulatory accounts there is a reproduction of scientistic treatments of risk and a continuation of trends that tend to normalise the place of risk in society.

The normalisation of credit risk management and structured finance

A number of IMF *Global Financial Stability Reports* produced in the five years (2006–2011) surrounding the crisis give an interesting account of how credit risk management appears to be increasingly 'normalised' as part of regulatory agendas. That is to say, the IMF depicts how risk management seems to be an ever-more pervasive activity in contemporary financialised societies and fundamental to how market agency is constituted. This appears to be the case even during the height of the crisis and remains largely unquestioned in the IMF's response in subsequent years. In 2006, the IMF (2006: 48) welcomed financial innovation because it contributes to growth in household credit. Indeed it celebrated how '[n]ew consumer lending technologies permit lenders to reach more consumers, better assess market and lending risks, price loans more accurately, and reduce the cost of lending' (IMF 2006: 48).

Then in 2007 as the credit crunch started in earnest the IMF (2007b: 74) opined that:

> One should not lose sight of the improvements in risk measurement and control over the last decade and the positive role of these improvements in reducing the likelihood of idiosyncratic failure from uninformed risk-taking. These advances should induce greater risk sensitivity on the part of financial institutions, leading to early unwinding of unanticipated exposures and better risk control.

Although at this time it also suggested that 'it is important not to place undue confidence in all aspects of firms' risk management systems' (IMF 2007b: 74), the IMF (2008a: 81) still reported in 2008 that structured products retain their utility if they can be 'standardised' in some way in order to facilitate 'the development of liquid secondary markets'. It argued: 'structured finance will recover, but . . . the products will likely be more standardized and transparent to both investors and regulators' (IMF 2008a: 54). By 2009, the IMF (2009b: 77) submitted that '[m]obilizing illiquid assets and transferring credit risk away from the banking system to a more diversified set of holders continues to be an important objective of securitization'. That is, even after the observable impact of structured finance at the height of the crisis in 2008, there was a firm belief held by the IMF (2009b: 77) that 'structuring technology in which different tranches are sold to various investors' helps to 'more finely tailor the distribution of risks and returns to potential end investors'. Further indicative of this outlook it suggested:

> Securitization technologies have also been instrumental in supporting a stable supply of housing funding and consumer credit in many emerging market countries. Several governments have pursued and continue to pursue securitization as a way to fund agency programs aimed at overcoming credit constraints for housing and consumer finance. In particular, mortgage securitization has removed constraints on domestic fixed-income markets by accommodating a growing investor base, particularly pension and insurance fund investors with the need for long-term, highly-rated local currency bond investments priced to a more liquid yield curve.
>
> (IMF 2009b: 79)

In 2010, the position appears to have remained largely the same: 'Starting securitization on a safer basis is . . . essential to support credit, particularly for households and small and medium-size enterprises' (IMF 2010a: xii). In 2011, again securitisation is understood as perfectly suitable for creating 'a strong housing finance system' as long as countries 'go back to basics' by 'ensuring safe loan origination and encouraging simple and transparent mortgage contracts' (IMF 2011a: xii).

The IMF's outlook here might be regarded as part of its inability to deal with the crisis in general. In line with many accounts of its performance over the period, Manuella Moschella (2012: 44) claims that 'the IMF conspicuously failed to spot the severe interconnected problems in the world's advanced economies or to provide clear warnings about the risks and vulnerabilities of the global financial system from 2004 to 2007'. Nevertheless, its place within the most significant group of international supervisory bodies, which includes the FSB, the BIS and the G20, remains largely the same, particularly as the IMF has also embraced the move to macroprudential regulation (Moschella 2012: 45). As with the state of global governance more broadly, though, the extent of this change at the IMF has largely been restricted to 'a tinkering around the edges of the mechanics of surveillance and conditionality' (Broome *et al.* 2012: 8). While there might have been some greater tolerance for unorthodox macroeconomic policies in the short-term of the crisis period (Broome 2010), on the whole the IMF's outlook towards risk management in general does not appear to have altered that much in light of the crisis and fits into the broader regulatory story of little radical change (Broome *et al.* 2012: 8).

Many other agenda-setting regulatory accounts of the GFC appear to reinforce this normalisation of credit risk management in general, and structured finance in particular, in the constitution of market agency. For instance, the United Kingdom's ICB (2011a: 7) argues that, '[f]or the most part, retail customers have no effective alternatives to their banks for vital financial services; hence the imperative to avert disruption to the system for their continuous provision'. It notes how important it is that 'ordinary depositors are protected' and suggests that one of the great merits of a 'ring-fencing' of retail from commercial banking is that it would 'isolate those banking activities where continuous provision of service is vital to the economy and to a bank's customers' (ICB 2011b: 8; 11). At first glance, these references to 'ordinary' depositors may seem far removed from the risk management techniques involved with structured finance, but actually the ICB makes clear that such activities could seemingly sit quite comfortably *inside* the retail ring-fence. It suggests that regulation must:

> not prevent a banking group from offering a 'one-stop shop' for customers who required services both from the ring-fenced bank and the rest of the group. One entity could sell products as an agent for other entities in the group. For example, the ring-fenced bank could sell to its customers complex risk management products originated in the non-ring-fenced bank.
>
> (ICB 2011b: 68)

This position chimes with the FSA's (2009: 43) view that a 'future system for credit intermediation will and should involve a combination of traditional on-balance sheet mechanisms and securitisation'. Quite clearly then, proposals for 'ring-fencing' bank operations do not constitute full 'Glass-Steagall' legislation, a reference to the US Banking Act of 1933 that set out provisions to separate retail from investment banking until its repeal in 1999.

At the time of writing, the Bank of England's Prudential Regulation Authority (PRA) (2014: 9), which took over the supervision of UK banks from the disbanded FSA, does not require ring-fencing to be implemented until 2019: eight years after the recommendation was made by the ICB and over a decade since the onset of the crisis itself. Given the length of the delay, the situation may well emulate the one in the United States with the passing of a much-diluted version of the 'Volcker Rule' for ring-fencing operations as part of the Dodd–Frank Wall Street Reform and Consumer Protection Act 2010 (Lavelle 2014). I return to this point in the next chapter.

Overall, regulatory accounts tend to echo the FSF's (2009: 15) initial outlook that while regulators will need to develop greater supervisory responsiveness to risk assessments, there is no urgent need to jettison or even roll-back on recent evolution and innovation in structured financial products. As revealed in the G20 (2009: 3) London Summit statement, a meeting of apparent lasting regulatory importance (Helleiner 2014: 5), the promotion of 'standardisation' and 'resilience' appears to be the length to which reform is acknowledged to be required: not a questioning of extant credit risk management or a halting of the normalisation of associated structured finance techniques. This general stance is also summed up well by the FCIC's (2011: 425) statement:

> Some argue that the conversion of a bundle of simple mortgages to a mortgage-backed security, and then to a collateralized debt obligation, was a problem. They argue that complex financial derivatives caused the crisis. We conclude that the details of this engineering are incidental to understanding the essential causes of the crisis. If the system works properly, reconfiguring streams of mortgage payments has little effect. The total amount of risk in a mortgage is unchanged if the pieces are put together in a different way.

Engaging a sympathetic political economy, it is highly problematic that the regulatory agenda here appears to normalise the place of credit risk management and structured finance, especially in Anglo-American societies. Even in the face of widely recognised forms of credit *mis*management in the build up to GFC, current approaches to – and techniques of – risk management appear to have avoided full scrutiny from within regulatory reform agendas. This might be because they continue to embody an economistic understanding of credit risk, which operates to exclude meaningful debate about the place of risk in society.

In other words, contestable interpersonal ethics at the level of the individual are excluded through assumptions about the basic appropriateness of living life through the ethos of financial risk management. By contrast, Smith's conception of mutual sympathy draws attention to the way in which such notions of 'risk' are constructed and contested within society as a matter of interpersonal ethics related to the inherently unequal nature of debt relations. Recognition of the 'constant balancing act' (Weinstein 2006: 86) involved in the sympathy procedure more fully problematises the place of risk in society. Read through the lens of Smith's sympathy, the major flaw contained within an economistic understanding of risk is that it attempts to exclude contestable interpersonal ethics at the level of the individual.

Scientistic risk management and the promise of structured finance

On what basis is the belief in structured finance maintained? Although it is recognised that the GFC 'represents the first significant test of several categories of innovative financial instruments' (IMF 2007b: 1), there appears to be continued admiration within regulatory agendas as to the benefits of extant risk management practices and the promise of structured finance based on a scientistic understanding of risk. One might suppose that faith in recent financial innovations in general and the securitisation model in particular would have been questioned in regulatory debates in light of the subprime crisis (Gotham 2009). As Julie Froud and Sukhdev Johal (2008: 107) suggest, 'much to the surprise of many whom had previously considered that the growth and reach of finance was a manifestation of its ability to manage risk . . . [the crisis] provides a reminder that finance is unstable and that uncertainty has not been eliminated by more complex financial innovations and models'.

Nevertheless regulatory agendas seemingly contain little by way of a fundamental questioning of the 'scientific' status of risk management practices. The FSF (2008: 9), for instance, provides an early response to the crisis that maintains great confidence in a key plank of recent securitisation trends, the 'originate-to-distribute' (OTD) model:

> When accompanied by adequate risk management and incentives, the OTD model offers a number of benefits to loan originators, investors and borrowers. Originators can benefit from greater capital efficiency, enhanced funding availability, and lower earnings volatility since the OTD model disperses credit and interest rate risks to the capital markets. Investors can benefit from a greater choice of investments, allowing them to diversify and to match their investment profile more closely to their risk preferences. Borrowers can benefit from expanded credit availability and product choice, as well as lower borrowing costs.

The FSF is thus still highly supportive of the OTD model and, in its eyes, the response to the crisis then becomes a question of how to ensure that the individuals and firms involved in securitisation can *make the model work better*. Originators, investors and borrowers just need to become better skilled at risk management. The FSF (2008: 10) points out, 'some firms seem to have handled . . . challenges better than others. This suggests that it is not the OTD model or securitisation per se that are problematic. Rather, these problems, and the underlying weaknesses that gave rise to them, show that the underpinnings of the OTD model need to be strengthened'. Although this is the response of the FSF which was disbanded and replaced by the FSB (2009: 11), the latter still holds essentially the same position in this regard: quite simply, it states that the 'revival of securitisation markets is needed in many countries to support the provision of credit to the real economy'.

The FSA (2009: 43 emphasis added) echoes the sustained belief in recent securitisation practices:

> The challenge is to design regulatory responses which will produce a safer version of the securitised credit model – less complex, more transparent to end investors, with less packaging and trading of securitised credit through multiple balance sheets, *more true distribution* to end investors and *more real risk diversification.*

Interestingly, rather than cast doubt on the securitisation model itself, regulatory responses tend to explicitly attach blame to the inadequate risk management practices of individuals and firms, bringing agendas back to the role of 'financial education' once again. So, the narrative goes, it was a failure on behalf of market participants 'to understand and manage' some of the new risks associated with credit risk transfer (CRT) and securitisation that contributed to the market turmoil (BIS 2008a: 1). Examples of this attempt to blame market participants themselves abound in regulatory accounts. The FSF (2008: 5; 7 emphasis added) reports how 'banks, investors and CRAs [credit rating agencies] *misjudged the level of risks*' involved in the US subprime mortgage market and that 'benign macroeconomic conditions gave rise to *complacency among many market participants* and led to an erosion of sound practices in important financial market segments'.

Crucially, the explanation of the crisis actually starts to appear as a pointed attack on market participants for not living up to the standard of an 'optimal' market agent in risk management (G20 2008: 1). Doubt is cast on the actual *ability* of people to perform their proper role as optimal risk managers:

> Some firms retained large exposures to super-senior tranches of CDOs that *far exceeded the firms' understanding of the risks* inherent in such instruments, and failed to take appropriate steps to control or mitigate those risks. When the turbulence started, *firms and investors misjudged or were unable* to rapidly assess their exposures.
>
> (FSF 2008: 7 emphasis added)

Thus, for the FSF (2008: 8; 20), investors were at fault for being *unwilling* (even those with the 'capacity' to undertake their own credit analysis, 'did not sufficiently examine the assets underlying structured investments') and *unable* (they 'seem to have had insufficient understanding of the risks of structured products in which they invested') to appropriately measure and manage credit risk.

The BIS (2008a: 13 emphasis added) concurs that '[s]ome investors appear to have entered the CRT market despite *lacking the capacity* to independently evaluate the risks of complex CRT products', which essentially meant that they were over-reliant on the CRAs. Moreover, blame is again attached to market participants because, although the CRAs clarified that their ratings are 'not intended to capture the risk of a decline in market value or liquidity, nor should it be considered an investment recommendation . . . *some investors do not seem to understand this point or simply ignore it*' (BIS 2008a: 13 emphasis added). As such, 'many market participants appeared not fully to appreciate how one type of risk (e.g. liquidity) can quickly evolve into another type (e.g. market and credit risk) in CRT' (BIS 2008a: 24). Notably, this account very much depends on treating the crisis as a problem *of* risk, but in such a way that does not question the 'probabilistic paradigm' of contemporary risk management itself (Langley 2015: 103).

The Senior Supervisors Group (SSG) (2009: 4) of the FSB also seems to maintain ultimate faith in pre-crisis risk management practices provided that market participants weed out that which prevents securitisation living up to its promise. Specifically, it points to market participant level problems including 'the *unwillingness or inability* of boards of directors and senior managers to articulate, measure, and adhere to a level of risk acceptable to the firm' and 'arrangements that favored risk takers at the expense of independent risk managers and control personnel' (SSG 2009: 4 emphasis added). This is echoed in country-based examples, such as in the case of the UK's Royal Bank of Scotland, where the FSA (2011: 21) reports that both its supervisory approach and the bank's strategy 'underestimated how bad losses associated with structured credit might be'. The problem was, it continues, that there was 'a consensus, among practitioners and policy-makers, which confidently asserted that financial innovation and complexity had made the financial system more stable' (FSA 2011: 29).

Notably, before the crisis proper, the BIS (2005: 3) recognised that 'the most important credit risk management issue' associated with CRT activity is 'the assessment of default correlation across different reference entities'. 'Correlation', it suggests, 'is critical to evaluating the risk of a portfolio of credit default swaps or the risk associated with CDO tranches' (BIS 2005: 3). Yet the BIS (2005: 14) understood the tranching of risk associated with synthetic CDOs to be 'appealing because it allows the credit risk associated with a pool of exposures to be divided up and allocated to parties based on their underlying risk preferences'. It later explains in a 2008 report how:

> CDOs are designed to diversify risk. The laws of probability imply that the average credit performance of a pool of similar assets will be less volatile and more predictable than the performance of a typical asset in the pool. Indeed, if the pool consists of a large number of relatively small assets, uncertainty in the pool-wide credit loss rate will arise almost entirely from correlations in default losses across assets. In this setting, idiosyncratic risk is diversified away. Only systematic risk factors that influence many assets at once are likely to influence pool-wide credit losses.
>
> (BIS 2008a: 49)

Somewhat calamitously, such a view allowed market participants to understand the poor performance of subprime loans as a 'low-probability economic event' (BIS 2008b: 5). Indeed, as Donald MacKenzie (2011: 1804) suggests, the assumption of low levels of default correlation was 'at the very core of the rationale for CDOs'. After all, the point of their creation was to use a diversified pool of loans with 'relatively modest ratings' and package them in such a way that would allow certain tranches to have much higher ratings (MacKenzie 2011: 1804). With the benefit of hindsight, it is now known that the seemingly small technical decision of how to model default correlation became central to the creation of the largest single category of estimated loss ($290 billion) during the crisis (MacKenzie 2011: 1779).

There was of course some recognition of the limitations of risk management techniques in regulatory accounts of the crisis, including a new emphasis on 'complex' systems (Datz 2013). The FSA (2009: 22) is at times explicit about some of the shortcomings:

> The very complexity of the mathematics used to measure and manage risk, moreover, made it increasingly difficult for top management and boards to assess and exercise judgement over the risks being taken. Mathematical

> sophistication ended up not containing risk, but providing false assurance that other prima facie indicators of increasing risk (e.g. rapid credit extension and balance sheet growth) could be safely ignored.

On a similar note, the FCIC (2011: xix emphasis added) suggests that '[f]inancial institutions and credit rating agencies embraced mathematical models as reliable predictors of risks, replacing judgment in too many instances. Too often, *risk management became risk justification*'. Likewise, the FSF (2008: 34) also points to how many investors erroneously 'took CRAs' ratings opinion of structured credit products as a seal of approval and looked no further' without recognising how 'structured finance ratings differ from traditional corporate debt ratings in that they are model-based and to a larger degree assumption-driven'. Nevertheless, this is not a questioning of the securitisation practices per se, but rather again the flawed market participants using such processes inappropriately.

In sum, a striking feature of regulatory accounts of the GFC is that there is little sense of a fundamental questioning of the securitisation model. Essentially, explanations of the crisis tend to point blame at the specific (in)action of market participants rather than criticise features of securitisation, such as the OTD model or CRT practices more broadly. Interestingly, such an understanding of the crisis contains remarkable implications for the constitution of financial market agency fostered by such depictions. That is to say, in pointing blame at market participants for not living up to the crowning promise of the model, the subsequent regulatory agenda appears to be indicating that individuals and firms ought to better perform the roles that securitisation dictates for them. So, in order to avoid future financial crises, market participants should become more *willing* and more *able* to carry out the kind of risk management practices that the securitisation model requires in order for it to operate 'properly'.

In terms of financial market agency, this essentially suggests that people ought to become better and more efficient risk managing machines. The notion that there might ethico-political contestation over a debt relation is therefore entirely overlooked. Put simply, in regulatory accounts of the GFC, there is nothing wrong with the securitisation model, so the task then becomes making market participants more capable of performing the subject position of optimal risk manager.

In certain ways, the articulation of this form of financial market agency might be successful, and an appropriate response to the GFC. Yet, alongside the ostensible promotion of optimal risk managers, much of the regulatory agenda also points to the significance of information problems in the practices associated with securitisation. Crucially, such problems might hinder the success of the market participant as optimal risk manager and, in those very same regulatory accounts, show some of the limitations and contradictions that come with a scientistic understanding of risk management. In fact, the *Stiglitz Report* (UN 2010: 90) states that securitisation 'opened up new information asymmetries' and the models used to assess risk 'overestimated the benefits of risk diversification and underestimated the costs of the information asymmetries and herd behavior by investors'. This echoes the concern highlighted by the BIS (2008: 27) which states that some products, such as ABS CDOs, may contain little or no 'credit message' because market pricing cannot operate properly in the face of an opaque dispersal of underlying credit risk. It also chimes with the SSG's (2009: ii) view that 'inadequate and often fragmented technological infrastructures . . . hindered effective risk identification and measurement' in the build up to the crisis.

Reading across the regulatory account of the GFC, the governance of credit risk appears to contain a rather problematic articulation of individual market agency as optimal risk management. This is because, on the one hand, the regulatory response seems to continue its strong support for securitisation and belief in the benefits of the science of risk management. It is in this sense that the regulatory agendas foster, or at least attempts to foster, financial market agency in the form of the ultra-*able* risk manager. Yet, on the other hand, in these very same regulatory responses, among other limitations to complete success, significant problems associated with access to information and information asymmetries are highlighted. On one level, then, financial market agency *as* optimal risk management is brought into doubt by the contradictory articulation of the market participant as necessarily limited in their access to information, or their ability to deal with immeasurable uncertainty.

Significantly, regulatory accounts tend to hold on to a belief in the benefits of the securitisation model such that they still place confidence in the *perfectibility* of risk management. In this sense, it is possible to suggest that the regulatory agenda appears to be dominated by a shared understanding as to the appropriateness of promoting financial market agency as optimal risk management. This prevailing view of the perfectibility of the science of risk management is sustained by a narrow scientistic understanding that accepts a legitimate focus on risk rather than immeasurable uncertainty (Blyth 2002), even though the promotion of individuals and firms as optimal risk managers is shot through with contradiction based on such uncertainty. Whereas a sympathetic political economy might call into question the place of risk in society by recognising it as a negotiated construct that is formulated as part of contestation over mutual sympathy, an economistic governance of credit risk relies on a scientistic and disembodied understanding of risk. This is perhaps why many regulatory accounts appears to foster optimal risk managers in order to perfect risk management, rather than fundamentally problematise contemporary risk management practices.

In all, faith in the science of credit risk management remains strong in the regulatory worldview. Yet, more generally concerning risk, there is continued belief in the promise of structured finance: the task is to just make the scientistic systems work more efficiently. Notably, this becomes embodied in constructs like 'Early Warning Exercises' that seek to identify the build up of macroeconomic and financial risks and the actions needed to address them (G20 2009: 1). The central idea of 'resilience' has become important to this post-crisis governance framework in this regard, informing the agendas of the FSB, the G20 and the World Economic Forum (Clarke 2015: 263).

Read through the lens of Smith's sympathy, the major flaw contained within this economistic understanding of credit risk is that it attempts to exclude contestable interpersonal ethics at the level of the individual. For Smith, 'the manner in which we judge' is an imaginative mental procedure and a process of negotiating and internalising standards of interpersonal ethics. In one sense, therefore, it is possible to contrast the ultra-able modern risk manager with the eighteenth-century Smithian subject. The former demonstrates ability through the development of their calculative rationalities, whereas the latter does so through the development of their moral faculties and their impartial spectator. The former is conceived in terms of the ability to embody a position of perfect calculation in terms of how to act in market-oriented behaviour, whereas the latter, while engaging in market-oriented behaviour, recognises it as negotiated and constructed through ongoing contestation over interpersonal ethics. In other words, as opposed to a static or predetermined standard of model individual behaviour alluded to above in economistic accounts of instrumental rationality, a sympathy perspective thus allows for interpersonal ethics to be formed and negotiated in particular ways at specific moments in time and space. This can be seen as a way of politicising risk and risk management by more fully problematising how the construction and contestation of risk takes place in society.

The regulatory governance of debt

There is little doubt as to the tremendous growth in size of debt in Anglo-American economies in the subprime era (Montgomerie 2009: 6; Soederberg 2014: 78–79). The ICB (2011b: 50) reports that between 1998 and 2008, sterling loans made by UK banks to households and private non-financial companies relative to GDP rose 50 percent and 60 percent respectively, while loans to financial companies grew by over 200 percent. As the United Nations Conference on Trade and Development (UNCTAD) (2009: 5) suggests, Anglo-American households borrowed and consumed 'far beyond the real incomes that they could realistically expect, given the productivity growth of the real economy and the dismal trends in personal income distribution'. Despite a general recognition of this over-indebtedness in financialised societies, in many of the regulatory depictions of the crisis there is arguably a depoliticisation of the place of debt in society. In basic terms, it is often completely overlooked that a debt relation is inherently unequal and in turn an ethico-political question.

Standards of appropriate financial market agency

On one level, the majority of regulatory accounts of the crisis clearly recognise that the enormous build up of private debt in the subprime era was highly problematic. In the main, this turns on the issue that when 'credit quality deterioration' occurred and exposed the risky nature of some contracts even 'previously credit worthy customers' were affected (FSA 2009: 35). Yet, on a deeper level, in regulatory accounts there is a sense in which the taking on of relatively high levels of personal debt remains to be seen as an entirely *appropriate* form of behaviour in order to secure a certain standard of living, or indeed to finance the costs of social reproduction (Roberts 2013). For instance, the FCIC (2011: 83 emphasis added) remarks:

> Increased access to *credit meant a more stable, secure life* for those who managed their finances prudently. It meant families could borrow during temporary income drops, pay for unexpected expenses, or buy major appliances and cars. It allowed other families to borrow and spend beyond their means. Most of all, *it meant a shot at homeownership, with all its benefits*; and for some, an opportunity to speculate in the real estate market.

This outlook appears to echo a 2006 IMF (2006: 46 emphasis added) report, which suggests that:

> Better access to credit reduces household consumption volatility, improves investment opportunities, eases the constraints on small and family businesses, and diversifies household and financial sector assets. The welfare gains from such expansion can be sizable, *making further growth of household credit desirable.*

The rationale behind this thinking appears to be that ever-increasing access to credit for households presents them with benign consumption and investment prospects and 'enables better diversification of household wealth' (IMF 2006: 47). Much of this thinking is explicitly based on the 'life cycle income hypothesis' which states that 'the availability of credit allows households to overcome liquidity constraints and permits consumption to be smoothed over periods of high and low income' (Ando and Modigliani cited in IMF 2006: 47).

According to many regulatory outlooks, then, the extension of household credit should be celebrated (Executive Office of the President 2013: 34), especially if it 'frees household equity tied in housing and other consumer durables' that can then be reinvested (IMF 2006: 47). Quite simply, 'access to loans is advantageous to borrowers – and to the economy in general – because capital is able to circulate, and be used in an efficient manner' (ICB 2011a: 16). Indeed, something of this normalisation of finance in general and of debt relations in particular is articulated by the UNCTAD (2009: 11 emphasis added):

> The financial sector acts as the central nervous system of modern market economies. It distributes liquidity and mobilizes the capital necessary to finance large investment projects; it allocates funds to the most dynamic sectors of the economy; *it provides households with the necessary funds to smooth consumption over time*; and, through its payment system, it allows managing the complex web of economic relationships that are necessary for economies characterised by a high degree of division and specialisation of labour.

Picking up on the notion of the normalisation of asset-based welfare outlined above, a similar dynamic appears to occur with the use of credit in regulatory agendas. Notably, claims are made about the importance of protecting banking services against disruption in order that financial services to customers are constantly maintained (ICB 2011b: 36–37). In fact, the ICB (2011a: 97) objects to the 'social costs' of a narrow banking model because the prevention of deposit taking banks from lending to individuals and businesses 'destroys the synergies of such financial intermediation'. It sees this as undesirable because the potential costs involved in 'increasing lending rates and credit rationing' (ICB 2011a: 97). It also states:

> The most visible function that banks undertake is to receive deposits from savers, including the general public. Households in the UK are the ultimate holders of wealth in the UK, yet they are not well placed to look after that wealth safely themselves and use it effectively. Furthermore, money that is not engaged in productive activity will devalue over time as a consequence of inflation. Interest-bearing deposit facilities therefore act to store value.
>
> (ICB 2011a: 16)

Moreover in another indicative step of how professional risk management techniques are deemed appropriate for household debt, the IMF (2006: 70) suggests:

> The regulation of household credit does not entail a fundamentally different approach from that for other credits, and the standard prudential apparatus – risk-weighting, capital adequacy, classification, and provisioning – should suffice. Household credit is also somewhat easier to evaluate and classify than corporate credit.

Arguably the very processes of debt evaluation and classification serve to normalise the use of personal debt within a financialised economy. The IMF (2006: 61) reports that household debt is generally considered 'sustainable' if a borrower has 'positive net worth' and 'can service debt at contractual terms'. The characteristics of a borrower which determine such factors include: 'future income; savings, interest, and exchange rates; access to refinancing; and whether loans are used purely for consumption, durable assets (such as housing), or productivity-enhancing investments (e.g., education)' (IMF 2006: 61). One problem noted in the assessment of credit histories, however, is the difficulty of distinguishing between a 'life event' (understood as incidents such as 'divorce, illness or involuntary redundancy'), on the one hand, and a borrower using credit to maintain an 'unaffordable lifestyle', on the other (FSB 2011: 18). Seemingly quite controversial and contestable questions, the FSB (2011: 18) suggests that although an automated underwriting process might not pick this up, an 'expert risk assessment' is presumed to be sufficient. Notably, though, the FSB (2011: 34) maintains that debt service 'metrics' can still appropriately assess affordability in order to ensure that the amount of discretionary income a borrower has is 'sufficient to maintain an adequate standard of living'.

Furthermore, as detailed above, the regulatory response to the crisis points to the well-known 'problem' of extending credit to borrowers who, in other circumstances not in the subprime era, would not have been granted mortgage credit. Some of the blame for this excessive risk-taking in the form of over-risky lending is attached to strong investor demand and the excessive compensation structures of the period. Yet, one of the most significant aspects of the regulatory representations of the GFC is that they appear to suggest that there is a way of distinguishing between those who deserved to be extended credit and those who do not. Seemingly, the creditworthy and the uncreditworthy can and should be clearly demarcated in a properly functioning financial system. So the interesting question then becomes, who are those creditworthy individuals? Who represents the model citizen of a credit-based, but not *overly* indebted, financialised economy?

One possible answer is contained within regulatory debates in the form of those groups who are presented as the 'victims' of the crisis: they are those who have successfully performed the position of the financially responsible individual. Incidentally, from a Smithian sympathy perspective, it is not really possible to attribute the personality of 'innocent victim' to a whole group of people in this way. This is because under the terms of a sympathy procedure, which emphasises the moral learning required for an *individual* to partake in market-oriented behaviour, the constitution of ethico-political categories such as 'blame' and 'victimhood' involve contestation over the appropriate forms of that market-oriented behaviour. So, if anything, to attribute these categories to groups in this way might close down contestation over appropriate standards of market-oriented behaviour rather than adequately problematise such standards as a response to the GFC.

Yet it is quite remarkable just how explicitly many regulatory accounts put forward certain people and groups as the *innocent* victims of the subprime crisis. The promotion of particular constructions of financial market agency might be unintentional, but a clear indication is given as to who is considered to be the 'prime' financially responsible individual who is suffering because of the subprime debacle. On this issue, the *Stiglitz Report* is particularly noteworthy. It refers to the need for continued efforts to identify those 'institutional innovations that might contribute to improvements in the well-being of ordinary citizens and to the functioning of the global economic system' (UN 2010: 198). Who are these 'ordinary citizens' to be protected? There are in fact numerous passages throughout the report that appear to indicate the character traits of these deserving groups. It notes how the crisis 'has shown how the failures of the financial system have imposed costs on others, such as *taxpayers, homeowners, and workers*, who were not directly party to the excessive risk-taking' (UN 2010: 68 emphasis added). Then, again, it reports that the 'failure of the financial system to perform its core functions has imposed huge costs on society – on the economy, *on taxpayers, on homeowners, on workers, on retirees*, on virtually everyone . . . Well-functioning globalization might have protected *them*' (UN 2010: 197 emphasis added).

Moreover, the *Stiglitz Report* (UN 2010: 59) suggests that '[w]hile "blame" should rest on the financial sector, government failed to protect the market from itself and to protect society from the kinds of excesses that have repeatedly imposed high costs on taxpayers, workers, homeowners, and retirees'. When considering some of the immediate effects of policy responses to the crisis, the last group come up for special mention as 'the unprecedented lowering of interest rates may have been the correct macroeconomic response to the crisis, but it has produced a sharp reduction in the incomes of retirees who did not gamble on risky securities and invested prudently in short- or medium-term government securities' and 'who are likely to see their *hard-earned pension funds* disappear' (UN 2010: 13; 106 emphasis added). This stance is particularly notable given that government interventions in response to the subprime crisis effectively served to 'protect wealth already accumulated on the housing market' by drawing empathetic boundaries around the 'middle-class homeowner constituted as the "responsible mortgage borrower"' (Watson 2009b: 423). Implicitly, of course, this also problematically tends to refer to the white, hetero-normative nuclear family.

Overall, it is possible to discern in some of the regulatory accounts of the GFC a characterisation of the financially responsible individual who constitutes the 'prime', as opposed to the subprime, individual. Essentially, they are depicted as a taxpayer, employed, a homeowner, and with a pension fund (and they are thus not in receipt of benefits, unemployed, unmortgaged, or without financial assets). In this manner, the regulatory agenda ostensibly promotes a financialised individual who in many ways lives up to the financially responsible individual who acted prudently in the subprime era and ended up as a 'victim'. Seemingly a financialised individual is thus fostered both *before* the GFC (as part of asset-based welfare agendas) and in the regulatory *response* to the GFC (as part of the process of attributing blame for the crisis which is clearly not focused on the financialised individual but more likely directed at the subprime borrower). This degree of continuity is a fundamental point to which I return in the next chapter to consider whether the everyday politics of the GFC offers any challenges to this enduring aspect of financialisation.

Moreover, although the disastrous consequences of extending credit might be quite clear in regulatory accounts, it is telling that the construction of financial market agency in terms of a financialised individual is still very much promoted. In this sense, there is very little shift in outlook on appropriate standards of behaviour from before the GFC. The sphere of sympathy in which there is a shared understanding about appropriate standards of 'good' market-oriented behaviour is thus limited to the financialised individual: the regulatory accounts extend their condolences to people who display the character traits of instrumental rationality by appropriately assuming personal responsibility for their wellbeing and attempt to secure it through systems of credit and debt. This arguably leaves little room for contestable interpersonal ethics at the level of the individual and recognition of the ethico-political nature of debt relations.

The depoliticisation of debt relations

Regulatory accounts of the GFC give a clear sense that financial and banking services are central to the maintenance of an 'advanced economy'. For instance, the BIS (2011: 1) argues that a 'strong and resilient banking system is the foundation for sustainable economic growth, as banks are at the centre of the credit intermediation process between savers and investors'. Similarly, the FSA

(2009: 47) reports that the relative importance of financial services tends to increase as incomes grow because the wealthier people become, 'the more life cycle consumption smoothing occurs, and the more diverse they become in their preferences for consumption at different points in their life'. In turn, it suggests, this leads to an increase in demand for both savings and borrowing products (FSA 2009: 47).

A pertinent issue in this regard though, especially in light of the crisis, is that if the place of financial services is recognised as increasingly important to an advanced financialised economy, then the highly politicised nature of creditor-debtor relations underneath the financial services industry is potentially overlooked. As discussed in the previous chapter, from a sympathetic political economy perspective such relations are part of contestable interpersonal ethics; after all, in basic terms, they are inherently unequal and have to be negotiated. Yet, on the whole, regulatory accounts tend to deny the political nature of debt relations by treating all instances of market-oriented behaviour as merely the expression of a 'voluntary exchange of equivalents between two consenting parties', whichever side of the relationship an individual happens to be situated (Soederberg 2014: 4). In the recognition and reinforcement of the centrality of financial services to Anglo-American societies, therefore, the regulatory agenda may erroneously serve to deny the politics of debt because to foster instrumental rationality is to exclude the ongoing contestable ethics of financial market agency.

There is a definite sense in regulatory accounts that the ostensibly vital services provided by banks and other financial institutions ought not to be threatened by such potential dangers as over-regulation or state interference. The 'safeguard' against high-risk products is understood in terms of reserve, liquidity and capital requirements (US Senate PSI 2011: 160). In the UK context, the recurrent theme is the importance of 'competition' to retail banking, with attendant stipulation that regulatory costs should not be too high (Bowman *et al*. 2014: 87). For instance, the ICB (2011b: 44) stresses the 'core economic function' of banks and so wants to avoid the 'high' economic costs of imposing too many restrictions on their activities. Perhaps for this reason, rather than call for more onerous regulation, as in much of the discussion on international banking reform, it places a good degree of confidence in capital buffers being a suitable response to prevent (or cushion the impact of) further crises. The ICB (2011b: 163) writes:

> A theme emphasised throughout this report has been that making banks better able to absorb losses, and easier to resolve if they still get into trouble, will help curb incentives for excessive risk taking in the first place. This was manifestly not the case in the run-up to the crisis.

The ICB's interest in countercyclical capital buffers here represents part of something of the new consensus in financial regulation. Andrew Baker (2013: 113) describes the move to macroprudential regulation (MPR) from late 2008 onwards among those in the financial regulatory networks centred around the Swiss city of Basel as a 'rapid ideational shift'. Crucially, the Basel III agreement contains a macroprudential component and a number of leading central banks and the FSB use MPR as a central idea shaping their proposals (Baker 2013: 127; Helleiner 2014: 100). Yet, these developments do not constitute a radical overhaul of what banks do and their motivations more broadly, with all this entails in terms of essential shortcomings for reform proposals (Froud *et al.* 2010; Rethel and Sinclair 2012). In Lena Rethel's (2014: 87) terms, 'there remains a tendency to focus on regulative rules, whilst refraining from more substantial debates about the purpose of banks in a world of disintermediated finance'.

When it does make slightly more onerous demands on banks for reform, such as the ring-fencing of retail operations, the ICB is still cautious about not taking this reform too far. Notably, both secured and *unsecured* lending is still allowed within the ring-fence proposal, including mortgage lending and credit cards (ICB 2011b: 54). What is more, the ICB (2011b: 18 emphasis added) openly admits on its terms 'banking reform':

> In many respects . . . *would be restorative of what went before in the recent past* – better-capitalised, less leveraged banking more focused on the needs of savers and borrowers in the domestic economy. Banks are at the heart of the financial system and hence of the market economy.

Other regulatory institutions appear guarded in making burdensome claims on banks and other financial institutions based on their supposed importance to a properly functioning economy. On the one hand, the FSB (2009: 1) claimed in 2009 that:

> In recent months, expectations have taken hold in some parts of the private financial sector that the financial and regulatory system will remain little changed from its pre-crisis contours. These expectations – that business will be able to go on just as before – need to be dispelled.

Yet, on the other hand, its recommendations for reform in light of the crisis do not stray very far away from a 'business as usual' scenario. For instance, the FSB (2011: 29) recommends a 'principles-based framework' rather than set international standards because it claims that households across jurisdictions will face 'different degrees of idiosyncratic risk' based on different systems of welfare, health care and employment protection. It therefore advocates that national regulators monitor lending standards 'across a range of dimensions' that take account of particular 'national circumstances' regarding lenders' funding patterns, housing supply flexibility, household 'resilience' and access to welfare (FSB 2011: 29). Indeed the FSB's overall message seems to be one of very mild reform, rather than a thorough questioning of the place of debt in Anglo-American society. It suggests:

> Innovation in the mortgage market to increase affordability for borrowers will likely continue but the layering of risks should be avoided. In particular,

> practices that combine aggressive underwriting parameters with aggressive mortgage products should be discouraged: for example, low-doc loans coupled with teaser rate or interest-only products, or loans with high LTV [loan-to-value] ratios that include negative amortisation.
>
> (FSB 2011: 20)

In a sense, then, the regulatory agenda in response to the GFC is about removing the 'aggressive' edge to lending, not altering in any significant way the financial systems through which credit and debt are allocated.

This position seems to be similar to the IMF's (2006: 68) suggestion that there are 'no easily identifiable global "best practice" parameters with respect to prudential regulation of household credit' so national regulators, although they may look to international benchmarks for guidance, should design 'country-specific rules' on issues like loan-to-value ratios. Along similar lines, rather than perhaps a downsizing of the place of banks in society, the BIS (2011: 5) speaks of making them 'more resilient' to procyclical dynamics and helping them serve as a 'shock absorber'. Principally in this respect it also merely recommends increasing capital buffers (BIS 2011: 7).

Moreover, there are other aspects of the regulatory debate that appear to reinforce existing debt relations and further deny ethico-political contestation over appropriate forms of financial market agency. For instance, on the one hand, the IMF (2009a: 27) recognises that the economic 'stress' put on 'household balance sheets and debt servicing' at the start of the crisis meant that US households 'borrowed more heavily on credit cards and other forms of consumer credit as other credit channels began to close'. Indeed, at times it expresses a significant degree of concern:

> Subprime mortgages are especially exposed to . . . payment shocks, since a disproportionate share originated as ARMs. Once faced with payment shock, borrowers with limited built-up equity may be unable to avoid default by extracting that equity to meet monthly payments. Similarly, they may be unable to pay off a mortgage by selling their home, particularly in an environment of weak home price appreciation.
>
> (IMF 2007a: 6)

Yet, on the other hand, the IMF is careful not to speak too harshly of existing debt relations in its reform recommendations. Indeed the IMF (2008a: 38) actually expresses concern that the US moratorium on interest rate resets for subprime borrowers, which seeks to limit foreclosures, might 'redistribute the cost from borrowers to lenders, servicers, and investors'. It also notes that responsive measures to the GFC will need to be 'weighed carefully' to ensure that a balance is struck between legitimate issues of consumer protection and the 'protection of legal contracts that underpin modern finance, as some of these measures may undermine existing contracts' (IMF 2008a: 38). Finally, the IMF (2010b: 21) also expresses surprise at the rise in 'strategic defaults' in which borrowers were up-to-date on their mortgage loan payments, but chose to default because they were in negative equity. As such action became 'more socially acceptable', it laments, lenders were 'ill-prepared for this risk, which is not well captured in most risk models and provisioning rules' (IMF 2010b: 23).

Perhaps in an attempt to 'correct' for such financially deviant behaviour, the IMF (2006: 62) expresses admiration for the way in which in some countries the collection of household debt is linked to payroll deductions. It views this as useful because it serves to 'inculcate a habit of prompt debt service' and also 'adjust consumption to post-debt service disposable income, thereby enabling lenders to offer more household credit' (IMF 2006: 62). In another similar move with paternalistic undertones, the FSB (2011: 36) recommends that regulators should allow lenders to 'consider combining easier terms in some dimensions with repayment arrangements that encourage extra principal repayments so as to encourage borrowers to build up equity more quickly than would normally be required'. Here, the agenda returns to one of financial education and the inculcation of good financial habits.

In the wake of the GFC, in what has been referred to as 'the age of austerity', governments around the world have sought to engage in significant and often unprecedented policies of fiscal retrenchment based on an individualisation of responsibility for that crisis. In the United Kingdom, as in many other instances, legitimation for cutting the large fiscal deficit was garnered through appeals to everyday experiences of perceived overspending and feelings of individual guilt associated with the crisis (Stanley 2014: 897). For many, austerity measures have involved a 'reassertion of the individual, the community and the market, and further renouncement of the role of the state' (Kennett *et al.* 2013: 18). Indeed as Mark Blyth (2013: 23) argues, the private-sector financial crisis was transformed into a financial crisis of the state in order to justify extraordinary cuts to welfare and public employment. In a sense, then, the responsibility for the debt fallout of the crisis has been placed firmly at the door of individual people under austerity politics. Thus while austerity discourse focuses on the need for fiscal retrenchment because of excessive collective (state) debt, it pays little attention to the highly contestable nature of that debt, given that it was originally largely private in kind (Dodd 2014: 124). Private bank debt was ultimately socialised, yet moral blame under the austerity era is still attached to individual debtors for behaving poorly in causing the crisis.

Overall, drawing these points together, I argue that in the regulatory governance of personal debt there is again an attempt to exclude interpersonal ethics from market-oriented behaviour. The ways in which the majority of regulatory accounts of the GFC serve to reinforce the dominant position of financial and banking services in Anglo-America is complicit in the exclusion of contestable ethics in terms of debt relations. In fact, a sizeable extension of credit in society even to simply maintain existing living standards is on the whole viewed as quite appropriate in an advanced economy. In turn, the regulatory agenda works to give a clear indication of the model citizen of such an economy: they are the people who are identified as innocent 'victims' of the crisis and essentially embody the characteristics of the financialised individual. The protection of 'normal' financial and banking services for these model citizens also serves to normalise debt relations to the exclusion of any meaningful discussion of fundamental banking reform in response to the GFC. This is especially problematic in the face of the idea that debt relations are inherently unequal. From a sympathetic political economy perspective, the regulatory governance of personal debt appears to rely heavily on a flawed economistic treatment of market-oriented behaviour, which might be improved by, at the very least, re-politicising questions of debt so as not to deny the contestable nature of the ethics of financial market-oriented behaviour.

Concluding remarks

I began this chapter by reflecting on the way in which Stiglitz, a leader in global financial governance, appears to uncritically reproduce at least one of Skinner's basic mythologies in his interpretation of Smith. Based on my contention that historiographical matters can perform a significant role in the construction of contemporary issues themselves, it is notable that Stiglitz's economistic outlook on the GFC, in this chapter represented in his UN report, mirrors a distinctly economistic interpretation of the work of Smith. Mobilising a sympathetic political economy I have tried to indicate some of the problems of continuing to treat financial market agency in economistic terms.

Specifically, at the three sites of finance explored at the regulatory level, the GFC has been explained as a crisis based on the denial of contestable ethics at the individual level. In the first section, I illustrated how asset-based systems of welfare enjoy a largely unquestioned position in regulatory accounts. Even with the issues of access to homeownership and financial security falling right at the heart of the crisis, there is a tendency to reinforce and rearticulate the need for asset-based welfare. In the second section, I argued that credit risk management practices remain largely unchallenged in the regulatory debates. If anything, along with the securitisation model, they are further normalised based on a continued faith in the 'science' and perfectibility of risk management. In the final section, I suggested that the regulatory view of personal debt appears to continue to depoliticise debt relations by insisting on the normalisation of financial services in an advanced economy and works to foster model financialised citizens. Again, despite the possible challenge to such an outlook posed by the GFC, a denial of the political contestability of debt appears to remain.

What unites the crisis of ethical imagination at each of these sites of finance is that on the whole the regulatory account of and response to the GFC relies on an economistic understanding of financial market agency that attempts to exclude contestable ethics at the individual level. Asset-based systems of welfare are based on societies made up of instrumentally rational individuals acting autonomously to secure their wellbeing through the financial market; extant risk management practices rely on assumptions about the individualisation of disembodied risk in society again dependent on instrumentally rational and autonomous individuals; and contemporary treatments of issues of debt depoliticise the creditor-debtor relation by assuming that all market-oriented behaviour is instrumentally rational on either side. By contrast, a sympathetic political economy, at the very least, problematises and opens up contestable ethico-political space at these important sites of finance.

In an extremely insightful comment submitted to the FCIC, the president and CEO of the National Community Reinvestment Coalition (NCRC), a US association that seeks to combat discrimination in access to credit, sums up impeccably the lingering problem for the regulatory account of the GFC (2011: 404 emphasis added):

> a few hundred thousand people, even a million people going into foreclosure, you can kind of blame and say, 'Well they should have known better.' But 15 [or] 16 million American families can't all be wrong. *They can't all be greedy and they can't all be stupid.*

In many ways, this intervention highlights the problem of assuming away ethico-political contestation at the individual level: it is simply unacceptable to explain the problem of subprime borrowing as one caused by *all* subprime borrowers acting in a 'greedy' or 'stupid' way (Seabrooke 2010). In the next and final chapter, I explore the extent to which voices in the everyday politics of the GFC – represented by interventions from organisations such as the NCRC – provide a challenge to the regulatory level of finance more congruent with a Smithian sympathetic political economy.

5 The everyday politics of finance in crisis

> Smith, wrongly cited as the father of free-market economics, constantly cautioned against the unregulated power of big business, warning that unchecked 'trade or manufacture' would engage in 'conspiracy against the public' . . . since business interest 'is always in some respects different from, and even opposite to, that of the public'.
>
> (Smith cited in *The Occupied Times* 2012a: 12)

This is how members of the Occupy movement claim Smith's name for their cause in protest against economic and political elites. Here Smith is appealed to *not* as 'the father of free-market economics', as an economistic reading of Smith might have it, but as a thinker concerned about how monopolistic business practices can be harmful to society. Notably the occupiers' interpretation is almost diametrically opposed to Joseph Stiglitz's (2007: 66) reading, such as when he argues that Smith was 'the founder of modern economics'. The rival interpretations here mirror the competing and drastically different responses to the GFC. Stiglitz is very much embedded in the regulatory level of financial governance discussed in the previous chapter. The occupiers who claim Smith's name in *The Occupied Times of London*, a newspaper founded in October 2011 during the first week of the occupation outside Saint Paul's Cathedral, have an ostensibly radical and anti-elite driven agenda which is deliberately positioned against this very same regulatory level of finance. Once again Smith's ideas, and the contest over them, appear to play a pivotal part in the regulatory and everyday accounts of the crisis itself.

I employ the term 'everyday' in this chapter to refer to the 'non-elite', in opposition to the regulatory level of finance discussed in the previous chapter. Used here as a provisional heuristic device, this draws upon John Hobson and Leonard Seabrooke's influential division of political economy. They suggest that 'everyday' actions are defined as:

> acts by those who are subordinate within a broader power relationship but, whether through negotiation, resistance or non-resistance, either incrementally or suddenly, shape, constitute and transform the political and economic environment around and beyond them.
>
> (Hobson and Seabrooke 2007: 15–16)

Seabrooke (2007: 83) further suggests that everyday political economy actions are those associated with questioning the legitimacy of government policies, complaining in public or private about how the economy should work and a general sense that government tends to intervene in the economy on behalf of the narrow interests of rentiers rather than the broader population. I think it is fair to consider groups like the Occupy movement a form of 'everyday' agency. It certainly fits earlier IPE discussions of 'global civil society' understood by many as a key source of ethical agency (e.g. Cox 1999; De Goede 2005; Gill 2000; Kaldor 2003; Scholte 2004). When considered alongside more traditionally structured Anglo-American movements and groups who have formulated substantial accounts of the crisis, it is possible to piece together a sketch of the types of interventions made in the everyday politics of the GFC. These include the New Economics Foundation (NEF), the National Community Reinvestment Coalition (NCRC), the Put People First (PPF) coalition of NGOs, and Wall Street Watch, together with more critical academic studies by the Centre for Research on Socio-Cultural Change (CRESC) and Democratic Audit. This survey is not meant to be comprehensive, but illustrative of what more everyday accounts provide. Paralleling the previous chapter, then, I present alternative representations of and responses to the crisis investigated at the same three sites of finance explored at the regulatory level.

Building on an interest in a sympathetic political economy, is it possible to identify elements of the everyday politics of the crisis that successfully challenge the regulatory representation and response? Do everyday interventions offer alternatives along more sympathetic lines? In the first section, I survey the place of asset-based systems of welfare. I assess the extent to which such representations of and responses to the crisis articulate a challenge to these systems. I look to the everyday politics of the GFC for articulations that open up ethico-political questions in a way that echoes a Smithian sympathy perspective. In the second section, I investigate the issue of credit risk management. I ask if everyday representations are more congruent with a Smithian sympathy perspective that accounts for how norms of risk might come to be formed and contested in society through moments of mutual sympathy. Finally, I examine treatments of indebtedness in the everyday politics of the GFC. I ask whether this politics provides a challenge to the depoliticisation of debt and whether it offers a fuller recognition of the contestable interpersonal ethics that make up credit-debt relations according to a sympathetic political economy.

If interventions into the everyday politics of the crisis do indeed offer alternatives to the economistic liberal outlook in terms of ethico-political contestation, this would surely be a significant success for those who seek to challenge existing regulatory financial market governance. Members of the Occupy movement, for instance, consciously position themselves as part of an attempt to reimagine and seek alternatives to the elitist and, in their eyes at least, failed 'system' of regulatory financial governance (*The Occupied Times* 2011a: 2; 2012b: 11). The fact that they occupied financial space as part of an intentional performative act, seeking to repoliticise finance by subverting the spaces it fills, draws attention to this line of challenging existing structures of finance. Offering alternatives to an economistic outlook thus might offer them, and others who provide exacting critiques of Anglo-American financial governance of the last 40 years or so, a substantial way to make the claim that the GFC was a crisis of ethical imagination that calls for a radical rethinking of finance. This is based on the notion that, from a sympathetic political economy at least, a denial of contestable ethics at the individual level *is a crisis of ethics*. The question for this chapter, then, is about the extent to which the everyday politics of the crisis contains a substantial challenge to the economistic liberalism embodied at the regulatory level of financial governance.

The everyday politics of asset-based welfare

Success in Anglo-America has long been defined in terms of the size and quality of one's home, such that the 'pecuniary and psychological benefits we attach to home ownership are unique' (Zandi 2009: 49). In this section, I illustrate the ways in which interventions into the everyday politics of the GFC offer challenges to this kind of 'homeowner ideology' rooted in systems of asset-based welfare. In the previous chapter, I argued that asset-based welfare enjoys a largely unquestioned position in regulatory accounts. In turn, I suggested, this has the effect of potentially excluding interpersonal ethics from market-oriented behaviour by inducing an economistic and autonomous individual detached from the rest of society. Might everyday accounts avoid such an economistic treatment of market-oriented behaviour? Does the everyday politics of the GFC open up ethico-political questions in a way that echoes a Smithian sympathetic understanding of market-oriented behaviour?

Financial responsibility and challenges to asset-based welfare

In a foundational statement, London occupiers assert that they are 'part of a global movement against corporate greed and unregulated banking systems, subverting hierarchies and creating a space where people are encouraged to join' (*The Occupied Times* 2011a: 1). It is also claimed that the Occupy movement is 'a soulful expression of a moral outrage at the ugly corporate greed that pushes our society and world to the brink of catastrophe' (*The Occupied Wall Street [OWS] Journal* 2011c: 1). In their 'Declaration of the Occupation of New York City' occupiers state '[w]e come to you at a time when corporations, which place profit over people, self-interest over justice, and oppression over equality, run our governments' (Occupy Wall Street [OWS] 2011a). They claim they are allied to 'all people who feel wronged by the corporate forces of the world' (OWS 2011a) and they 'protest the blatant injustices of our times perpetuated by the economic and political elites' (OWS 2011b).

Within everyday political groups and movements like Occupy, there is often a sustained critique of the housing finance systems found in Anglo-America expressed in terms of condemnation of the place of financiers in those systems. A typical sentiment expressed is that '[*t*]*hey have taken our houses* through an illegal foreclosure process, despite not having the original mortgage' (OWS 2011a emphasis added). Indeed occupiers frequently condemn the place of mortgage-related debt and speak of attempting to 'reclaim our mortgaged future' (OWS 2011b). This line of criticism is echoed by the advocacy project Wall Street Watch (2009: 14 emphasis added) in their account of the GFC:

> *They engaged in unconscionable predatory lending* that offered huge profits for a time, but led to dire consequences when the loans proved unpayable. And *they created, maintained and justified a housing bubble*, the bursting of which has thrown the United States and the world into a deep recession.

The direct vilification of financiers works alongside a critique of the homeowner ideology also identified as playing a fundamental role in the subprime debacle. For Wall Street Watch (2009: 65):

> There were reasons why [former Chair of the Federal Reserve Alan] Greenspan and other top officials did not act to pop the bubble. They advanced expanded home ownership as an ideological goal. While this objective is broadly shared across the political spectrum, the Bush administration and Greenspan's ideological commitment to the goal biased them to embrace growing home buying uncritically – without regard to whether new buyers could afford the homes they were buying, or the loans they were getting.

It further suggests that 'Wall Street grew rich on mortgage-related securities and exotic financial instruments' and 'people borrowed en masse against the rising value of their homes to spend more and keep the economy functioning' (Wall Street Watch 2009: 66).

Notably though, in direct contrast to regulatory accounts, in everyday interventions there is much less blame attached to the 'subprime' borrower, much less emphasis put on the 'flawed' characteristics that the subprime borrower displayed in the period preceding the crisis and how they might be financially 'educated' out of displaying such characteristics again. Instead, attention tends to focus on financiers, as well as on the governments and regulatory bodies that promote systems of asset-based welfare (Chomsky 2012: 29). For instance in the pages of *Tidal* (2011: 17 emphasis added), a publication of the Occupy movement, there is an account of how borrowers were in a sense cheated by a homeowner ideology, with the argument made that '[s]uburban sprawl and home ownership have *deceived us into debt* and a twisted sense of control, success, and identity'. Moreover in another instance of blaming mortgage lenders, but not borrowers, the NCRC (2008: 3) reports that significant numbers of adjustable-rate mortgage borrowers were defaulting even before the first interest rate adjustment on their loans, which clearly points towards 'unsatisfactory underwriting practices'. In a further attribution of blame, it also documents that nearly 35 percent of subprime loans were issued to borrowers who could have qualified for fixed rate 'prime' loans (NCRC 2010c: 3).

Similarly, in the United Kingdom, the ills of asset-based welfare also appear to get attached to the financial sector itself, rather than borrowers specifically. For instance CRESC, a research centre that has produced 'public interest' reports such as *An Alternative Report on UK Banking Reform*, provides interesting interventions into the politics of the crisis coming from the perspective of practitioners and academics. CRESC (2009: 64) suggests that '[i]ndiscriminate lending for consumers loaded revolving debt onto the household balance sheet and caused the housing bubble'. In turn, it notes that the debt burden was pushed up for new entrants and low income households who spent 40 percent of disposable income on mortgages, while those already 'on the [property] ladder' were encouraged to withdraw equity to fuel further consumption (CRESC 2009: 64). For CRESC (2009: 68), then, the GFC represents a 'social turning point', a 'change in the economic conjuncture' and something of a direct challenge to the asset-based welfare model. It argues that the crisis 'discredited the social promise' that people could find economic security through property, particularly in old age (CRESC 2009: 68).

Echoing Wall Street Watch and members of the Occupy movement, CRESC (2009: 40) is of the opinion that '[t]wenty years of innovation in wholesale finance did very little for anybody outside finance, except for those who wanted to trade assets and through luck or judgement took their money off the table before the asset price bubble popped'. Ben Dyson, founder of the research and campaign group Positive Money, and his collaborators from NEF seemingly concur in their publication *Towards a 21st Century Banking and Monetary System* (2011). They report that in the United Kingdom the house price boom and excessive lending 'more than doubled the cost of housing relative to income': a huge problem in terms of affordability which ultimately means that households have to pay much more, via mortgage interest, to the banking sector (Dyson *et al.* 2011: 21).

Given these complaints, it is perhaps unsurprising that many everyday interventions contain significant direct challenges to established models of asset-based welfare. First, on one level, there are direct proposals put forward that seek to question the current politics of homeownership. For instance, one contributor to *The Occupied Times* makes a call for 'networked community based investment in housing' (Cook 2012). The call for collective action here also echoes PPF's (2009a: 5) suggestion that it is necessary to 'work towards universal achievement of the human right to adequate housing'. It argues that the role of private finance and reduced social provision in housing markets has prompted 'insecurity and indebtedness for low and middle-income earners' and looks to investment in social housing as a remedy (PPF 2009a: 5).

Moreover an interviewee for occupiers recommends that if someone is in negative equity they should 'stop being a debt slave to [their] banker and default on [their] mortgage and become a renter' (Interview with James G. Rickards in *The Occupied Times* 2011d: 8). Further, they claim, homeownership 'is a myth perpetuated by bankers who profit from mortgages' and that renting 'is a perfectly acceptable economic arrangement between those who need housing and those who provide it' (Interview with James G. Rickards in *The Occupied Times*

2011d: 8). The NCRC (2010e: 10) also picks up on renting as an important alternative to homeownership by welcoming calls in the United States for 'right to rent' arrangements, which allow owner-occupiers to stay in their homes even if they are threatened with foreclosure. Seemingly, the outcome of sympathetic moral structures here are activated to suggest that the 'right to housing' ought to be a central aspect of welfare states given that the social provision of housing has dignifying effects.

Second, on a deeper level, rather than emphasise the different 'proposals' and 'policy ideas' of the movement, Occupy constitutes a direct challenge to current systems of property by the physical act or *performance* of occupation itself (Calhoun 2013: 37; Cobbett and Germain 2012: 111; Mitchell 2012: 10). Occupy is thus not part of a 'representative' politics, but what has been referred to as an 'event-movement' (Tormey 2012: 135). As Judith Butler (2011a) said in her speech at OWS:

> there are no demands that you can submit to arbitration here because we are not just demanding economic justice and social equality. We are assembling in public, we are coming together as bodies in alliance, in the street and in the square. We're standing here together making democracy, enacting the phrase 'We The People!'

In direct defiance of property as financial asset, occupiers were able to claim:

> The space we are occupying in the heart of London has huge financial value, but we've shown that it has a value to people beyond money . . . Occupy is reinstating some of the human value back into buildings and spaces by making them democratic, inclusive political spaces.
>
> (*The Occupied Times* 2012a: 4)

Though not an uncontroversial issue, one of the consequences of this ethos was that the reclamation of space in Zuccotti Park, the site of OWS, and at the many other occupation sites around the world, had immediate practical benefits to the permanently urban homeless who were often welcomed into the camps (Herring and Glück 2011: 167; Roth 2011: 27). While still camping, occupiers also suggested that the movement should move to indoor spaces 'such as foreclosed houses and abandoned buildings' because this 'politicizes individual struggles' (*Tidal* 2011: 10). Thus, in important ways the very act of occupying symbolic spaces is a form of resisting the financial value attached to that space. As Manual Aalbers (2012: 3) argues:

> If the financial crisis was about privatizing profit and socializing risk, OWS is about politicizing state/market relations and socializing space. OWS targets both the financialization of the economy and the privatization of public space as well as the neoliberal logic and market fundamentalism that underlies both.

Alongside a focus on the role of homeowner ideology in the inflation of the subprime bubble and the destructive consequences of foreclosure, there are also criticisms made in the everyday politics of the crisis directly related to other forms of state restructuring towards asset-based welfare systems. Most explicitly, asset-based pension provision is identified as a significant problem related to the GFC. As Wall Street Watch (2009: 6) points out, in the United States, even those 'lucky enough to have had pensions or retirement funds have watched helplessly as 25 percent of their value evaporated in 2008'. Writing in *The Occupied Times*, Owen Jones (2011), the author and commentator, claims that UK private sector pension restructuring is 'one of the great scandals of our age'. He reports how for the low-paid, only 20 percent of private sector workers have an employer sponsored pension scheme and notes the problem of how this is used by some as justification for reforming public sector pensions in a 'race to the bottom' (Jones 2011). More broadly, occupiers protest that pensions, alongside other social goods such as health, housing, and education, are currently 'controlled by global banks, markets, tax havens, corporations and financial crises' (Occupy LSX 2011b).

Asset-based systems of welfare are also criticised by CRESC (2009: 8) that suggests at the regulatory level the 'language of social innovation' is often used to 'argue that new financial products can address "unmet social needs" such as care in old age'. For CRESC (2009: 69), pension contributions from low-paid individuals often represent a 'failure' in terms of not building a sufficient personal fund for security through 'property in coupons'. It contrasts this individualised asset-based welfare system with a more 'social' arrangement, which might include 'pooled contributions' that could be organised along more collective lines to build a 'social fund for infrastructure renewal' (CRESC 2009: 69). CRESC (2009: 68) finds the denial of 'comfortable retirement in the UK' based on employment history and status 'entirely unacceptable'. On this account, the right to an adequate pension might come from the outcome of the activation of sympathetic moral structures that stress the need for social provisioning in pensions because of their dignifying effects.

Relatedly, in her contribution to the Occupy literature, Butler (2011b) criticises 'prevailing attitudes toward health insurance and social security' in the US which suggest that 'market rationality should decide whose health and life should be protected, and whose health and life should not'. She writes:

> this neo-liberal morality, as it were, demands self-sufficiency as a moral ideal at the same time that it works to destroy that very possibility at an economic level. Those who cannot afford to pay into health care constitute but one version of population deemed disposable.
>
> (Butler 2011b)

Again, this argument also appears to stress a right to adequate healthcare based on an appeal to the outcome of sympathetic moral structures that are activated to stress the need for the social provision of healthcare because of its dignifying effects: people cannot be just left without healthcare based on individualised market rationale.

The potential to reject the economistic worldview is summarised well in an intervention into the Occupy literature by Christopher Herring and Zoltán Glück

(2011) on what they term 'the homeless question'. This refers to the issue of how in the Occupy camps the urban homeless were often either viewed as an asset or a risk to the movement depending on whether or not such individuals were making a 'contribution' to 'dissent' (Herring and Glück 2011: 166). They ultimately reject such a distinction and make an argument for a new politics of inclusion based on solidarity, in such a way as to link the issue of homelessness with the failed financialisation of US society:

> We must understand that a common logic underlies the mass foreclosures, the expulsion of low- and middle-income earners from their homes, the emergence of an indebted and seemingly economically redundant generation of students, the growth of mass incarceration as a tool for containing impoverished populations, the widespread and growing homelessness of the past forty years, and the racial dynamics that play out in these processes.
>
> (Herring and Glück 2011: 169)

Drawing these points together, there are clear ways in which everyday interventions offer sharp challenges to asset-based welfare. The roles of homeowner ideology and state restructuring towards individualised responsibility in particular both seem to form central parts of everyday accounts of the GFC. Interestingly, unlike at the regulatory level, there is little blame attached to the subprime borrower because culpability for the crisis, as might be expected from movements like Occupy, is much more directly attributed to financiers and the capitalist state. In the previous chapter, I argued that asset-based systems of welfare enjoy a largely unquestioned position in the regulatory accounts, even though they are widely identified as so central to the crisis. By contrast, mobilising a sympathetic political economy interested in opportunities to recognise the contestation of interpersonal ethics, in the everyday politics of the crisis there is a greater degree of questioning of asset-based welfare. In turn, this means there is also *potentially* more space for ethico-political contestation at the individual level.

Such a position is at least seemingly more congruent with a sympathetic political economy, especially compared to the economistic liberalism of the regulatory accounts that tends to encourage the reproduction of atomistic and instrumentally rational market-oriented behaviour. However, it is also important to interrogate the limits of this questioning, particularly with regard to how financialisation trends and asset-based welfare systems might still be partially reinforced in everyday interventions themselves. What are the limits of the everyday challenge to economistic liberalism?

Financialised citizenship and the reinforcement of asset-based welfare

It is possible to discern elements of legitimation for asset-based systems of welfare, including a nascent homeowner ideology, in certain interventions into what is understood here as the everyday politics of the GFC. As with the regulatory account, one way in which this is articulated is in the identification of 'victims' of the crisis. Notably, it is the very same groups in society that display certain financialised character traits that tend to be identified. For instance, writing in *The Occupied Times*, Matt Taibbi (2011), the author and journalist famous for describing the investment bank Goldman Sachs as 'a great vampire squid wrapped around the face of humanity', argues that the GFC and its response from governments represent 'the biggest heist in the history of robberies' with *homeowners*, *pensioners*, *taxpayers* and *savers* all singled out as victims who have been 'fleeced'.

Again directing blame at financiers in particular, Wall Street Watch (2009: 9 emphasis added) claims that 'the enemies of American *consumers, taxpayers and small investors* live in multimillion-dollar palaces and pull down seven-, eight- or even nine-figure annual paychecks'. It claims that 'consumers are not to blame for this debacle', certainly not those who used credit 'in an attempt to have a decent quality of life', and US subprime borrowers should not be blamed simply because they faced misleading loan conditions (Wall Street Watch 2009: 9). Wall Street Watch (2009: 110) argues that 'the American economy cannot be based on finance and the trading of paper' because rather than increase national wealth, Wall Street 'siphoned profits from the real economy' and from 'consumers, workers and investors' who were then 'asked to foot the bill'. Thus as with regulatory accounts, at least in part, a particular financialised depiction of citizenship appears to be articulated in everyday interventions.

The NCRC also presents an interesting intervention with regard to tendencies to reinforce financialised citizenship and asset-based welfare. On the one hand, given that it considers itself the US 'trade association for economic justice whose members consist of local community based organizations' and claims to have since its inception in 1990 'spearheaded the economic justice movement', it might be expected that its views would depart quite significantly from regulatory accounts, especially on issues such as subprime lending (NCRC 2003: 2). However, on the other hand, the NCRC (2003: 2) views its 'mission' as building 'wealth in traditionally underserved communities' and bringing low- and moderate-income populations 'into the financial mainstream'. Seemingly, it is this latter mission that tends to take precedence and set the limits of its critique of existing systems of finance. This is because in a number of important ways it promotes asset-based welfare in much the same way as the regulatory accounts in response to the crisis and in fact reinforces something of a homeowner ideology.

As discussed above, despite presenting renting as an alternative to homeownership, the NCRC also appears to suggest that it is merely a step on the way to the ultimate goal of owner-occupation. It also speaks of 'lease-to-purchase' options as providing an important 'stepping stone' to homeownership while people build up 'the credit and capital needed to buy a home' (NCRC 2010e: 18). Such suggestions are part of the NCRC's overall position on homeownership, which it seems to promote almost above all else. It speaks approvingly of shared equity schemes because they provide an 'opportunity for *wealth building creation* [that] can be passed on to countless future generations' (NCRC 2010e: 20 emphasis added). It welcomes 'resident ownership mechanisms' that provide 'low- and moderate-income residents with opportunities to *enhance their financial assets* and gain ownership stakes in redevelopment initiatives' (NCRC 2010e: 32 emphasis added). What is more, the NCRC (2011a: 1–3) expresses concern about 'shutting out future generations of working Americans from homeownership' on a number of counts, including issues of private credit provision, debt-to-income ratios and down payment criteria.

In many ways the NCRC (2011a: 2) appears to prefer an improved system of, but not a distinct departure from, relatively easy credit conditions: a move away from the 'risk factors such as no income documentation, prepayment penalties and adjustable rates that plagued subprime loans', yet not a fundamental and thoroughgoing rethink of finance. In fact, it claims that the Community Reinvestment Act 'ensured that lending conducted by banks is safe and sound' and it speaks highly of the US Government Sponsored Enterprises which it claims 'encouraged the origination of safe and sustainable loans' (NCRC 2010d: 1; 2010c: 3). Perhaps most revealingly, it suggests that '[r]esponsible subprime lending has an important role to play in the marketplace' and if a significantly increased level of advice can be offered to customers, it would prevent them 'falling victim to predatory lending' (NCRC 2008: 30).

This line of thinking actually echoes a number of other interventions in the everyday politics of the GFC. One contributor to *The Occupied Times* appears to suggest that in the United Kingdom the problem was not subprime lending per se, but the distortion of credit provision through criminal practice. He writes, 'the single most important factor behind the catastrophic global insolvency of the banking industry' was a 'failure to enforce existing laws' because it was the 'systematic resort to mortgage fraud perpetrated by the financial sector' that caused the massive accumulation of bad debts (Shutt 2011). Moreover, Stiglitz (2011) speaks enthusiastically about homeownership in *The Occupied Times*, somewhat blurring the lines between the regulatory and the everyday, by pointing to the 87 percent owner-occupation rate in Mauritius that has been achieved without fuelling a housing bubble. Proposals coming from Occupy more generally of course have to grapple with their own limits of imagination; occupiers themselves for instance claim that the 'upshot of the necessary turn to financialisation is that it is simply not possible to turn back the clocks and revert to a form of capitalism premised upon manufacturing and a chastened financial sector' (*The Occupied Times* 2011d: 9).

Overall, interventions into the everyday politics of the crisis offer a complex and variegated attitude with regard to systems of asset-based welfare. On the one hand, they offer a sharp critique of homeowner ideology and state restructuring towards individualised responsibility. As such, they potentially avoid an economistic treatment of market-oriented behaviour and enunciate representations much more in line with a Smithian sympathy perspective than the regulatory accounts. This is found most forcefully in interventions that question an 'atomistic view of society' (*The Occupied Times* 2011b: 3). However, on the other hand, there are certain limits to the reimagining of financial market agency. In important ways, they still display notable instances where there is a perceived *need* for asset-based welfare and a reproduction of a homeowner ideology. Even the NEF (2011b: 21 emphasis added), otherwise extremely critical of extant financialised citizenship, identifies the ability to 'build assets' and tools and services, such as insurance and pensions, '*to protect aspects of life*' as financial needs that are 'equally valid for Joe Public and Vulnerable Groups'.

For a sympathetic political economy, ethico-political contestation at the individual level is closed down if asset-based welfare and systems of individualised financial responsibility go unquestioned. This is what makes it so remarkable that even in the face of issues of access to homeownership and financial security falling right at the heart of the financial crisis, asset-based welfare systems still seem to be reproduced certainly at the regulatory level and, at least in part, at the everyday level. Outside a financialised society, it might be possible for the sympathy procedure to be unhindered by the ethos of individualised financial responsibility such that more collective forms of welfare provision become important to meet the demands of the outcome of negotiation of interpersonal ethics between people, as some of the everyday interventions imply. Within parts of everyday politics, though, it appears as though a commitment to asset-based welfare still produces a somewhat financialised outcome for any sympathetic reimagining of finance.

However, it is important to note the argument made here is not that there is anything necessarily 'wrong' with the promotion of homeownership by associations such as NCRC, especially perhaps when the very explicit intention is to further the position of low-income groups. Rather, the point is to dig a little deeper to question what ethico-political space is being opened up or closed down in this very act of fostering asset-based welfare and financial citizenship. On the one hand, it might be that the deeply ingrained aspects of financialisation in contemporary Anglo-American societies simply limit the possibilities of the operation of the sympathy procedure in the current era. That is, even if everyday interventions do provide political space to rethink notions of financial responsibility in less individualised terms, they still ask people to perform the imaginative act of sympathy in terms which are shot through with ideas that are associated with a financialised society, such as asset-based welfare.

On the other hand, more empowering for a sympathetic political economy, the use of sympathy here might actually serve as a form of immanent critique. That is, given that everyday politics provides opportunities to rethink finance in less financialised terms, while still speaking to ideas such as homeownership that people recognise as so central to their lives, it could provide an even more important feature of a counter-political culture to transcend economistic liberalism. Thus everyday interventions might serve to challenge the economistic understanding of market-oriented behaviour, while still speaking to ideas about empowerment in terms of homeownership, pension provision and healthcare. In a sense, the sympathy procedure here works not to provide collective resistance to finance, but subversion (De Goede 2005). This is a significant point to which I return in the concluding chapter because it speaks directly to the issue of how economistic market-oriented behaviour might be challenged under contemporary economic governance.

The everyday politics of risk

> Market finance became a new form of worship: What would the market think? What would the market say? Without even knowing why, the common person was suddenly exhorted to care very deeply about how the market 'felt' about something. If the market was upset, something so unspeakably terrible would happen!
>
> (*The Occupied Times* 2011b: 3)

This intervention is illustrative of how in some discussions of the power of financial markets occupiers work to denaturalise 'the market', which is something that is essential to a sympathetic political economy. As opposed to being naturally occurring between innately instrumentally rational individuals, markets are *made* as people perform the character traits of market-oriented behaviour. There is no such thing as 'the market' itself *saying*, *doing*, or *feeling* anything from such a perspective (Watson 2005a: 163). People embody the roles of market 'makers' when they engage in market-oriented behaviour, but such behaviour is always contingent, contestable and involved in the negotiation of interpersonal ethics. It is not a uniform and homogenous process that results in a dogmatic structured outcome called 'the market'. Yet, are there other deeper ways in which everyday political interventions offer distinctly Smithian insights into the ethics of financial market agency? Are there forms of resistance to financial market governance that serve to open up ethico-political contestability about the place of risk in society?

Resistance to the normalisation of credit risk management and structured finance

> There is a shared feeling on the streets around the world that the global economy is a Ponzi scheme run by and for Big Finance.
>
> (White and Lasn 2011)

There are many indictments levelled at financial institutions in general and practices associated with modern risk management systems and structured finance in particular. For instance, in the United Kingdom, occupiers state '[w]e refuse to pay for the banks' crisis' and as such 'do not accept the cuts as either necessary or inevitable' (Occupy LSX 2011a). Occupiers protest that the 'complex gambling inherent in today's institutions of high finance is also all about using money to beget money' and that 'the gamblers risk not their own livelihoods but ours' (*The Occupied Times* 2011e: 10). They ask how it is acceptable for large financial institutions to benefit from staggering government bailouts 'after handing out countless high-risk loans', while the 'recipients of these loans have to default' (*The OWS Journal* 2011a: 2). Adopting a similar perspective, the NEF (2011b: 8) claims that the activities that 'created' the GFC 'deliver little social value' because those in the banking sector 'operated for themselves'. Specifically, it blames the way in which they 'created a new sectoral business model that fused retail and wholesale through securitization and turned banking into a giant "transaction generating machine"' (NEF 2011b: 8).

'Occupy the SEC' is a group within the OWS movement that submitted a 325-page letter to the regulatory agencies involved in considering the Volcker Rule in the United States. They do not claim to represent the viewpoints of OWS as a whole, but one of their key criticisms of contemporary risk management is that while major investment banks used to operate as partnerships, they now tend to utilise a public company structure that 'leads to a striking moral hazard in the manner in which these banks conduct trades' (Occupy the SEC 2012: 78). In essence, the problem is that since traders have no personal liability in such a structure, there is 'little real downside [for them] to incurring monumental losses' (Occupy the SEC 2012: 78). This of course relates to the widely discussed issue of 'moral hazard' in the crisis (Wade 2008: 32–33). Speculation using structured financial products is effectively encouraged because '[p]rovided that no fraud occurs, the worst-case scenario for a trader who loses millions or billions of dollars of depositor-backed money is the loss of a job' (Occupy the SEC 2012: 78). 'In effect', as Dyson *et al.* (2011: 12) also suggest, this means that 'while the potential upside of an investment goes to the bank and the saver/investor, the potential losses fall upon the taxpayer'.

Such appraisals of the banking and financial services sectors tend to sit alongside attempts at a fundamental 'rethink' of the desired function and place of banks and other financial institutions in society. For instance David Beetham (2011: 7), social theorist and author of *Unelected Oligarchy*, argues that the 'dominance of the financial sector has been detrimental to other sectors of the economy, since it has generally been more profitable to invest in financial trading than in domestic businesses'. Likewise, the NEF (2010: 14) suggests that 'it stretches credulity to imagine that trading in assets can ever be an engine of economic growth as it does not add much to the productive capacity of the economy'. It is in fact a 'fallacy', the NEF (2010: 25) claims, to suggest that 'banks are middlemen between depositors and borrowers' because in actuality while banks do instigate lending 'they are not constrained by deposits'.

This is an element of recent banking practices identified as hugely problematic based on the argument that when a loan is made, it 'doesn't actually come from anyone else's savings', but rather is a simple process of *creating* an account on a computer system (Interview with Ben Dyson in *The Occupied Times* 2011b: 7). From this perspective, Ben Dyson reports that the creation of 'brand new money' by banks, shown in Bank of England figures, largely goes towards 'pushing up house prices and speculating on commodities' (Interview with Ben Dyson in *The Occupied Times* 2011b: 7). In 2010 the Positive Money campaign was launched in an attempt to address the perceived problems of fractional reserve banking, which they claim 'underpins the global economy' but is little understood by politicians, the media and the authorities (Dyson *et al.* 2011: 2–4).

On this issue, the NEF (2010: 25 emphasis in original) explains that '[n]othing is closer to alchemy than the creation of credit' and as it is precisely this process that allows private banks to generate income and profit, it always comes with the 'powerful temptation' to over-lend. By way of response, Dyson *et al.* (2011: 9 emphasis in original) look to a 'full-reserve' system, in which banks 'would continue to play an allocatory and maturity transformation role but as genuine intermediaries that transfer existing purchasing power, not as credit *creating* entities that expand the money supply'. This criticism is part of NEF's (2010: 6) general argument that the 'economic history of the world indicates that crisis after crisis arises from financial failures' and that these failures 'follow from one simple cause: the over-extension of credit'.

Concerning over-lending, CRESC (2009: 44) agrees that the banking sector made 'easy loans for non-productive purposes' on residential and commercial property or to other financial firms 'because property and finance were the only sectors which had an insatiable demand for loans'. It argues that central banks and regulatory agencies in the United Kingdom and the United States were 'as culpable as everybody else' because their 'experts and technocrats had accepted the wholesale bankers' story about the benefits of financial innovation, credited Black-Scholes algebra with a heroic role and misrepresented derivatives as a "marketisation of risk" which made the financial system more robust' (CRESC 2009: 19).

Remarkably in this regard, as the NEF reports, the former Chairman of the Federal Reserve, Ben Bernanke, boasted in 2006 that the 'management of market risk and credit risk has become increasingly sophisticated . . . Banking organizations of all sizes have made substantial strides over the past two decades in their ability to measure and manage risks' (Ben Bernanke cited in NEF 2010: 6). In stark contrast, CRESC (2009: 54) calls the idea that 'traders at a node in a complex circuit can calculate the risks of what they do' a 'fundamental misapprehension'. In its view, risk calculation is much more inexact, uncertain, and characterised by a 'system which is smart at the links and dumb through the chains' (CRESC 2009: 54). Along similar lines, Wall Street Watch (2009: 40) claims that the GFC has, quite simply, 'exposed how poorly the sellers and the buyers understood the value of the derivatives they were trading'.

For such reasons Max Keiser, a former Wall Street broker, financial analyst, and broadcaster interviewed in *The Occupied Times*, identifies the subprime bubble as one 'of swapped and re-swapped risk, floating around above the "real world"', which became 'utterly abstracted from the layer of asset-value which actually determines the value of the derivatives' (Max Keiser cited in *The Occupied Times* 2012c: 9). In a sense, as the NEF (2010: 28) argues, it is 'highly complex to even ascertain where associated securities ended up' because of opaque structured financial products and more broadly because, as the subprime debacle reveals, 'some assets simply go round and round the banking system'.

That there was a fundamental mismanagement of risk in the subprime era, according to everyday political actors at least, did not inhibit financiers from making significant use of structured finance. The NCRC (2011b: 2) reports that many US lenders operated 'almost without regard to risk' because when they made loans it was solely 'to sell the loan to other market players'. Taibbi (2011) suggests that the financial system was much healthier 20 years ago when 'banks didn't make risky loans because they worried about collecting on them', as opposed to more recently when 'the loans were designed to be sold off as soon as the ink was dry'. Wall Street Watch (2009: 74) complains that acquirers of a mortgage did not have 'any duty to investigate the terms of the loan and [were] effectively immunized . . . from liability for the initial loan'. All these ideas seem to point towards agreement with the NEF's (2011b: 4) lament that surely a 'criterion' of 'good banking' is that financiers 'take responsibility for what they do'.

In some of its recommendations for reform and response, everyday interventions contain further significant damning assessments of extant credit risk management practices and the use of structured finance. The NCRC (2011a: 1), for instance, notes that if Fannie Mae and Freddie Mac were abolished and large private banks assumed the functions of securitising and guaranteeing mortgages, it would be 'like the fox running the hen house' because it was exactly 'the securitization practices of Wall Street banks financing toxic mortgages that was a major factor plunging this country into the current foreclosure crisis'. Furthermore, Occupy the SEC (2012: 131) claims that credit derivatives, which constitute 'insurance products free from the protections of insurance regulation', and synthetic securities, which 'derive their value from other assets or liabilities', should be designated as 'high risk assets' because of the threats they pose.

A number of other everyday accounts look to fundamental reform of the regulation of structured finance. Of course such proposals do not come without their own set of problems, one of which as discussed below is the notion of looking to a financialised capitalist state for action. PPF (2009a: 3) calls for greater control of derivatives trading, credit securitisation, and other complex financial instruments in a 'globally coordinated way'. Specifically, it demands rules that 'discourage or ban short-term, non-productive or damaging investment, while promoting longer term socially productive and environmentally sustainable investment' (PPF 2009a: 3). Likewise, Wall Street Watch (2009: 112) claims financial institutions 'should be specifically required to explain why [an] instrument does not worsen financial systemic risk, taking into account recent experience where purported diversification of risk led to its spread and exponential increase'. In other words, it suggests that a 'precautionary principle' should be adopted for 'exotic financial instruments' such that the 'burden should be placed on those urging the creation or trade of exotic financial instruments – existing and those yet to be invented – to show why they should be permitted' (Wall Street Watch 2009: 112). In addition, one interviewee in the Occupy literature suggests banning 'derivatives and other structured financial products that serve no purpose other than to deceive customers and enrich bankers' (Interview with James G. Rickards in *The Occupied Times* 2011d: 8).

This chimes with the broader demand made by occupiers for '[i]ndependent and effective regulation' that works for 'the good of our society' given that the GFC shows that '[d]angerous and highly leveraged trading practices have not been regulated properly' (Occupy LSX 2011c). Similarly, for Occupy the SEC (2012: 220):

> Financial innovation goes hand-in-hand with increased concentrations of risk and pricing opacity. The banking model has shifted away from 'old-fashioned'

> prudential banking of the George Bailey variety, in favor of an 'originate and distribute' model that revels in risk-taking . . . From a Pareto-optimal, macro-economic perspective, the markets would actually benefit if the Volcker Rule were to reduce 'financial innovation' by government-backstopped banking entities.

In this spirit, CRESC makes a number of interesting demands for regulatory reform. Essentially, it argues for 'a presumption in favour of simplification' on the issue of derivatives regulation (CRESC 2009: 55). It notes how financial innovation is 'mutable', so the object of reform should be 'to simplify wholesale finance' by encouraging 'short, direct chains' in finance 'where the location of risk and the identity of the holder is *much more knowable*' (CRESC 2009: 55 emphasis added). This is part of CRESC's (2009: 66) 'structural circuits explanation of the pre-2007 bubble', which it sees as resisting many of the very definitions of the GFC to be found in regulatory accounts.

Drawing these points together, in many ways the accounts point towards simplifying securitisation, de-linking chains of finance and more broadly almost a sense of *de-financialisation*. Broadly speaking, such ideas speak to the concerns discussed in this section about taking responsibility for financial market actions, reducing the powerful place of banks in society, and making issues of credit risk more *knowable*. This itself is of course a limited form of resistance and certainly some everyday voices would want to go much further: for instance, proposals for 'full-reserve' banking might require an even larger 'rethinking' of finance.

Yet, collectively, the everyday interventions articulate a promising form of resistance to economistic treatments of issues of credit risk and structured finance. Simplification, de-linking and de-financialisation are certainly aspirant themes that are much more congruent with a sympathy perspective than an economistic governance agenda that serves to normalise the place of risk and risk management in society. Specifically, the crucial point here is that simplification and de-linking make finance more *knowable* in the sense of people knowing with whom they are in a market relationship when they perform market-oriented behaviour. In other words, without knowing about the content of this relationship – or at least the possibility of 'imagining' that relationship because finance is deemed too 'complex' to think about such things – then it becomes difficult for people to engage in a sympathetic procedure, to activate their impartial spectator at all. As Aalbers (2012: 5) argues, the reason why OWS did not produce a 'shared agenda' is because as compared to many other social movements 'it fights against something that is much harder to identify: the contemporary, internationalized, financialized economy'. Indeed, '[o]ne of the many things the current global financial and economic crisis demonstrates is that *large parts of our economy are really beyond our control and often even beyond our imagination*' (Aalbers 2012: 5 emphasis in original)

Making known finance would thus seem to be a basic demand of reorienting economy and society towards recognising the contestable interpersonal relations that make up markets according to a sympathy perspective. Put simply, Smith's sympathetic imaginative acts depend on knowing the situation of another's position in order to activate sympathy. By challenging the dominant place of risk in Anglo-American finance, everyday interventions at the very least open up ethico-political space in which the desired place of risk management in society can be contested. This starts to recognise the contestable nature of interpersonal ethics, as a sympathetic political economy insists, rather than assuming a society of atomised instrumentally rational individuals all working to 'perfect' risk management.

What is more, the outcome of more space for negotiations over appropriate forms of market-oriented behaviour might result in novel ways of rethinking finance, perhaps in terms of finding ways of financial market participants exercising more responsibility for their actions. Certainly to challenge the way in which the powerful place of financiers in Anglo-American societies allows them to avoid responsibility would appear to be an important outcome of the activation of a sympathy procedure in this regard, at least according to some everyday interventions. However, as with asset-based welfare, it is also important to interrogate the limits of this questioning of risk, particularly with regard to the extent to which securitisation and structured finance can be tamed, regulated or abolished in a financialised capitalist economy.

Reinforcement of credit risk management practices

> To facilitate the allocation and deployment of economic resources, both spatially and temporally, to ecological sustainable activities that maximise long-term financial and social returns under conditions of uncertainty.
>
> (NEF 2011b: 2)

This is the NEF's (2011b: 2) response to the question of 'what do we expect the financial system to deliver?' On one level, it appears to be a fairly standard account of what might be expected of an Anglo-American financial system, broadly understood. Yet, on another level, even this short statement is full of allusions to a position that, at least in part, serves to reinforce existing approaches to and practices of credit risk management.

First, most obviously, as might be expected to some degree, if the financial system (here presumably made up of *private* financial institutions if they are maximising financial returns) is still responsible for facilitating the 'allocation and deployment of economic resources', there is no radical change proposed in terms of socialising risk or fostering collectivised sources of credit, for example. Second, it is difficult to envisage a great departure from existing structures of credit allocation if banks and other financial institutions are understood to be seeking to 'maximise' financial returns. The words 'long-term' and ecologically 'sustainable' are obviously important here, but if this is part of the agreed purpose of a financial system, it still appears that 'financial' and 'social' 'returns' are understood to be at least complementary, if not equivalent. This is a point that would surely be contested by other everyday interventions. Finally, the phrase 'under conditions of uncertainty' might provide a significant qualification for the definition. Put simply it suggests that it is expected that a financial system, if operating properly, will be able to successfully measure and manage 'uncertainty', or 'risk' proper, and will not be operating within or producing conditions of 'Knightian uncertainty' (Blyth 2002) or even 'radical ambiguity' (Best 2005).

The NEF is not necessarily somehow misguided in its understanding of how a financial system might work, but the point is that even one of the most critical voices in the everyday politics of the crisis contains elements of reasoning in its position that serve to reinforce existing risk management practices. The question then becomes one of how much everyday politics as a whole tends to be limited in its reimagining of risk. One issue clearly concerns the extent of envisaged reform and the degree to which a radical 'rethinking' of systems of credit emerges. As noted, the NEF (2010: 72) clearly wishes to revisit the question of the desired 'function' of banks and other financial firms, but its views of how a financial system needs to facilitate exchange, allocate capital, and '[r]edistribute and share risk' do not mark a radical departure, at least not in terms of how risk is understood and presumed to be managed.

Moreover, in its proposals, the NEF (2011a: 16; 2011b: 21) advocates the introduction of a 'Statement of Purpose' requirement and 'a social contract element' for banks and banking activities. This might be a useful and progressive reform in response to the GFC, but it is also notable that it depends on a 'consumer protection' agenda that does not differ that markedly from that which is found in the regulatory accounts. The NEF (2011a: 16 emphasis added) suggests that such measures would 'allow regulators and *customers* to assess' the activities of financial institutions. In a similar suggestion that places faith in informed consumers, the NEF (2011b: 18 emphasis added) also calls for the introduction of 'licensing of financial products that are stress tested and *given a kite mark like food*'.

Notably, Wall Street Watch (2009: 110) also advocates a new framework for financial sector regulation organised around a consumer protection agenda. It calls for a new 'financial consumer protection agency' to be established and suggests giving 'consumers the tools to organize themselves' in order to produce independent financial consumers associations that could 'hire their own independent representatives to review financial players' activities, scour their books, and advocate for appropriate public policies' (Wall Street Watch 2009: 113–114). Yet a consumer protection agenda might sit quite comfortably within existing understandings of risk. In fact, it could even serve to induce a model form of financialised consumer citizen able to behave in an instrumentally rational way to ensure that the market provides 'good' and 'safe' financial products. That it does fit within such a vision might be part of the reason why, as Sarah Anderson (2010: 4) reports, one area in which '[p]ublic interest advocates overcame intense Wall Street lobbying to win some important reforms through the Dodd-Frank legislation' was in the area of 'consumer protection'.

Overall, interventions into the everyday politics of the crisis present an interesting challenge to both existing understandings of credit risk management and uses of structured finance. On the one hand, ideas about taking responsibility for financial market actions, reducing the powerful place of banks in society and making finance better known all work against the normalisation of 'risk' in Anglo-America. By problematising risk management, everyday politics begins to provide a means of recognising the contestable nature of interpersonal ethics on which a Smithian sympathy perspective insists. In particular, proposals based on notions of simplification, de-linking and de-financialisation are more congruent with a sympathetic political economy, especially compared to an economistic governance that serves to normalise the place of risk and risk management in society. At the very least, it presents fruitful ideas that are worthy of consideration, especially with regard to the ethos of making finance 'better known' which seems to be desirable and realisable from a sympathy perspective.

However, on the other hand, there are clearly limits to the level of resistance offered here. In this regard, even at the most critical edge of the everyday interventions, it is possible to identify the persistence of economistic ways of thinking about risk. This is especially the case when there is a tendency to rearticulate the existing architecture of credit allocation systems and posit mild reform proposals based on a consumer protection agenda backed by the state. Outside a financialised society, it might be possible for the sympathy procedure to be less restricted by existing understandings of risk in society such that alternative forms of credit provision become important to meet the demands of the outcome of negotiation of interpersonal ethics between people, as some of the everyday interventions imply. The basic demand of making finance better known would certainly seem to be fundamental to reorienting finance towards recognising the (contestable) interpersonal relations that make up markets according to a sympathy perspective in the first place. Within parts of everyday politics, though, it appears as though a commitment to the extant ethos of risk management still produces a somewhat economistic outlook for any sympathetic reimagining of finance.

In a sense, though, this might still provide the operation of sympathy working within everyday politics a way of intervening quite directly into existing understandings of finance. Indeed on a productive note, CRESC (2009: 56) claims it wishes to avoid 'Luddism about securitisation of loans', which is 'an entirely acceptable practice as long as transaction chains are short and transparent': the point is to moderate in some way the 'national supply of feedstock from retail savers and their funds'. Likewise Occupy the SEC (2012: 85) supports the implementation of the Volcker Rule because it envisions a 'shift in banking' towards a focus on more 'safe, "plain vanilla," customer-focused transactions'. Such proposals are limited in vision, but they at least speak more directly to issues of concern from a sympathy perspective. I return to them in the concluding chapter.

The everyday politics of debt

> More and more of us – through a combination of college loans, credit cards, mortgages and bank loans – are being stealthily habituated to debt. We end up feeling that it's an inevitable and mundane part of life – *like blisters and bus stops*.
>
> (*The Occupied Times* 2011c: 8 emphasis added)

In the United Kingdom, occupiers protest that '[m]any within society are burdened with crippling debt' (Occupy LSX 2011c). In the United States, occupiers claim that their efforts 'will not stop until foreclosures and bank repossessions stop . . . and families no longer have to plunge into bankruptcy to pay medical bills' (*The OWS Journal* 2011b: 1). The Occupy movement may have 'rejected conventional rationality, discourse, and strategies', but it *did* constitute a form of 'political disobedience' that interrupted the existing politics and governance of debt (Harcourt 2012: 34).

The way in which occupiers politicise questions of debt is highly significant for developing a sympathetic political economy. Rather than treat debt as a necessary and normal part of life, devoid of political content, a sympathy perspective draws attention to how the negotiation of positions of debt is part of the contestable interpersonal ethics of market-oriented behaviour. In the previous chapter, I suggested that regulatory accounts tend to depoliticise creditor-debtor relations by insisting on the normalisation of financial services in an advanced economy and working to articulate model financialised citizens. In this section, I make the case that many everyday interventions, by contrast, successfully repoliticise such issues and in turn offer a fuller recognition of the contestable interpersonal ethics that make up credit-debt relations.

The re-politicisation of debt

> We must forge our own ethics and our own future. This is an ethic opposed to rights and wrongs and fairness. This is an ethic that says, 'end all debt,' and the other concrete material conditions of our existence that oppress us. We must stress a revolutionary character
>
> (*The Occupied Times* 2012c: 7)

In the everyday politics of the crisis, an important way in which issues of debt are politicised is through discussions of democracy and finance, broadly understood (Calhoun 2013: 33). Such debates are clearly more thoroughgoing than notions of the 'promise' of 'financial democracy' put forward by more mainstream commentators (Shiller 2008). In terms of the Occupy movement, occupiers claim to be taking on the 'global Mubarak' of 'undemocratic global institutions and financialised capitalism', a reference to the overthrow of the former President of Egypt during the Arab Spring (*The Occupied Times* 2011a: 7). For some, efforts to overthrow financialised capitalism begin with a very direct politicisation of questions relating to the regulatory governance of debt.

Various contributions to *The Occupied Times* speak to this idea. As David Wearing (2011) points out, 'protesters understand that neoliberal capitalism is not ordained by God, but sustained by human beings through a series of choices'. Occupiers have thus 'taken up the duty abrogated by the political class to subject those choices, and that system, to proper critical scrutiny and challenge' (Wearing 2011). A similar point is made by Michael Richmond (2012), who suggests that there 'are choices to be made in political economy, not that you'd know it from most politicians and the media'. On one level then, the Occupy movement is involved in a process of constructing discursive democratic space to treat issues of financial governance, which before the GFC tended to be increasingly depoliticised, in much more overtly politicised terms by recognising that there are 'choices' to be made. This might be viewed in relation to how the production of economic and financial knowledge is an important site where power is exercised.

Occupiers posit a deeply political critique of the financialisation of British economy and society. They claim that financialisation 'did not arise as an aberration of capitalism; it was instead a necessary outgrowth' (*The Occupied Times* 2011d: 9). This is based on the idea that there were clear 'systemic' pressures leading to the rise of finance from the 1970s onwards when 'investment in productive sectors of the economy was becoming increasingly difficult to generate a profit from' and so finance 'arose precisely to resolve the problems of declining manufacturing profits and declining profitable investments' (*The Occupied Times* 2011d: 9). Occupiers claim that these original problems 'have not been solved, but only displaced into the financial sector' (*The Occupied Times* 2011d: 9).

CRESC (2009: 21) gives a similar account of financialisation by suggesting that 'every UK government since Thatcher . . . has presided over an anaemic private sector and needs economic success stories so that it can claim to preside over a strong, successful economy, thereby justifying the pain of marketisation and growing inequality'. Since that time, it argues, sectors like finance have had 'an opportunity to tell stories of economic purpose and social achievement to politicians and civil servants, who wanted to believe and deferred to business success' (CRESC 2009: 21). However, CRESC (2009: 8) also reports that the financial sector in actuality 'undermined sustainable growth by inflating asset price bubbles rather than underwriting any kind of productive investment'. Specifically, it notes how '[p]roductive business investment remained at a steady 10 percent of GDP between 1996–2008, but declined sharply from 30 percent of all bank lending towards 10 percent as banks expanded their lending on property and to other financial institutions' (CRESC 2009: 8). For this reason, CRESC (2009: 8) argues that the United Kingdom has 'an economic co-ordination problem' because the financial sector 'allocated capital to (leveraged and unsustainable) asset price growth and not into productive, socially useful investment that might generate the sustainable returns to support debt repayments'.

In addition to this account of the rise of finance, everyday interventions also suggest that financialisation brings about significant questions in terms of the size and power of banks and other financial institutions in society. For instance, occupiers protest that financial institutions 'have increased in size to dominate our economy but have not become socially accountable in line with their increased power' (Occupy LSX 2011c). The 'accent of free-market or neoliberal conceptions of capitalism' is said to have meant that 'social control over banks and corporations became virtually impossible, and we are now paying the costs' (Interview with David Ruccio in *The Occupied Times* 2012a: 13). This echoes PPF's (2009a: 1) argument that '[b]lind faith in the virtues of markets, and inadequate public control, regulation and accountability of finance are at the heart of the financial crisis'.

Of considerable concern in this regard, CRESC (2009: 5) suggests that 'inaction' on behalf of the UK government actually 'results from the influence of the "distributive coalition" in and around the City of London, which has co-opted the political leadership of both major parties'. In a similar claim, Beetham (2011: 21) reports how the levels of lobbying involved in the ICB's interim report mean that ultimately, rather than providing significant proposals on bank restructuring in the United Kingdom, it was 'dismissed as a victory for the banks'. This actually parallels Paul Volcker's opinion that in the United States, his own Volcker Rule as it eventually made its way into the Dodd-Frank bill had been significantly diluted and made much more complex than it needed to be. On the topic, Volcker (cited in Reuters 2011) stated: 'There is no set of lobbyists in the United States bigger, more important and more rewarded than the financial lobbyists'.

As discussed in the previous section, major criticisms are also levelled at Anglo-American systems of credit based on the way in which banks are said to enjoy a 'virtual monopoly' in creating the credit supply (NEF 2011b: 14). Yet this is not just a critique based on the problem of the overextension of credit and how it is an easy way of profiteering by lending institutions. It is also highlighted as potentially emblematic of a highly unequal set of power relations in Anglo-American societies. This is a foundational element of NEF's (2010: 17) call to review the monetary system 'that puts the power of credit creation almost entirely in the hands of commercial banks'. As Chris Cook (2012) describes, the unequal relation is unmistakeable in such a system because as soon as a loan is 'provided out of thin air by the bank . . . interest will start to be charged'. One interviewee thus claims that occupiers must 'fight . . . until fractional reserve banking' is eliminated (Interview with Mike Ruppert in *The Occupied Times* 2011f: 8).

Instead of fractional reserve banking, it is often claimed that a system of full-reserve banking 'would be more stable and robust' and in which, in basic terms, 'the transactional function of banking (the payments system) is separated from the lending function' (Dyson *et al.* 2011: 2–4). In support of full-reserve banking, fractional reserve banking is criticised very much in terms of the redistributive politics of debt. Given that effectively the entire money supply is created as a debt by banks, Dyson *et al.* (2011: 23) claim, those banks can extract interest on all deposits to transfer to their own staff via salaries and bonuses. A redistributive effect of this, they argue, is that the 'baseline' of poverty is shifted downwards because those on the lowest incomes are the people most indebted and they in effect pay interest to the banking sector and those richer than themselves (Dyson *et al.* 2011: 23).

On the one hand, these popular critiques are limited to the extent that they assume that fractional reserve banking is the 'essence of what banks do', whereas often it is other financial institutions that carry out many of the activities that previously banks did (Dodd 2014: 113). On the other hand, they are successful at least in the sense that they draw attention to the power that is bestowed on those with the ability to create credit at little or no cost. Even Martin Wolf (2014), chief economics commentator at the *Financial Times*, has become an influential supporter of Positive Money's arguments and the general outlook has shifted considerably such that the Bank of England has subsequently published on the issue in such a way that challenges much conventional economic wisdom (McLeay *et al.* 2014). For the first time in 170 years, money creation was even debated in Parliament in 2014.

While the ultimate goal of such campaigns might be limited in vision, they still represent an important set of new public discussions in light of the crisis. The point is that there are clear examples of attempts to repoliticise the place of debt in society. From a sympathy perspective, this repoliticisation is important because it makes clear that credit-debt relations are between at least two market participants who are involved in an unequal relationship. What is more, usually, the creditor will have ethico-political *choice* over how they act in the marketplace and so their capacity to activate an imaginative reconstruction of the situation of a debtor is crucial in coming to understandings of appropriate market-oriented behaviour.

In terms of shifts in notions of appropriate behaviour, Anderson (2010: 8) reports how the Move Your Money campaign estimates that two million people 'pulled out of big banks' in the first three months of 2010. In the United States, occupiers have also been involved in promoting the relocation of private funds away from large financial institutions towards local credit unions (*The OWS Journal* 2011c: 3). Given the higher level of banking consolidation in the United Kingdom compared with the United States, there are not as many alternatives available to savers, but the NEF (2010: 71) speaks approvingly of the existence of 'deep ethical' banks and credit unions. In recent years, this trend towards the use of 'alternatives' to mainstream financial institutions has gathered pace. As Dodd (2014: 316 emphasis in original) explains, '[e]vidence of the progressive *de*centralization of money can be found as alternative monetary forms', which include time banking, mutualism, digital currencies and peer-to-peer lending.

Another case of politicising debt relations would be Keiser's argument that if someone is 'at the top of the tree' they 'can borrow money at close to zero, and in some cases below zero percent' while for 'everyone else, interest costs are considerably higher, reaching annualized rates of over 300 percent for "payday" loans' (Interview with Max Keiser in *The Occupied Times* 2011a: 8). This is the case even though Wall Street banks and top clients who have low borrowing costs 'have a horrible track record paying back their loans', while for micro-lending shops serving 'the poorest of the poor' the rate of paying back loans 'is over 97 percent', which he claims is 'financial apartheid' (Interview with Max Keiser in *The Occupied Times* 2011a: 8). In light of the GFC, the redistributive politics of debt are brought to the fore here in a way that is distinctly lacking in the regulatory accounts.

Notably occupiers appear to echo such critiques of the place of debt in a financialised economy. They claim that 'there is an underlying story at play within the kind of debt-oriented transactions engulfing our lives: the extension of the role of debt commitments on both the individual and on wider society' (*The Occupied Times* 2011g: 11). What is more, occupiers argue, unlike money spent on more 'tangible' goods and services, money spent on debt-related transactions such as mortgages, credit cards and student loans, 'represents an agreement by the consumer to honour these commitments throughout the course of their lives' (*The Occupied Times* 2011g: 11). In this light, 'debt can be seen to be a part of the environment of our future' (*The Occupied Times* 2011g: 11). Relatedly, the NEF (2011b: 21) also politicises such claims by making the suggestion that 'the basic question . . . of what it costs to live in society' must also be addressed because '[i]f people are living on such low income that they have to rely on credit to live, there is a broader political and economic failure to do with basic levels of poverty to correct'. For many, then, the crisis represents a call to action to reconsider the place of debt in Anglo-America and why it is that so many people are in need of debt in the first place.

In 2012, an anonymous collective of members of Strike Debt/OWS released *The Debt Resistors' Operations Manual*, which provides practical advice on dealing with various forms of common debt in the United States, consumer reporting agencies and fringe finance issues. It is designed specifically to be 'a political act of mutual aid' to confront the way – in the United States in particular – the debt industry works to 'keep debtors confused and afraid' (Strike Debt/OWS 2012: iii). The attitude adopted here is one of challenging dominant personalised narratives about what it means to be indebted:

> We are told all of this is our own fault, that we got ourselves into this and that we should feel guilty or ashamed. But think about the numbers: 76 percent of Americans are debtors. How is it possible that three-quarters of us could all have just somehow failed to figure out how to properly manage our money, all at the same time? And why is it no one is asking, "Who do we all owe this money to, anyway?" and "Where did they get the money they lent?"
>
> (Strike Debt/OWS 2012: 1)

The *Manual* explains that US household debt as a share of income has grown from 60 percent in the early 1980s to over 100 percent by the time of the GFC (Strike Debt/OWS 2012: 13). The implication is that debt has increased directly because wages have not kept up with living costs and there is little public welfare support left 'to pick up the slack' (Strike Debt/OWS 2012: 13). Access to credit has become much easier, the *Manual* reports, yet in such a way as to ensure that high risk ratings are no longer used to *deny* credit but to 'charge more for it', which has the tendency of producing a self-fulfilling prophecy whereby the designation of being 'risky' exposes someone to more 'unfair and abusive financial practices' (Strike Debt/OWS 2012: 15). Fortunately, however, Strike Debt/OWS emphasise that there are ways out of this situation as forms of debt resistance are proliferating. They point to their own education initiatives, debtors' assemblies, the Occupy Student Debt campaign, the Rolling Jubilee and direct actions against predatory lenders throughout the United States (Strike Debt/OWS 2012: 105).

Overall, the everyday politics of the crisis offers sharp criticisms of the place of debt in a financialised society and in many cases serves to repoliticise questions of debt. Specifically the politicised treatment of debt involves, among other aspects, drawing attention to: the sizable power of banks and other financial institutions in a financialised economy; the redistributive politics of credit-debt relations; and something of the underlying material or resource capacity struggles that debt might conceal. These interventions are highly significant from a Smithian sympathy perspective because, rather than treat debt as a necessary part of life devoid of political content, they serve to highlight how the negotiation of debt is part of the contestable interpersonal ethics of market-oriented behaviour. Whereas regulatory accounts tends to depoliticise creditor-debtor relations by insisting on the normalisation of finance and work to articulate model financialised and even indebted citizens, everyday interventions repoliticise debt and potentially offer a fuller recognition of the contestable interpersonal ethics that make up debt relations.

For a sympathetic political economy this matters because it allows for the potential imaginative reconstruction of another's position in the credit-debt relationship, which could lead people to reorient their market-oriented behaviour, especially on the creditor side, along more progressive lines. For instance, at least according to a number of everyday interventions, there is a need to rethink finance because of the way in which taking on personal debt merely serves to conceal the disparities of material capabilities that exist in Anglo-America. Allowing for a fuller operation of sympathy might produce further challenges to these dilemmas. Nevertheless, as with the previous two sections, it is necessary to interrogate the limits of this vision, particularly in relation to how everyday politics may still serve, perhaps inadvertently, to promote certain financialised forms of citizenship and also reinforce structures of creditor-debtor relations as they currently stand.

Standards of financial market agency and the reinforcement of credit-debt relations

> The starting point has to be that retail banking is a utility because households and firms must have access to reasonable payment services, deposit facilities, and savings and loans which are as socially and economically necessary as electricity supply or telephony.
>
> (CRESC 2009: 56)

This is CRESC's 'starting point' in a search for effective financial regulation in response to the GFC. On the one hand, the general view that retail banking facilities are an undemanding 'utility' is not particularly contentious. As the former Governor of the Bank of England Mervyn King (2009) suggests, utility aspects of banking are 'quite different in nature from some of the riskier financial activities that banks undertake, such as proprietary trading'. Yet, on the other hand, although this *might* hold true for 'payment services' and 'deposit facilities', as soon as the move is made to 'savings and loans' the question of whether retail services are 'as necessary as electricity supply or telephony' starts to become a little more problematic, especially in light of some of the other politicising moves made in everyday politics. The problem is that in enunciating saving and borrowing as somehow 'necessary', credit-debt relations with regard to personal debt might start to be depoliticised and rearticulated as a normal feature of everyday life once again: merely one of those 'inevitable and mundane' parts of life, '*like blisters and bus stops*' (*The Occupied Times* 2011c: 8 emphasis added).

That CRESC (2009: 39) views retail banking as 'a worthy utility which provides essential services for all households' does not necessarily undermine its otherwise highly politicised critique of the place of debt in a financialised economy, but it does blunt it somewhat by serving, in part, to naturalise relations of debt in banking finance. While the false promise of 'competition' is severely questioned in this approach (Bowman *et al.* 2014: 88), the retail bank as utility model still works to entrench the place of banks in British society. Other areas of everyday politics follow a somewhat similar trajectory. For instance, the NEF (2011b: 2) bemoans a 'lack of consumer choice and universal service in high street banking' because 'as with utility companies, all citizens need a banking service'. Moreover the NCRC (2008: 7) claims that 'responsible high-cost lending often serves legitimate credit needs of borrowers with credit imperfections, thus, high-cost lending does not always constitute a predatory lending practice'. While seemingly harmless when framed in terms of progressive politics and concerns about marginalised groups, the point is that these standpoints on the 'necessity' of access to credit, at least in part, serve to dampen the repoliticising of credit-debt relations by in part naturalising the place of debt in everyday life.

Moreover a related limitation to the challenge presented to the depoliticisation of debt centres on the implicit endorsement of certain forms of model financialised citizenship within everyday interventions. In a direct mirroring of regulatory accounts, 'savers, retirees, annuity and insurance policy holders and others living on fixed incomes' are singled out as *innocent victims* as they are 'robbed while the financial mavens are properly hedged' (Interview with James G. Rickards in *The Occupied Times* 2011d: 8). Moreover, notably, Occupy the SEC (2012: 1–2 emphasis added) reports that '[l]ike much of the 99 percent, *we have bank deposits and retirement accounts that are in need of the protection* of the Volcker Rule'. Furthermore, Occupy the SEC (2012: 81) offers its support partly because if an 'expansive' interpretation of proprietary trading is used this 'would reduce the risk of bank failure because only the most basic, customer-focused trades would make it through the Volcker Rule's gauntlet'. In turn, this would serve to '*increase both depositor and investor confidence* in banking entities, which in turn would increase real liquidity in the banking industry, and as a consequence, the overall market for credit' (Occupy the SEC 2012: 81 emphasis added). Along similar lines, Strike Debt/OWS (2012: 102) concludes:

> We should be clear: we are not against all debt nor are we against credit. Rather, we call for new, fair arrangements that help us exceed the boundaries of the present (as credit does) without burdening the future in chains of compound interest.

Everyday political accounts articulate a significant, cutting, yet partially limited encounter with the politics of debt. On one level, they offer an unforgiving repoliticisation of credit-debt relations by drawing attention to, among other things, the sizable power of banks and other financial institutions in a financialised economy, the redistributive politics of credit-debt relations and the underlying material or resource capacity struggles that personal debt might conceal. A typical intervention in this regard is made by occupiers who ask, given that 'housing is increasingly unaffordable and the social costs of homelessness are enormous', why the Bank of England does not use 'quantitative easing' to fund housebuilding as it does to prop up the financial system (Occupy London 2012). As such, everyday interventions tend to repoliticise issues of debt and potentially offer a fuller recognition of the contestable interpersonal ethics that make up debt relations. In this regard, such voices are highly significant for a sympathetic political economy; rather than treating debt as a necessary and inevitable part of life devoid of political content, they serve to highlight how the negotiation of debt is part of the contestable interpersonal ethics of market-oriented behaviour.

However, on another level, there are certain limits to this repoliticisation particularly in relation to how everyday politics may still serve, perhaps inadvertently, to promote certain model forms of citizenship and reinforce creditor-debtor relations as they currently stand. In particular, there are elements of everyday politics that work to normalise the place of personal debt in everyday life through appeal to its 'necessity' and almost unquestionably 'legitimate' place in a financialised society. What is more, at times, certain forms of model financialised citizenship are endorsed in everyday interventions, which although not on the same scale as in the regulatory accounts, does blunt somewhat the otherwise highly charged politicalised critique of debt.

Perhaps the activation of the sympathy procedure outside the confines of existing forms of financialisation and widespread uses of debt is to a large extent extremely difficult in the present conjuncture. In a less financialised society, it might be possible for the sympathy procedure to escape such boundaries by reimagining finance along more radical lines. Within parts of everyday politics, though, it appears as though an acceptance of the inevitability of debt still produces a somewhat economistic outlook for any sympathetic reimagining of finance. This might seem entirely appropriate given a pragmatic acceptance that reform has to start from within financialised capitalism. It is unlikely that debt can be removed altogether from society: the point is to repoliticise finance in this regard. Given the partial successes of this politicisation in everyday politics – actually embodied of course in the Occupy movement itself – I return to the foundational issue of contestation over the nature of debt in the concluding chapter.

Concluding remarks

> The problem is not capitalism, the problem is financial rape by bankers. Capitalism, the Adam Smith kind, grew out of the Enlightenment which gave birth to the ideals shared by all #occupy participants.
>
> (Interview with Max Keiser in *The Occupied Times* 2011a: 8)

I end this chapter in the same way I began it: with an appeal to Smith made in the Occupy literature. This time, the invocation appears to replicate one of Skinner's mythologies. For surely it is a mythology of parochialism to associate Smith with a 'kind' of 'capitalism', even though he was writing in a manifestly *pre*-capitalist era? Nonetheless, the invocation is fascinating given the way in which Keiser seemingly appeals to a kind of capitalism, before the onset of recent processes associated with financialisation 30 years ago or so, that is in some sense less dominated by 'bankers': a pre-financialised or de-financialised reimagining of economy and society perhaps? The association of this as one of the 'ideals' of occupiers with Smith is very thought-provoking because it alludes to exactly the point on which I wish to conclude: the prospects for an everyday politics of finance congruent with a sympathetic political economy.

In the first section, I illustrated how many everyday interventions articulate a complex and variegated attitude with regard to systems of asset-based welfare, which offers a sharp critique of homeowner ideology and state restructuring. While there are certain limits to the reimagining of financial market agency based on notable instances of where there is a need expressed for asset-based welfare and a partial reproduction of a homeowner ideology, on the whole they avoid an economistic treatment of market-oriented behaviour and enunciate a representation much more in line with a Smithian sympathy perspective.

In the second section, I argued that everyday interventions present an interesting challenge to both existing understandings of credit risk management and uses of structured finance. Crucially, ideas about taking responsibility for financial market actions, reducing the powerful place of banks in society, and making credit risk 'better known' all work against the normalisation of risk in Anglo-America. Even though there is a tendency to rearticulate the existing architecture of credit allocation systems and posit somewhat mild reform proposals, by problematising risk management everyday politics begins to provide a means of recognising the contestable nature of market-oriented behaviour on which a Smithian sympathy perspective insists.

In the final section, I suggested that many everyday interventions provide a significant, cutting, yet partially limited encounter with the politics of debt. Although tempered somewhat at times by tendencies to reinforce the 'necessity' of debt and certain model forms of financialised citizenship, they offer an unforgiving repoliticisation of credit-debt relations by drawing attention to, among other things, the sizable power of banks and other financial institutions in a financialised society, the redistributive politics of credit-debt relations, and the underlying material or resource capacity struggles that personal debt might conceal.

A sympathetic sensibility is at least partially embodied in the everyday politics of the crisis and it offers up fruitful lines of enquiry for efforts to rethink finance with a sympathetic political economy in mind. Such a task is not too far removed from certain stated aspirations associated with the Occupy movement: some speak of 'changing the underlying values that govern our society' (Klein 2011); others 'a total rethinking of western consumerism that throws into question how we measure progress' (White and Lasn 2011); and yet others still a move to 'occupy the teaching of economics' to rubbish economic theory that is 'based on a singular methodology' and 'divorced from ethical concerns' (Interview with David Ruccio in *The Occupied Times* 2012a: 13). The important point is that some of these interventions might work towards a fuller recognition of ethico-political contestation at the individual level.

Conclusion

Occupy Adam Smith

At the heart of the GFC lay a crisis of ethical imagination. Economistic liberalism denies the very existence of contestable interpersonal ethics, which places limits around how market-oriented behaviour is understood and theorised. It also bounds the extent to which economy and society can be reimagined in the wake of crisis. The constitution of individual selfhood depends on contest and any attempt to deny or marginalise this idea produces inadequate understandings of the crisis itself. A sympathetic political economy provides a different outlook. Adopting a sympathy perspective does not produce a 'tension-free' ethics of finance. To the contrary, a sympathetic sensibility recognises the very possibility of ethical negotiation of existing financial market relations.

Sympathy refers to a procedure in which 'self' engages in an imaginative reconstruction of the situation of 'other' in order to make ethical judgement of both self and other. It denotes 'fellow-feeling' with the situation of another and suggests a route to a conventionalist-relational interpersonal ethics (*TMS* I.i.1.5). Sympathy can be tutored or improved, but also corrupted or deactivated in different contexts. A sympathetic political economy recognises the sympathy procedure as central to the making of market-oriented behaviour. Rethinking the ethics of global finance from such a perspective therefore begins from the position that market-oriented behaviour is made up of contestable interpersonal ethics.

However, those accounts of instrumentally rational forms of market-oriented behaviour implicated in the crisis often cite the intellectual authority of Adam Smith. This interpretation can only be sustained through an economistic historiography of his work. The work of Stiglitz (2007: 66) comes to mind here in his attempts to use Smith in response to the GFC, while viewing him as 'the founder of modern economics'. Notably, members of the Occupy movement appeal to him in a diametrically opposed way. On this occasion as on so many others, the competing historiographies of Smith help constitute the rival and drastically different responses to the crisis itself. Historiographical matters thus perform a significant role in the very construction and negotiation of contemporary political economy.

Many of the major problems of interpretation relating to Smith can be understood through reference to Skinner's ideas about different interpretive mythologies

(Chapter 1). Contemporary political economy interpretations of Smith often uncritically accept the mythologies of doctrine, prolepsis and parochialism, while having very little to say on the Adam Smith Problem. A more robust reading pays close attention to Smith's *intentions* in writing his work (Chapter 2). The cultivation of standards of moral behaviour in the emerging commercial society of his time emerges as central to Smith's work (Fitzgibbons 1995; Force 2003; Teichgraeber 1986). A sympathetic political economy developed out of this reading offers a reframing of the crisis.

An encounter between three core themes of *TMS* (sympathy, mutual sympathy and the sympathy procedure) and three principal sites of finance implicated in the GFC (asset-based welfare, risk management and indebtedness) permit an illustration of the crisis of ethical imagination at hand (Chapter 3). At the regulatory level: asset-based systems of welfare remain unquestioned; credit risk management practices continue unchallenged and are further normalised based on faith in the 'science' and 'perfectibility' of risk management; and the view of debt continues to depoliticise creditor-debtor relations by insisting on the normalisation of financial services and operating to induce model financialised citizens (Chapter 4). The regulatory account of and response to the GFC thus relies on an economistic understanding of financial market agency that serves to exclude contestable interpersonal ethics.

The everyday politics of the crisis provides forms of subversion more congruent with a sympathetic sensibility (Chapter 5). Within these interventions there is often: an oppositional attitude with regard to systems of asset-based welfare, which offers a severe critique of homeowner ideology and state restructuring towards notions of individual financial responsibility; a destabilising encounter with the current theory and practice of credit risk management; and a repoliticisation of credit-debt relations through providing a critique of the sizable power of banks and other financial institutions in a financialised economy, the redistributive politics of indebtedness, and the underlying material or capacity struggles obscured by personal debt.

A sensibility to sympathy is at least partially embodied in some everyday politics and offers fruitful lines of enquiry for efforts to rethink finance. First and foremost, everyday interventions serve to confront individualised financial responsibility, disembodied risk for which no one assumes responsibility and the normalised place of indebtedness. As such, at the very least, they can conceive of allowing the sympathy procedure to operate. They conceptualise and mobilise financial agency in a way that allows for people to act as *attentive impartial spectators*, rather than as atomised and *unsighted onlookers*. The very sentiment 'We are the 99 percent', for instance, invokes an imaginative capacity to relate to others and negotiate standards of appropriate behaviour in a society in which one would want to live (*The Occupied Times* 2011c: 9).

Drawing from everyday interventions, a sympathetic finance might involve fostering a recognition that: (1) in terms of individual responsibility, it is necessary to think 'outside of the self' given that market relations always have consequences for others; (2) in terms of credit risk and structured finance, risk is always 'embodied' and borne by people who potentially suffer or profit in an interdependent society; and (3) in terms of debt, that creditor-debtor relations are always inherently unequal positions of power and that an imaginative act might be involved in setting the appropriate standards for and place of debt in society.

In some of the everyday interventions, notions of de-linking, de-financialisation and making financial chains more accountable speak to this theme of a sympathetic sensibility. Practically speaking, this points to a fundamental overhaul of institutional market design in finance to make it more *knowable*. Though a huge shift in ethos, simplifying chains in personal finance, for instance, might be as straightforward as cultivating more direct forms of savings and loans between people. One such route forward might be the space for negotiation provided by peer-to-peer networks online.

Beyond 'recognition' and 'opening up', what might be the possible *content* of the outcome of a sympathetic ethos operating in a radically overhauled finance? On the one hand, Smith's conventionalist-relational ethics does not necessarily produce straightforward solutions in this regard. Yet, on the other hand, adopting a sympathy perspective in the current conjuncture, what might be the most likely outcomes for economic governance today? Much of the answer here relates to Smith's sympathy attending to people's psychological capacities, as well as their economic or material needs. Concretely, the outcome of a sympathetic sensibility might involve routes to fostering forms of solidarity for those worst affected by the crisis. The collective action of Strike Debt and the efforts of Occupy groups to prevent foreclosures come to mind here.

Notably, in this regard, a sympathetic finance *does not* have to commit to the ideas: (1) that given the calamitous outcome of homeowner ideology in the GFC, homeownership is *necessarily* a bad thing; (2) that given the abuses of securitisation in the GFC, structured finance should be prohibited *completely*; or (3) that given the unequal positions of power that lie behind all credit-debt relations revealed in the GFC, that *all* debt must be ended. Everyday interventions do not challenge asset-based welfare, structured finance and personal debt entirely – that is, they still operate within certain limits of 'reimagining' finance, certain relational boundaries of the sympathy procedure – but they do make the more modest attempt to *repoliticise* these issues and serve to make them *a question of ethics*. The point is to escape the confines of market-oriented behaviour viewed and constituted *solely* in economistic terms.

Making known finance

This might most productively be sought in arrangements that allow one market participant to perceive more fully the situation of another. Imaginative acts of sympathy might then be performed that foster different forms of market-oriented behaviour. Put simply, Smith's sympathy perspective indicates that it is *not* ingrained into 'human nature' that people *have* to act in one particular way, even though economistic forms of governance imply that this *is* the case. Ways of knowing finance *differently* then become routes to radical change.

There is a vast array of ways to build on this agenda. For instance, a challenge to the current regulatory architecture might be driven by continuing efforts to democratise the institutions of global financial governance and make them more inclusive. Notably, as Sarah Anderson (2010: 16) reports, the Stiglitz Commission actually proposed the establishment of an 'UN Global Economic Coordination Council' as a more democratic alternative to the G20. Such ambitions are not easily attained, but groups such as the Jubilee USA Network and the New Rules for Global Finance Coalition represent key coalitions that continue to pursue this agenda (Anderson 2010: 17).

Another reform imperative holding synergies with a sympathy perspective might be to find ways to *simplify* finance so that it can be made more knowable. This of course is no small task, but there are voices in the contemporary politics of financial restructuring that offer interesting prospects along these lines. One might be the policy-oriented forms of academic analysis that organisations like CRESC (2009) produces in its 'public interest' report. For his part, Paul Volcker's banking reforms also essentially look to reduce financial innovation, which might also serve this agenda. Although, as noted, the kinds of resistance that banks and other financial institutions are able to mobilise may well curb the impact of such regulatory proposals.

Despite a degree of inaction at the regulatory level, as Occupy the SEC shows, there are radical everyday voices demanding more robust and thoroughgoing regulatory reforms willing to work within the existing regulatory architecture. Such voices are embellished by action groups such as the Move Your Money campaign, which serves to simplify finance through encouraging people to pull their money from large banks and put it into local credit unions and smaller financial institutions. These are speculative illustrations, but certainly it is possible to identify existing political action that might help to re-orient finance, at least implicitly, along more sympathetic lines.

The prospects for a 'sympathetic finance' might be extended by carrying out further research into how 'simplification' and 'de-linking' imperatives can be introduced in practice. One aspect of this could be to start by, to borrow a phrase from Donald MacKenzie (2005), 'opening the black boxes of global finance' to show how claims to technical and specialist knowledge might serve to sustain technocratic and elite structures of finance. A sympathetic political economy is furthered when these claims are brought into doubt so people can see the ethico-political aspects of financial markets themselves, can understand how their economic agency is involved in sustaining the structural power of markets, and can be provided with the opportunity to exercise their *own* judgement. In brief, further research might therefore ask: how can participation in decision making in financial governance be radically overhauled? How can the entrenched power of large financial institutions be reduced to allow for other forms of localised participatory finance? How can financial 'education' agendas be shifted from a focus on producing financialised citizens to making the structures of finance – and how to change them – more knowable?

Further historiographical endeavours might build on the interests driving this book. On the one hand, my focus has been on using a pragmatic historiography in relation to the 'Crisis in the Heartland' of Anglo-American financial capitalism (Gowan 2008). This could equally be built into approaches that scrutinise other areas and aspects of the world economy to allow political economy scholars to 'stand outside' their current disciplinary structures. On the other hand, future historiographical work could help firm up exactly what a sympathetic political economy might entail. Indeed there is certainly scope to consider Smith's work in relation to other thinkers of his time, aside from the major Enlightenment figures on which I focused in this book. The study of more of his intellectual influences, adding more depth to the Skinnerian endeavour, might provide for an expanded historicised account of what a sympathetic political economy can offer.

The GFC has demonstrated yet again that a novel rethinking of market economy and society is in order. In short, it is a rethinking that works to recognise and make known that there are decisions to be made in political economy and, therefore, market-oriented behaviour is always subject to ethico-political intervention and change. As occupiers claim:

> The economic and political are dovetailing together once more . . . we are rediscovering the economic sphere as a political project – something that can be altered and *shaped by our hands*.
>
> (*The Occupied Times* 2012c: 7 emphasis added)

Rather than the natural outgrowth of instrumentally rational behaviour deeply inbuilt in human nature, markets are made by people, by us – and, as Adam Smith might help remind us, are *not* the outcome of some unknowable, invisible hand.

Bibliography

Aalbers, M. B. (2008) 'The Financialization of Home and the Mortgage Market Crisis', *Competition & Change*, 12 (2), pp. 148–166.

Aalbers, M. B. (2012) 'Socializing Space and Politicizing Financial Innovation/Destruction: Some Observations On Occupy Wall Street', *Belgeo: Belgian Journal of Geography*, 1–2, pp. 1–8.

Abbott, J. P. and Worth, O. (2002) 'Introduction: The "Many Worlds" of Critical International Political Economy', in Abbott, J. P. and Worth, O. (eds) *Critical Perspectives on International Political Economy* (Basingstoke: Palgrave).

Acocella, N. (2005) *Economic Policy in the Age of Globalization* (Cambridge University Press).

Adam, B. and van Loon, J. (2000) 'Introduction: Repositioning Risk: the Challenge for Social Theory', in Adam, B., Beck, U. and van Loon, J. (eds) *The Risk Society and Beyond: Critical Issues for Social Theory* (London: Sage).

Agathangelou, A. M. (2004) *The Global Political Economy of Sex: Desire, Violence, and Insecurity in Mediterranean Nation States* (Basingstoke: Palgrave Macmillan).

Aggarwal, V. K. (1985) *Liberal Protectionism: The International Politics of Organized Textile Trade* (Berkley, CA: University of California Press).

Agnew, J. A. (1994) 'Timeless Space and State-Centrism: The Geographical Assumptions of International Relations Theory', in Rosow, S. J., Inayatullah, N., and Rupert, M. (eds) *The Global Economy as Political Space* (Boulder, CO: Lynne Rienner).

Aitken, R. (2005) '"A Direct Personal Stake": Cultural Economy, Mass Investment and the New York Stock Exchange', *Review of International Political Economy*, 12 (2), pp. 334–363.

Aitken, R. (2007) *Performing Capital: Toward a Cultural Economy of Popular and Global Finance* (New York: Palgrave).

Akerlof, G. A. and Shiller, R. J. (2009) *Animal Spirits: How Human Psychology Drives the Economy, and Why It Matters for Global Capitalism* (Princeton, NJ: Princeton University Press).

Amin, A. and Palan, R. (1996) 'Editorial: The Need to Historicize IPE', *Review of International Political Economy*, 3 (2), pp. 209–215.

Amoore, L. (2004) 'Risk, Reward and Discipline at Work', *Economy and Society*, 33 (2), pp. 174–196.

Amoore, L., Dodgson, R., Germain, R. D., Gills, B. K., Langley, P. and Watson, I. (2000) 'Paths to a Historicized International Political Economy', *Review of International Political Economy*, 7 (1), pp. 53–71.

Anderson, S. (2010) *Civil Society Responses to the Global Economic Crisis: White Paper Prepared for FNTG* (Funders Network on Transforming the Global Economy).
Atwood, M. (2008) *Payback: Debt and the Shadow Side of Wealth* (Toronto, ON: Anansi).
Austin, J. L. (1975) *How To Do Things With Words: The William James Lectures Delivered at Harvard University in 1955 Second Edition*, edited by J. O. Urmson and M. Sbisà (Oxford University Press).
Bagolini, L. (1975) 'The Topicality of Adam Smith's Notion of Sympathy and Judicial Evaluations', in Skinner, A. S. and Wilson, T. (eds) *Essays on Adam Smith* (Oxford University Press).
Baker, A. (2005) '3D Governance in the Advanced Capitalist World', in Baker, A., Hudson, D. and Woodward, R. (eds) *Governing Financial Globalization: International Political Economy and Multi-level Governance* (London: Routledge).
Baker, A. (2013) 'The New Political Economy of the Macroprudential Ideational Shift', *New Political Economy*, 18 (1), pp. 112–139.
Balaam, D. N. and Veseth, M. (2008) *Introduction to International Political Economy Fourth Edition* (Harlow: Pearson).
Bauman, Z. (2005) *Work, Consumerism and the New Poor Second Edition* (Maidenhead: Open University Press).
Beard, J. (2007) *The Political Economy of Desire: International Law, Development and the Nation State* (Abingdon: Routledge-Cavendish).
Beck, U. (1992) *Risk Society: Towards a New Modernity* (London: Sage).
Becker G. S. (2011) 'The Great Recession and Government Failure', *The Wall Street Journal*, September 2.
Beetham, D. (2011) *Unelected Oligarchy: Corporate and Financial Dominance in Britain's Democracy* (Liverpool: Democratic Audit).
Bell, D.S.A. (2001) 'The Cambridge School and World Politics: Critical Theory, History and Conceptual Change', *First Press Global Site*, pp. 1–22, Available online: http://www.theglobalsite.ac.uk/press/103bell.pdf [accessed 09/11/09].
Bell, D.S.A. (2003) 'Political Theory and the Functions of Intellectual History: A Response to Emmanuel Navon', *Review of International Studies*, 29 (1), pp. 151–160.
Bernanke, B. S. (2007) Speech: The Subprime Mortgage Market, At the Federal Reserve Bank of Chicago's 43rd Annual Conference on Bank Structure and Competition, Chicago, Illinois, May 17, Available online: http://www.federalreserve.gov/newsevents/speech/bernanke20070517a.htm [accessed 03/02/12].
Best, J. (2005) *The Limits of Transparency: Ambiguity and the History of International Finance* (Ithaca, NY: Cornell University Press).
Best, J. (2007) 'Why the Economy is Often the Exception to Politics as Usual', *Theory, Culture and Society*, 24 (4), pp. 87–109.
Best, J. (2009) 'How to Make a Bubble: Towards a Cultural Political Economy of the Financial Crisis', *International Political Sociology*, 2 (4), pp. 461–465.
Best, J. (2010) 'The Limits of Financial Risk Management: Or What we Didn't Learn from the Asian Crisis', *New Political Economy*, 15 (1), pp. 29–49.
Bhutta, N. and Ringo, D. (2014) 'The 2013 Home Mortgage Disclosure Act Data', *Federal Reserve Bulletin*, 100 (6), pp. 1–32.
Bieler, A. and Morton, A. D. (2006) 'Globalization, the State and Class Struggle: A "Critical Economy" Engagement with Open Marxism', in Bieler, A., Bonefeld, W., Burnham, P. and Morton, A. D. (eds) *Global Restructuring, State, Capital and Labour: Contesting Neo-Gramscian Perspectives* (Basingstoke: Palgrave Macmillan).
BIS (2005) *Credit Risk Transfer* (Basel: Bank for International Settlements).

BIS (2008a) *Credit Risk Transfer: Developments from 2005 to 2007* (Basel: Bank for International Settlements).

BIS (2008b) 'Ratings in Structured Finance: What Went Wrong and What Can be Done to Address Shortcomings?', *Committee on the Global Financial System Papers*, No. 32, July 2008 (Basel: Bank for International Settlements).

BIS (2011) *Basel III: A Global Regulatory Framework for More Resilient Banks and Banking Systems* (Basel: Bank for International Settlements).

Blaney, D.L. and Inayatullah, N. (2010) 'Undressing the Wound of Wealth: Political Economy as a Cultural Project', in Best, J. and Paterson, M. (eds) *Cultural Political Economy* (London: Routledge).

Blinder, A. S. (2010) 'When Greed Is Not Good', *The Wall Street Journal*, January 12.

Block, F. (1990) 'Political Choice and Multiple "Logics" of Capital', in Zukin, S. and Dimaggio, P. (eds) *Structures of Capital: The Social Organization of the Economy* (Cambridge University Press).

Blyth, M. (2002) *Great Transformations: Economic Ideas and Institutional Change in the Twentieth Century* (Cambridge University Press).

Blyth, M. (2013) *Austerity: The History of a Dangerous Idea* (Oxford University Press).

Blyth, M. and Spruyt, H. (2003) 'Our Past as Prologue: Introduction to the Tenth Anniversary Issue of the Review of International Political Economy', *Review of International Political Economy*, 10 (4), pp. 607–620.

Boltanski, L. (2004) *Distant Suffering: Morality, Media and Politics* (Cambridge University Press).

Bonefeld, W. (2006) 'Social Constitution and the Spectre of Globalization', in Bieler, A., Bonefeld, W., Burnham, P. and Morton, A.D. (eds) *Global Restructuring, State, Capital and Labour: Contesting Neo-Gramscian Perspectives* (Basingstoke: Palgrave Macmillan).

Bowman, A., Froud, J., Johal, S., Law, J., Leaver, A., Moran, M., and Williams, K. (2014) *The End of the Experiment?: From Competition to the Foundational Economy* (Manchester University Press).

Boyer, R. (1996) 'State and Market: A New Engagement for the Twenty-First Century?', in Boyer, R. and Drache, D. (eds) *States Against Markets: The Limits of Globalization* (London: Routledge).

Brassett, J. and Clarke, C. (2012) 'Performing the Sub-Prime Crisis: Trauma and the Financial Event', *International Political Sociology*, 6 (1), pp. 4–20.

Brassett, J., Rethel, L. and Watson, M. (2010) 'The Political Economy of the Subprime Crisis: The Economics, Politics and Ethics of Response', *New Political Economy*, 15 (1), pp. 1–7.

Broome, A. (2010) 'The International Monetary Fund, Crisis Management and the Credit Crunch', *Australian Journal of International Affairs*, 64 (1), pp. 37–54.

Broome, A., Clegg, L. and Rethel, L. (2012) 'Global Governance and the Politics of Crisis', *Global Society*, 26 (1), pp. 3–17.

Brown, C. and Ainley, K. (2009) *Understanding International Relations Fourth Edition* (Basingstoke: Palgrave Macmillan).

Brown, V. (1994) *Adam Smith's Discourse: Canonicity, Commerce and Conscience* (London: Routledge).

Buchan, J. (2006) *Adam Smith and the Pursuit of Perfect Liberty* (London: Profile Books Limited).

Buchanan, J. M. (1979) 'The Justice of Natural Liberty', in O'Driscoll, G. (ed) *Adam Smith and Modern Political Economy: Bicentennial Essays on The Wealth of Nations* (Iowa City, IA: Iowa State University Press).

Bucks, B. and Pence, K. (2006) 'Do Homeowners Know Their House Values and Mortgage Terms?', *The Federal Reserve Board Finance and Economics Discussion Series*, 2006–03 (March).

Bukovansky, M. (2006) 'Civilizing the Bad: Ethical Problems with Neo-Liberal Approaches to Corruption', in Bowden, B. and Seabrooke, L. (eds) *Global Standards of Market Civilization* (London: Routledge).

Bunn, P. and Rostom, M. (2014) 'Household Debt and Spending', *Bank of England Quarterly Bulletin 2014 Q3*, 54 (3), pp. 304–315.

Burch, K. (1997) 'Constituting IPE and Modernity' in Burch, K. and Denemark, R.A. (eds) *Constituting International Political Economy* (London: Lynne Rienner).

Burchill, S. (2005) 'Liberalism', in Burchill, S., Devetak, R., Donnelly, J., Linklater, A., Paterson, M., Reus-Smit, C. and True, J. (eds) *Theories of International Relations Third Edition* (Basingstoke: Palgrave Macmillan).

Butler, J. (1993) *Bodies That Matter: On the Discursive Limitations of 'Sex'*(London: Routledge).

Butler, J. (2011a) 'Bodies in Public: Remarks at Zuccotti Park, October 23', in Taylor, A., Gessen, K. and editors from *n+1, Dissent, Triple Canopy* and *The New Inquiry* (eds) *Occupy! Scenes from Occupied America* (London: Verso), p.193.

Butler, J. (2011b) 'For and Against Precarity', *Tidal: Occupy Theory, Occupy Strategy, Issue 1*.

Calhoun, C. (2013) 'Occupy Wall Street in Perspective', *The British Journal of Sociology*, 64 (1), pp. 26–38.

Carlsson, J., Köhlin, G. and Ekbom, A. (1994) *The Political Economy of Evaluation: International Aid Agencies and the Effectiveness of Aid* (Basingstoke: Macmillan).

Carter, M.R. (1997) 'Intellectual Openings and Policy Closures: Disequilibria in Contemporary Development Economics', in Cooper, F. and Packard, R. (eds) *International Development and the Social Sciences: Essays on the History and Politics of Knowledge* (Berkeley, CA: University of California Press).

Chomsky, N. (2012) *Occupy* (London: Penguin).

Clark, J.M. (1989 [1928]) 'Adam Smith and the Currents of History', in Clark, J.M., Douglas, P.H., Hollander, J.H., Morrow, G.R., Palyi, M. and Viner, J. (eds) *Adam Smith, 1776–1926: Lectures to Commemorate the Sesquicentennial of The Wealth of Nations* (New York: Augustus M. Kelley Publishers).

Clarke C. (2015) 'Learning to Fail: Resilience and the Empty Promise of Financial Literacy Education', *Consumption Markets & Culture*, 18 (3), pp. 257-276.

Clift, B. (2014) *Comparative Political Economy: States, Markets and Global Capitalism* (Basingstoke: Palgrave).

Clift, B. and Rosamond, B. (2009) 'Lineages of a British International Political Economy', in Blyth, M. (ed.), *Routledge Handbook of International Political Economy: IPE as a Global Conversation* (Abingdon: Routledge).

Coats, A.W. (1975) 'Adam Smith and the Mercantile System', in Skinner, A.S. and Wilson, T. (eds) *Essays on Adam Smith* (Oxford: Clarendon Press).

Cobbett, E. and Germain, R. (2012), '"Occupy Wall Street" and IPE: Insights and Implications', *Journal of Critical Globalisation Studies*, 5, pp. 110–113.

Cohen, B.J. (1974) *The Question of Imperialism: The Political Economy of Dominance and Dependence* (London: Macmillan).

Cohen, B.J. (2008) *International Political Economy: An Intellectual History* (Princeton, NJ: Princeton University Press).

Cook, C. (2012) 'Occupy the EU', *The Occupied Times of London, Issue 10*, February 8.

Cox, R. (1999) 'Civil Society at the Turn of the Millennium: Prospects for an Alternative World Order', *Review of International Studies*, 25 (1), pp. 3–28.

Cox, R. (2000) 'Political Economy and World Order: Problems of Power and Knowledge at the Turn of the Millennium', in Stubbs, R. and Underhill, G.R.D. (eds) *Political Economy and the Changing Global Order Second Edition* (Oxford University Press).

Crane, G.T. and Amawi, A. (1997) *Theoretical Evolution of International Political Economy: A Reader Second Edition* (Oxford University Press).

CRESC (2009) *An Alternative Report on UK Banking Reform: A Public Interest Report from CRESC* (University of Manchester: Centre for Research on Socio-Cultural Change).

Cropsey, J. (1975) 'Adam Smith and Political Philosophy', in Skinner, A. S. and Wilson, T. (eds) *Essays on Adam Smith* (Oxford: Clarendon Press).

Crouch, C. (2009) 'Privatised Keynesianism: An Unacknowledged Policy Regime', *British Journal of Politics and International Relations*, 11 (3), pp. 382–399.

Crouch, C. (2011) *The Strange Non-death of Neoliberalism* (Cambridge: Polity).

Dasgupta, B. (1998) *Structural Adjustment, Global Trade and the New Political Economy of Development* (London: Zed).

Datz, G. (2013) 'The Narrative of Complexity in the Crisis of Finance: Epistemological Challenge and Macroprudential Policy Response', *New Political Economy*, 18 (4), pp. 459–479.

De Goede, M. (2005) 'Carnival of Money: Politics of Dissent in an Era of Globalizing Finance', in Amoore, L. (ed) *The Global Resistance Reader* (London: Routledge).

Diaz-Alejandro, C.F. (1978) 'Delinking North and South: Unshackled or Unhinged?', in Fishlow, A., Diaz-Alejandro, C.F., Fagen, R.R. and Hansen, R.D. (eds) *Rich and Poor Nations in the World Economy* (New York: McGraw-Hill).

Dickey, L. (1986) 'Historicizing the "Adam Smith Problem": Conceptual, Historiographical, and Textual Issues', *Journal of Modern History*, 58 (3), pp. 579–609.

Dobb, M. (1937) *Political Economy and Capitalism: Some Essays in the Economic Tradition* (London: Routledge).

Dodd, N. (2014) *The Social Life of Money* (Princeton, NJ: Princeton University Press).

Dunn, B. (2009) *Global Political Economy: A Marxist Critique* (London: Pluto Press).

Dunne, T. (2005) 'Liberalism', in Baylis, J. and Smith, S. (eds) *The Globalization of World Politics: An Introduction to International Relations Third Edition* (Oxford University Press).

Dyson, B., Greenham, T., Ryan-Collins, J. and Werner, R.A. (2011) *Towards a 21st Century Banking and Monetary System: Submission to the Independent Commission on Banking*. Available online: http://neweconomics.org/publications/towards-a-21st-century-banking-and-monetary-system [accessed 09/02/12].

Endres, A.M. (1991) 'Adam Smith's Rhetoric of Economics: An Illustration Using "Smithian" Compositional Rules', *Scottish Journal of Political Economy*, 38 (1), pp. 76–95.

Evensky, J.M. (1987) 'The Two Voices of Adam Smith: Moral Philosopher and Social Critic', *History of Political Economy*, 19 (3), pp. 447–468, reprinted in Cunningham Wood, J. (1994) *Adam Smith: Critical Assessments Second Series Volume VI* (London: Routledge).

Evensky, J.M. (1989) 'The Evolution of Adam Smith's Views on Political Economy', *History of Political Economy*, 21 (1), pp. 123–145, reprinted in Cunningham Wood, J. (1994) *Adam Smith: Critical Assessments Second Series Volume VI* (London: Routledge).

Executive Office of the President (2013) *The Financial Crisis: Five Years Later* (Washington).

FCA (2014) *FCA Risk Outlook 2014* (London: Financial Conduct Authority).

FCIC (2011) *The Financial Crisis Inquiry Report: Final Report of the National Commission on the Causes of the Financial and Economic Crisis in the United States* (Washington, DC: Financial Crisis Inquiry Commission).
Federal Reserve Board of Governors (2007) *Statement on Subprime Mortgage Lending* (Washington, DC: Board of Governors of the Federal Reserve System).
Federal Reserve Board of Governors (2014) *100th Annual Report 2013* (Washington, DC: Board of Governors of the Federal Reserve System).
Femia, J. (1988) 'An Historicist Critique of "Revisionist" Methods for Studying the History of Ideas' in Tully, J. (ed) *Meaning and Context: Quentin Skinner and his Critics* (Cambridge: Polity).
Finlayson, A. (2009) 'Financialisation, Financial Literacy and Asset-Based Welfare', *British Journal of Politics and International Relations*, 11 (3), pp. 400–421.
Fitzgibbons, A. (1995) *Adam Smith's System of Liberty, Wealth, and Virtue: The Moral and Political Foundations of The Wealth of Nations* (Oxford: Clarendon Press).
Fleischacker, S. (2004) *On Adam Smith's Wealth of Nations: A Philosophical Companion* (Princeton, NJ: Princeton University Press).
Fleischacker, S. and Brown, V. (2010) 'Introduction', in Fleischacker, S. and Brown, V. (eds) *The Philosophy of Adam Smith: Essays Commemorating the 250th Anniversary of The Theory of Moral Sentiments* (Abingdon: Routledge).
Force, P. (2003) *Self-Interest before Adam Smith: A Genealogy of Economic Science* (Cambridge University Press).
Foster, J. (2001) 'Competition, Competitive Selection and Economic Evaluation', in Garrouste, P. and Ioannides, S. (eds) *Evolution and Path Dependence in Economic Ideas: Past and Present* (Cheltenham: Edward Elgar).
Foucault, M. (2008) *The Birth of Biopolitics: Lectures at the College De France, 1978–79* (Basingstoke: Palgrave Macmillan).
Fourcade-Gourinchas, M. and Babb, S (2002) 'The Rebirth of the Liberal Creed: Paths to Neoliberalism in Four Countries', *American Journal of Sociology*, 108 (9), pp. 533–579.
French, S. Leyshon, A. and Wainwright, T. (2011) 'Financializing Space, Spacing Financialization', *Progress in Human Geography*, 35 (6), pp. 798–819.
Frieden, J.A. and Lake, D.A. (2000) 'Introduction: International Politics and International Economics', in Frieden, J.A. and Lake, D.A. (eds) *International Political Economy: Perspectives on Global Power and Wealth Fourth Edition* (London: Routledge).
Froud, J. and Johal, S. (2008) 'Editorial: "Questioning Finance": A Special Issue of Competition & Change', *Competition and Change*, 12 (2), pp. 107–109.
Froud J., Johal, S. and Williams, K. (2002) 'Financialisation and the Coupon Pool', *Capital and Class*, 26, pp. 119–151.
Froud, J., Moran, M., Nilsson, A. and Williams, K. (2010) 'Wasting a Crisis? Democracy and Markets in Britain after 2007', *The Political Quarterly*, 81 (1) pp. 25–38.
Fry, M. (ed) (1992) *Adam Smith's Legacy: His Place in the Development of Modern Economics* (London: Routledge).
FSA (2009) *The Turner Review: A Regulatory Response to the Global Banking Crisis* (London: Financial Services Authority).
FSA (2011) *The Failure of the Royal Bank of Scotland: Financial Services Authority Board Report* (London: Financial Services Authority).
FSB (2009) *Improving Financial Regulation: Report of the Financial Stability Board to G20 Leaders* (Basel: Financial Stability Board).
FSB (2011) *Thematic Review on Mortgage Underwriting and Origination Practices Peer Review Report* (Basel: Financial Stability Board).

FSF (2008) *Report of the Financial Stability Forum on Enhancing Market and Institutional Resilience* (Basel: Financial Stability Forum).

FSF (2009) *Report of the Financial Stability Forum on Enhancing Market and Institutional Resilience: Update on Implementation* (Basel: Financial Stability Forum).

G20 (2008) *Declaration on Financial Markets and the World Economy: Washington Summit*, November 15.

G20 (2009) *Declaration on Strengthening the Financial System: London Summit*, April 2.

Gallagher, K.P. (2015) 'Contesting the Governance of Capital Flows at the IMF', *Governance: An International Journal of Policy, Administration, and Institutions*, 28 (2), pp. 185–198.

Gamble, A. (1983) 'Critical Political Economy', in Jones, R.J.B. (ed) *Perspectives on Political Economy* (London: Frances Pinter).

Gamble, A. (2010) 'The Political Consequences of the Crash', *Political Studies Review*, 8 (1), pp. 3–14.

Germain, R.D. (1996) 'The Worlds of Finance: A Braudelian Perspective on IPE', *European Journal of International Relations*, 2 (2), pp. 201–230.

Germain, R.D. (1997) *The International Organisation of Credit: States and Global Finance in the World-Economy* (Cambridge University Press).

Germain, R.D. (2000) 'Globalization in Historical Perspective', in Germain, R.D. (ed) *Globalization and its Critics: Perspectives from Political Economy* (Basingstoke: Macmillan).

Germain, R.D. (2010) *Global Politics and Financial Governance* (Basingstoke: Macmillan).

Germain, R.D. and Kenny, M. (1998) 'Engaging Gramsci: International Relations Theory and the New Gramscians', *Review of International Studies*, 24 (1), pp. 3–21.

Gill, S. (1997) 'Finance, Production and Panopticism: Inequality, Risk and Resistance in an Era of Disciplinary Neo-liberalism', in Gill, S. (ed) *Globalization, Democratization and Multilateralism* (Basingstoke: Macmillan).

Gill, S. (2000) 'Toward a Postmodern Prince? The Battle in Seattle as a New Moment in the Politics of Globalisation', *Millennium. Journal of International Studies*, 29 (1), pp. 131–140.

Gilpin, R. (1987) *The Political Economy of International Relations* (Princeton, NJ: Princeton University Press).

Gotham, K. (2009) 'Creating Liquidity out of Spatial Fixity: The Secondary Circuit of Capital and the Subprime Mortgage Crisis', *International Journal of Urban and Regional Research*, 33 (2), pp. 355–371.

Gowan, P. (2008) 'Crisis in the Heartland: Consequences of the New Wall Street System', *New Left Review*, 55, pp. 5–29.

Glaze, S. (2008) 'The Gordon Brown Problem: New Labour and the Two "Adam Smiths"', *The Political Quarterly*, 79 (3), pp. 377–387.

Glaze, S. (2015) 'Schools Out: Adam Smith and Pre-disciplinary International Political Economy', *New Political Economy*, 20 (5), pp. 679–701.

Graham, K. (1977) *J.L. Austin: A Critique of Ordinary Language Philosophy* (Hassocks: Harvester Press).

Greenspan, A. (2008) 'The World Must Repel Calls to Contain Competitive Markets', *The Financial Times*, August 5.

Greenspan, A. (2011) 'How Dodd-Frank Fails to Meet the Test of Our Times', *The Financial Times*, March 30.

Griffin, P. (2007) 'Refashioning IPE: What and How Gender Analysis Teaches International Political Economy', *Review of International Political Economy*, 14 (4), pp. 719–736.

Griswold, C. (1999) *Adam Smith and the Virtues of Enlightenment* (Cambridge University Press).

Haakonssen, K. (1981) *The Science of the Legislator: The Natural Jurisprudence of David Hume and Adam Smith* (Cambridge University Press).

Haakonssen, K. (2003) 'Natural Jurisprudence and the Theory of Justice', in Broadie, A. (ed) *The Cambridge Companion to the Scottish Enlightenment* (Cambridge University Press).

Hall, S. (2011) 'Geographies of Money and Finance II: Financialization and Financial Subjects', *Progress in Human Geography*, 36 (3), pp. 403–411.

Harcourt, B. (2012) 'Political Disobedience', *Critical Inquiry*, 39 (1), pp. 33–55.

Harpham, E.J. (1983) 'Liberalism, Civic Humanism, and the Case of Adam Smith', *The American Political Science Review*, 78 (3), pp. 764–774.

Harrod, J. (2006) 'The Century of the Corporation', in May, C. (ed) *Global Corporate Power* (Boulder, CO: Lynne Rienner).

Haufler, V. (2006) 'Global Governance and the Private Sector', in May, C. (ed) *Global Corporate Power* (Boulder, CO: Lynne Rienner).

Hay, C. (2009) 'Good Inflation, Bad Inflation: The Housing Boom, Economic Growth and the Disaggregation of Inflationary Preferences in the UK and Ireland', *British Journal of Politics and International Relations*, 11 (3), pp. 461–478.

Helleiner, E. (2014) *The Status Quo Crisis: Global Financial Governance After the 2008 Meltdown* (Oxford University Press).

Herring, C. and Glück, Z. (2011) 'The Homeless Question', in Taylor, A., Gessen, K. and editors from *n+1, Dissent, Triple Canopy* and *The New Inquiry* (eds) *Occupy! Scenes from Occupied America* (London: Verso), pp.163–169.

Higgott, R. (1994) 'International Political Economy', in Groom, A.J.R. and Light, M. (eds) *Contemporary International Relations: A Guide to Theory* (London: Pinters).

Hirsch, P., Michaels, S. and Friedman, R. (1990) 'Clean Models vs. Dirty Hands: Why Economics is Different from Sociology', in Zukin, S. and Dimaggio, P. (eds) *Structures of Capital: The Social Organization of the Economy* (Cambridge University Press).

Hite, A.B. and Roberts, J.T. (2007) 'Development and Globalization: Recurring Themes', in Roberts, J.T. and Hite, A.B. (eds) *The Globalization and Development Reader: Perspectives on Development and Global Change* (Oxford: Blackwell).

HM Treasury (2012) *Review of HM Treasury's Management Response to the Financial Crisis* (London: HM Treasury).

HM Treasury (2014) *The Financial Policy Committee's Housing Market Tools* (London: HM Treasury).

Hobson, J.M. and Seabrooke, L. (2007) 'Everyday IPE: Revealing Everyday Forms of Change in the World Economy', in Hobson, J.M. and Seabrooke, L. (eds) *Everyday Politics of the World Economy* (Cambridge University Press).

Holden, G. (2002) 'Who Contextualizes the Contextualizers? Disciplinary History and the Discourse about IR Discourse', *Review of International Studies*, 28 (2), pp. 253–270.

Hollander, S. (1973) *The Economics of Adam Smith* (London: Heinemann).

Hollander, S. (1987) *Classical Economics* (Oxford: Basil Blackwood).

Holton, R.J. (1992) *Economy and Society* (London: Routledge).

Hont, I. and Ignatieff, M. (1983) 'Needs and Justice in the Wealth of Nations: An Introductory Essay' in Hont, I. and Ignatieff, M. (eds) *Wealth and Virtue: The Shaping of Political Economy in the Scottish Enlightenment* (Cambridge University Press).

Hoogvelt, A. (2001) *Globalization and the Postcolonial World: The New Political Economy of Development Second Edition* (Basingstoke: Palgrave).

Hume, D. (1751) *An Enquiry Concerning the Principles of Morals* (London: A. Millar).
Hutcheson, F. (2002 [1742]) *An Essay on the Nature and Conduct of the Passions and Affections, with Illustrations on the Moral Sense*, The Collected Works of Francis Hutcheson, edited by Garrett, A. (Indianapolis, IN: Liberty Fund).
ICB (2011a) *Independent Commission on Banking Interim Report: Consultation on Reform Options April 2011* (London: ICB).
ICB (2011b) *Independent Commission on Banking Final Report: Recommendations September 2011* (London: ICB).
IMF (2006) *Global Financial Stability Report: Market Developments and Issues September 2006* (Washington, DC: International Monetary Fund).
IMF (2007a) *Global Financial Stability Report: Market Developments and Issues April 2007* (Washington, DC: International Monetary Fund).
IMF (2007b) *Global Financial Stability Report: Financial Market Turbulence Causes, Consequences, and Policies October 2007* (Washington, DC: International Monetary Fund).
IMF (2008a) *Global Financial Stability Report: Containing Systemic Risks and Restoring Financial Soundness April 2008* (Washington, DC: International Monetary Fund).
IMF (2008b) *Global Financial Stability Report: Financial Stress and Deleveraging Macrofinancial Implications and Policy October 2008* (Washington, DC: International Monetary Fund).
IMF (2009a) *Global Financial Stability Report: Responding to the Financial Crisis and Measuring Systemic Risks April 2009* (Washington, DC: International Monetary Fund).
IMF (2009b) *Global Financial Stability Report: Navigating the Financial Challenges Ahead October 2009* (Washington, DC: International Monetary Fund).
IMF (2010a) *Global Financial Stability Report: Meeting New Challenges to Stability and Building a Safer System April 2010* (Washington, DC: International Monetary Fund).
IMF (2010b) *Global Financial Stability Report: Sovereigns, Funding, and Systemic Liquidity October 2010* (Washington, DC: International Monetary Fund).
IMF (2011a) *Global Financial Stability Report: Durable Financial Stability Getting There from Here April 2011* (Washington, DC: International Monetary Fund).
IMF (2011b) *Global Financial Stability Report: Grappling with Crisis Legacies September 2011 Summary Version* (Washington, DC: International Monetary Fund).
Isaak, R.A. (1995) *Managing World Economic Change: International Political Economy Second Edition* (London: Prentice-Hall International).
Jones, O. (2011) 'Protests, Strikes and Occupations Are All the Same Struggle', *The Occupied Times of London, Issue 6*, November 30.
Jørgensen, K. E. (2000) 'Continental IR Theory: The Best Kept Secret', *European Journal of International Relations*, 6 (1), pp. 9–42.
Kaldor, M. (2003) *Global Civil Society: An Answer to War* (Cambridge: Polity).
Keane, J. (1988) 'More Theses on the Philosophy of History' in Tully, J. (ed) *Meaning and Context: Quentin Skinner and his Critics* (Cambridge: Polity).
Kennedy, G. (2005) *Adam Smith's Lost Legacy* (Basingstoke: Palgrave).
Kennett, P., Forrest, R. and Marsh, A. (2013) 'The Global Economic Crisis and the Reshaping of Housing Opportunities', *Housing, Theory and Society*, 30 (1), pp. 10–28.
Kindleberger, C.P. (1976) 'The Historical Background: Adam Smith and the Industrial Revolution', in Wilson, T. and Skinner, A. S. (eds) *The Market and the State: Essays in Honour of Adam Smith* (Oxford University Press).
King, M. (2009) Speech by Mervyn King to Scottish business organisations, Edinburgh, October 20, Available online: http://www.bankofengland.co.uk/publications/Documents/speeches/2009/speech406.pdf [accessed 19/03/12].

Kirshner, J. (2009) 'Realist Political Economy: Traditional Themes and Contemporary Challenges', in Blyth, M. (ed) *Routledge Handbook of International Political Economy: IPE as a Global Conversation* (London: Routledge).

Klein, N. (2011) 'The Most Important Thing in the World', *The Occupied Wall Street Journal, Issue 2*, October 8.

Kline, J.M. (2005) *Ethics for International Business: Decision Making in a Global Political Economy* (New York: Routledge).

Krugman, P. (2010) 'Financial Reform Endgame', *The New York Times*, March 1.

Lal, D. (2006) *Reviving the Invisible Hand: The Case for Classical Liberalism in the Twenty-First Century* (Princeton, NJ: Princeton University Press).

Lamb, R.B. (1974) 'Adam Smith's System: Sympathy not Self-Interest', *Journal of the History of Ideas*, 35 (4), pp. 671–682.

Lanchester, J. (2010) *Whoops!: Why Everyone Owes Everyone and No One Can Pay* (London: Penguin).

Langley, P. (2006) 'The Making of Investor Subjects in Anglo-American Pensions', *Environment and Planning D: Society and Space*, 24 (6), pp. 919–934.

Langley, P. (2007) 'Everyday Investor Subjects and Global Financial Change: The Rise of Anglo-American Mass Investment' in Hobson, J.M. and Seabrooke, L. (eds) *Everyday Politics of the World Economy* (Cambridge University Press).

Langley, P. (2008a) 'Sub-prime Mortgage Lending: A Cultural Economy', *Economy and Society*, 37 (4), pp. 469–494.

Langley, P. (2008b) *The Everyday Life of Global Finance: Saving and Borrowing in Anglo-America* (Oxford University Press).

Langley, P. (2015) *Liquidity Lost: The Governance of the Global Financial Crisis* (Oxford University Press).

Lavelle, K. (2014) 'Implementing the Volcker Rule in National and International Politics', in Porter, T (ed) *Transnational Financial Regulation after the Crisis* (London: Routledge).

Lipschutz, R.D. (2005) *Globalization, Governmentality and Global Politics: Regulation for the Rest of Us?* (Abingdon: Routledge).

Little, R. (1999) 'Historiography and International Relations', *Review of International Studies*, 25 (2), pp. 291–299.

Macfie, A.L. (1967) *The Individual in Society: Papers on Adam Smith* (London: Allen and Unwin).

MacKenzie, D. (2005) 'Opening the Black Boxes of Global Finance', *Review of International Political Economy*, 12 (4), pp. 555–576.

MacKenzie, D. (2011) 'The Credit Crisis as a Problem in the Sociology of Knowledge', *American Journal of Sociology*, 116 (6), pp.1778–1841.

MacLean, J. (2000) 'Philosophical Roots of Globalization and Philosophical Routes to Globalization', in Germain, R.D. (ed) *Globalization and its Critics: Perspectives from Political Economy* (Basingstoke: Macmillan).

Mandeville, B. (1732) *An Enquiry into the Origin of Honour and the Usefulness of Christianity in War, by the Author of the Fable of the Bees* (London: John Brotherton).

Mandeville, B. (1988 [1732]) *The Fable of the Bees or Private Vices, Publick Benefits Volume 2* (Indianapolis: Liberty Fund).

Martin, R. (2002) *Financialization of Daily Life* (Philadelphia, PA: Temple University Press).

Martinez, M.A. (2009) *The Myth of the Free Market: The Role of the State in a Capitalist Economy* (Sterling, VA: Kumarian Press).

Marron, D. (2013). '"Informed, Educated and More Confident": Financial Capability and the Problematization of Personal Finance Consumption', *Consumption Markets and Culture*, 17 (5), pp. 491–511.

McKenna, S.J. (2006) *Adam Smith: The Rhetoric of Propriety* (Albany, NY: State University of New York Press).

McLean, I. (2006) *Adam Smith, Radical and Egalitarian: An Interpretation for the 21st Century* (Edinburgh University Press).

McLeay, M., Amar, R. and Thomas, R. (2014) 'Money Creation in the Modern Economy', *Bank of England Quarterly Bulletin 2014 Q1*, 54 (1), pp. 14–28.

McWilliams, W.C. and Piotrowski, H. (2001) *The World Since 1945: A History of International Relations Fifth Edition* (Boulder, CO: Lynne Rienner).

Mew, P. (1971) 'Conventions on Thin Ice', *The Philosophical Quarterly*, 21 (85), pp. 352–356.

Miller, R.C. (2008) *International Political Economy: Contrasting World Views* (London: Routledge).

Minogue, K. (1988) 'Method in Intellectual History: Quentin Skinner's Foundations' in Tully, J. (ed) *Meaning and Context: Quentin Skinner and his Critics* (Cambridge: Polity).

Mirowski, P. (2013) *Never Let a Serious Crisis Go to Waste: How Neoliberalism Survived the Financial Meltdown* (London: Verso).

Mitchell, W.J.T. (2012) 'Image, Space, Revolution: The Arts of Occupation', *Critical Inquiry*, 39 (1), pp. 8–32.

Mittelman, J.H. (1997) 'Restructuring the Global Division of Labour: Old Theories and New Realities', in Gill, S. (ed) *Globalization, Democratization and Multilateralism* (Basingstoke: Macmillan).

Mittelman, J.H. and Pasha, M.K. (1997) *Out From Underdevelopment Revisited: Changing Global Structures and the Remaking of the Third World Second Edition* (Basingstoke: Macmillan).

Montes, L. (2004) *Adam Smith in Context: A Critical Reassessment of Some Central Components of His Thought* (Basingstoke: Palgrave).

Montgomerie, J. (2006) 'Giving Credit where it's Due: Public Policy and Household Debt in the United States, the United Kingdom and Canada', *Policy and Society*, 25 (3), pp. 109–141.

Montgomerie, J. (2009) 'The Pursuit of (Past) Happiness? Middle-class Indebtedness and American Financialisation', *New Political Economy*, 14 (1), pp. 1–24.

Montgomerie, J. (2013) 'America's Debt Safety-Net', *Public Administration*, 91 (4), pp. 871–888.

Morgan, M.S. (2006) 'Economic Man as Model Man: Ideal Types, Idealization and Caricatures, *Journal of the History of Economic Thought*, 28 (1), pp. 1–27.

Morrow, G. (1989 [1928]) 'Adam Smith: Moralist and Philosopher', in Clark, J.M., Douglas, P.H., Hollander, J.H., Morrow, G.R., Palyi, M. and Viner, J. (eds) *Adam Smith, 1776–1926: Lectures to Commemorate the Sesquicentennial of The Wealth of Nations* (New York: Augustus M. Kelley Publishers).

Moschella, M. (2012) 'IMF Surveillance in Crisis: The Past, Present and Future of the Reform Process', *Global Society*, 26 (1), pp. 43–60.

Muller, J.Z. (1995) *Adam Smith in His Time and Ours* (Princeton, NJ: Princeton University Press).

Murphy, C.N. and Nelson, D.R. (2002) 'Conclusions: Explaining a Thriving Heterodoxy', in Abbott, J.P. and Worth, O. (eds) *Critical Perspectives on International Political Economy* (Basingstoke: Palgrave).

Murphy, C.N. and Tooze, R. (1991a) 'Introduction', in Murphy, C.N. and Tooze, R. (eds) *The New International Political Economy* (Boulder, CO: Lynne Rienner).
Murphy, C.N. and Tooze, R. (1991b) 'Getting Beyond the "Common Sense" of the IPE Orthodoxy', in Murphy, C.N. and Tooze, R. (eds) *The New International Political Economy* (Boulder, CO: Lynne Rienner).
NCRC (2003) *The Broken Credit System: Discrimination and Unequal Access to Affordable Loans by Race and Age* (Washington, DC: National Community Reinvestment Coalition).
NCRC (2008) *Income is No Shield: Against Racial Differences in Lending II* (Washington, DC: National Community Reinvestment Coalition).
NCRC (2010a) *Home Affordable Modification Program Survey 2010* (Washington, DC: National Community Reinvestment Coalition).
NCRC (2010b) *Foreclosure Rescue Scams: A Nightmare Complicating the American Dream* (Washington, DC: National Community Reinvestment Coalition).
NCRC (2010c) *Foreclosure in the Nation's Capital: How Unfair and Reckless Lending Undermines Homeownership* (Washington, DC: National Community Reinvestment Coalition).
NCRC (2010d) *Safe and Sound Lending in Neighborhoods: An Examination of the Community Reinvestment Act (CRA) at Work in Washington, DC and Houston, TX* (Washington, DC: National Community Reinvestment Coalition).
NCRC (2010e) *Rebuilding Communities in Economic Distress: Local Strategies to Sustain Homeownership, Reclaim Vacant Properties, and Promote Community-Based Employment* (Washington, DC: National Community Reinvestment Coalition).
NCRC (2011a) 'Analysis of the Obama Administration's Housing Finance Proposals', *National Community Reinvestment Coalition Issue Brief*, February 2011.
NCRC (2011b) *The Impact of the Proposed Qualified Residential Mortgage Definition on Home Opportunity in America* (Washington, DC: National Community Reinvestment Coalition).
NEF (2010) *Where Did Our Money Go? Building a Banking System Fit for Purpose* (London: New Economics Foundation).
NEF (2011a) *Subverting Safer Finance: How the UK Holds Back Global Financial Regulation* (London: New Economics Foundation).
NEF (2011b) *Good Banking: Why We Need a Bigger Public Debate on Financial Reform* (London: New Economics Foundation).
Nesvetailova, A. (2010) *Financial Alchemy in Crisis: The Great Liquidity Illusion* (London: Pluto).
Nieli, R. (1986) 'Spheres of Intimacy and the Adam Smith Problem', *Journal of the History of Ideas*, 47 (4), pp. 611–624.
Nitzan, J. and Bichler, S. (2000) 'Capital Accumulation: Breaking the Dualism of "Economics" and "Politics"', in Palan, R. (ed) *Global Political Economy: Contemporary Theories* (London: Routledge).
O'Brien, D.P. (2004) *The Classical Economists Revisited* (Oxford University Press).
O'Brien, R. and Williams, M. (2007) *Global Political Economy: Evolution and Dynamics Second Edition* (Basingstoke: Palgrave).
Occupy London (2012) 'How Hayek Helped Us to Find Capitalism's Flaws', *The Financial Times*, January 25.
Occupy LSX (2011a) Statement: 'Initial Statement', Available online: http://occupyLSX.org/?page_id=575 [accessed 08/02/12].
Occupy LSX (2011b) Statement: 'United for Global Democracy', Available online: http://occupyLSX.org/?page_id=2958 [accessed 08/02/12].

Occupy LSX (2011c) Statement: 'Economics Statement', Available online: http://occupyLSX.org/?page_id=2855 [accessed 08/02/12].

Occupy the SEC (2012) 'Comment Letter on the Notice of Proposed Rulemaking for the Volcker Rule' to the Securities Exchange Commission, the Federal Reserve Board, the Federal Deposit Insurance Corporation, and Office of Comptroller of the Currency, January 13, Available online: http://www.occupythesec.org/ [accessed 27/02/12].

Occupy Wall Street (2011a) Statement: 'Declaration of the Occupation of New York City', Available online: http://www.nycga.net/resources/declaration/ [accessed 08/02/12].

Occupy Wall Street (2011b) Statement: 'Principles of Solidarity', Available online: http://www.nycga.net/resources/principles-of-solidarity/ [accessed 08/02/12].

OECD (2009) *The Financial Crisis: Reforms and Exit Strategies* (Paris: Organisation for Economic Co-operation and Development).

Ormerod, P. (1994) *The Death of Economics* (London: Faber and Faber).

Otteson, J.R. (2002) *Adam Smith's Marketplace of Life* (Cambridge University Press).

Palan, R. and Cameron, A. (2003) *The Imagined Economies of Globalization* (London: Sage).

Panić, M. (2003) *Globalization and National Economic Welfare* (Basingstoke: Palgrave).

Parekh, B. and Berki, R.N. (1973) 'The History of Political Ideas: A Critique of Q. Skinner's Methodology', *Journal of the History of Ideas*, 34 (2), pp. 163–184.

Payne, A. (2005) *The Global Politics of Unequal Development* (Basingstoke: Palgrave).

Peil, J. (1989) 'A New Look at Adam Smith', *International Journal of Social Economics*, 16 (1), pp. 52–72, reprinted in Cunningham Wood, John (1994) *Adam Smith: Critical Assessments Second Series Volume VI* (London: Routledge).

Peil, J. (1999) *Adam Smith and Economic Science: A Methodological Reinterpretation* (Cheltenham: Edward Elgar).

Pettman, R. (1996) *Understanding International Political Economy: With Readings for the Fatigued* (Boulder, CO: Lynne Rienner).

Phillipson, N. (1983) 'Adam Smith as Civic Moralist' in Hont, I. and Ignatieff, M. (eds) *Wealth and Virtue: The Shaping of Political Economy in the Scottish Enlightenment* (Cambridge University Press).

Pocock, J.G.A. (1983) 'Cambridge Paradigms and Scotch Philosophers: A Study of the Relations between the Civic Humanist and the Civil Jurisprudential Interpretation of Eighteen-Century Social Thought' in Hont, I. and Ignatieff, M. (eds) *Wealth and Virtue: The Shaping of Political Economy in the Scottish Enlightenment* (Cambridge University Press).

Pocock, J.G.A. (1985) *Virtue, Commerce and History: Essays on Political Thought and History, Chiefly in the Eighteenth Century* (Cambridge University Press).

Polanyi, K. (2001 [1944]) *The Great Transformation: The Political and Economic Origins of Our Time* (Boston, MA: Beacon).

Porter, T. (2005) *Globalization and Finance* (Molden, MA: Polity Press).

Posner, R. (2009) *A Failure of Capitalism* (Cambridge, MA: Harvard University Press).

Power, M. (2007) *Organized Uncertainty: Designing a World of Risk Management* (Oxford University Press).

PPF (2009a) *Put People First: Ensuring a Response to the Economic Crisis that Delivers Democratic Governance of the Economy*, Available online: http://www.putpeoplefirst.org.uk/about-us/policy-platform/ [accessed 08/02/12].

PPF (2009b) *Beyond the London Summit: Assessing the UK Government's Response to the Financial Crisis and Charting a Way Forward*, Available online: http://www.putpeoplefirst.org.uk/about-us/beyond-the-london-summit/ [accessed 08/02/12].

PRA (2014) *The Implementation of Ring-Fencing: Consultation on Legal Structure, Governance and the Continuity of Services and Facilities* (London: Bank of England Prudential Regulation Authority).

Prestowitz, C. (2005) *Three Billion New Capitalists: The Great Shift of Wealth and Power to the East* (New York: Basic).

Raphael, D.D. (1975) 'The Impartial Spectator', in Skinner, A.S. and Wilson, T. (eds) *Essays on Adam Smith* (Oxford University Press).

Raphael, D.D. (2007) *The Impartial Spectator: Adam Smith's Moral Philosophy* (Oxford University Press).

Raphael, D. D. and Macfie, A. L. (1982) 'Introduction' to Smith (1982 [1759]) *The Theory of Moral Sentiments*, The Glasgow Edition of the Works and Correspondence of Adam Smith, edited by Raphael, D. D. and Macfie, A. L. (Indianapolis, IN: Liberty Fund).

Rasmussen, D.C. (2008) *The Problems and Promise of Commercial Society: Adam Smith's Response to Rousseau* (University Park, PA: Pennsylvania State University Press).

Ravenhill, J. (2005) 'The Study of Global Political Economy', in Ravenhill, J. (ed) *Global Political Economy* (Oxford University Press).

Recktenwald, H.C. (1978) 'An Adam Smith Renaissance anno 1976? The Bicentenary Output – A Reappraisal of His Scholarship', *Journal of Economic Literature*, 16, pp. 56–83.

Reddy, S.G. (1996) 'Claims to Expert Knowledge and the Subversion of Democracy: The Triumph of Risk over Uncertainty', *Economy and Society*, 25 (2), pp. 222–254.

Rethel, L. (2014) 'Bank Regulation after the Global Financial Crisis: The Case of Regulatory Arbitrage', in Porter, T (ed) *Transnational Financial Regulation after the Crisis* (London: Routledge).

Rethel, L. and Sinclair, T. (2012) *The Problem with Banks* (London: Zed Books).

Reuters (2011) 'Paul Volcker Says Volcker Rule Too Complicated', *Reuters.com*, November 9 Available online: http://www.reuters.com/article/2011/11/09/us-regulation-volcker-idUSTRE7A83KN20111109 [accessed 19/02/12].

Richmond, M. (2012) 'How Do You Solve a Problem Like TINA?', *The Occupied of London, Issue 8*, January 4.

Roberts, A. (2013) 'Financing Social Reproduction: The Gendered Relations of Debt and Mortgage Finance in Twenty-first-century America', *New Political Economy* 18 (1): pp. 21–42.

Ronald, R. (2008) *The Ideology of Home Ownership: Homeowner Societies and the Role of Housing* (Basingstoke: Palgrave).

Rosenberg, N. (1979) 'Adam Smith and Laissez-faire Revisited', in O'Driscoll, G. (ed) *Adam Smith and Modern Political Economy: Bicentennial Essays on The Wealth of Nations* (Iowa City, IA: Iowa State University Press).

Rosow, S.J. (1997) 'Echoes of Commercial Society: Liberal Political Theory in Mainstream IPE' in Burch, K. and Denemark, R.A. (eds) *Constituting International Political Economy* (London: Lynne Rienner).

Roth, M. (2011) 'Letters of Resignation from the American Dream', in Taylor, A., Gessen, K. and editors from *n+1, Dissent, Triple Canopy* and *The New Inquiry* (eds) *Occupy! Scenes from Occupied America* (London: Verso), pp. 23–29.

Rothschild, E. (2001) *Economic Sentiments: Adam Smith, Condorcet and the Enlightenment* (Cambridge, MA: Harvard University Press).

Rousseau, J.J. (1997) *The Discourses and Other Early Political Writings By Jean-Jacques Rousseau*, edited by Gourevitch, V. (Cambridge University Press).

Rupert, M. and Solomon, M. S. (2006) *Globalization and International Political Economy: The Politics of Alternative Futures* (Oxford: Rowman & Littlefield).

Sally, R. (1998) *Classical Liberalism and International Economic Order: Studies in Theory and Intellectual History* (London: Routledge).

Samuels, W.J., Johnson, M.F. and Perry, W.H. (2011) *Erasing the Invisible Hand: Essays on an Elusive and Misused Concept in Economics* (Cambridge University Press).

Samuelson, P.A. (1969) 'Presidential Address: The Way of an Economist', in Samuelson, P.A. (ed) *International Economic Relations: Proceedings of the Third Congress of the International Economic Association* (London: Macmillan).

Santiso, J. (2003) *The Political Economy of Emerging Markets: Actors, Institutions, and Financial Crises in Latin America* (New York: Palgrave).

Scholte, J.A. (2004) 'Civil Society and Democratically Accountable Global Governance', *Government and Opposition*, 39 (2), pp. 211–233.

Schrecker, T. (1997) 'Introduction: Sustainability, Globalization and Moral Imagination', in Schrecker, T. (ed) *Surviving Globalism: The Social and Environmental Challenges* (Basingstoke: Macmillan).

Schwartz, H.M. (2009) *Subprime Nation: American Power, Global Capital, and the Housing Boom* (Ithaca, NY: Cornell University Press).

Schwartz, H.M. and Seabrooke, L. (2009) 'Varieties of Residential Capitalism in the International Political Economy: Old Welfare States and the New Politics of Housing', in Schwartz, H.M. and Seabrooke, L. (eds) *The Politics of Housing Booms and Busts* (Basingstoke: Palgrave).

Seabrooke, L. (2006) *The Social Sources Of Financial Power: Domestic Legitimacy And International Financial Orders* (Cornell University Press).

Seabrooke, L. (2007) 'The Everyday Social Sources of Imperial and Hegemonic Financial Orders', in Hobson, J.M. and Seabrooke, L. (eds) *Everyday Politics of the World Economy* (Cambridge University Press).

Seabrooke, L. (2010) 'What Do I Get? The Everyday Politics of Expectations and the Subprime Crisis', *New Political Economy*, 15 (1), pp. 51–70.

Sen, A. (2009) *The Idea of Justice* (London: Allen Lane).

Shaw, M. (2000) 'Historical Sociology and Global Transformations', in Palan, R. (ed) *Global Political Economy: Contemporary Theories* (London: Routledge).

Shiller, R. (2008) *The Subprime Solution: How Today's Global Financial Crisis Happened, and What to Do about It* (Princeton, NJ: Princeton University Press).

Shiller, R. (2009) 'A Failure to Control the Animal Spirits', *The Financial Times*, March 9.

Shutt, H. (2011) 'On the Criminality of the Financial Sector', *The Occupied Times of London, Issue 5*, November 23.

Simmel, G. (1910) 'How is Society Possible?', *American Journal of Sociology*, 16 (3), pp. 372–391.

Skinner, A. (1996) *A System of Social Science: Papers Relating to Adam Smith Second Edition* (Oxford: Clarendon Press).

Skinner, Q. (1969) 'Meaning and Understanding in the History of Ideas', *History and Theory*, 8 (1), pp. 3–53.

Skinner, Q. (1974) 'Some Problems in the Analysis of Political Thought and Action', *Political Theory*, 2 (3), pp. 277–303.

Skinner, Q. (1988a) 'Motives, Intentions and the Interpretation of Texts' in Tully, J. (ed) *Meaning and Context: Quentin Skinner and his Critics* (Cambridge: Polity).

Skinner, Q. (1988b) 'A Reply To My Critics' in Tully, J. (ed) *Meaning and Context: Quentin Skinner and his Critics* (Cambridge: Polity).

Smith, A. (1981 [1776] *WN*) *An Inquiry into the Nature and Causes of the Wealth of Nations*, The Glasgow Edition of the Works and Correspondence of Adam Smith, edited by Campbell, R. and Skinner, A. (Indianapolis, IN: Liberty Fund).

Smith, A. (1982a [1759] *TMS*) *The Theory of Moral Sentiments*, The Glasgow Edition of the Works and Correspondence of Adam Smith, edited by Raphael, D. D. and Macfie, A. L. (Indianapolis, IN: Liberty Fund).

Smith, A. (1982b [1756]) 'A Letter to the Authors of the Edinburgh Review', in *Essays on Philosophical Subjects*, The Glasgow Edition of the Works and Correspondence of Adam Smith, edited by Wightman, W.P.D. and Bryce, J. C. (Indianapolis, IN: Liberty Fund).

Smith, S. (2008) 'Owner-occupation: At Home with a Hybrid of Money and Materials' *Environment and Planning A*, 40 (3), pp. 520–535.

Soederberg, S. (2014) *Debtfare States and the Poverty Industry: Money, Discipline and the Surplus Population* (New York: Routledge).

SSG (2008) *Observations on Risk Management Practices during the Recent Market Turbulence* (Basel: Senior Supervisors Group).

SSG (2009) *Risk Management Lessons from the Global Banking Crisis of 2008* (Basel: Senior Supervisors Group).

Stanley, L. (2014) '"We're Reaping What We Sowed": Everyday Crisis Narratives and Acquiescence to the Age of Austerity' *New Political Economy*, 19 (6), pp. 895–917.

Steger, M. B. (2002) *Globalism: The New Market Ideology* (Lanham, MD: Rowman & Littlefield).

Stigler, G. J. (1976) 'The Successes and Failures of Professor Smith', *The Journal of Political Economy*, 84 (6), pp. 1199–1213.

Stiglitz, J. (2007) *Making Globalization Work* (London: Penguin).

Stiglitz, J. (2010a) 'Needed: A New Economic Paradigm', *The Financial Times*, August 20.

Stiglitz, J. (2010b) *Freefall: America, Free Markets, and the Sinking of the World Economy* (New York: W. W. Norton & Company).

Stiglitz, J. (2011) 'The Mauritius Miracle', *The Occupied Times of London, Issue 8*, January 4.

Strange, S. (1994) *States and Markets Second Edition* (London: Pinter).

Strike Debt/Occupy Wall Street (2012) *The Debt Resistors' Operations Manual*, Available online: http://strikedebt.org/The-Debt-Resistors-Operations-Manual.pdf [accessed 21/11/14].

Swedberg, R., Himmelstrand, U. and Brulin, G. (1990) 'The Paradigm of Economic Sociology', in Zukin, S. and Dimaggio, P. (eds) *Structures of Capital: The Social Organization of the Economy* (Cambridge University Press).

Swift, A. (1993) *Global Political Ecology: The Crisis in Economy and Government* (London: Pluto Press).

Tabb, W. K. (1999) *Reconstructing Political Economy: The Great Divide in Economic Thought* (London: Routledge).

Taibbi, M. (2011) 'Why We Fight', *The Occupied Wall Street Journal, Issue 5*, November.

Tarcov, N. (1988) 'Quentin Skinner's Method and Machiavelli's Prince' in Tully, J. (ed) *Meaning and Context: Quentin Skinner and his Critics* (Cambridge: Polity).

Taylor, C. (1988) 'The Hermeneutics of Conflict' in Tully, J. (ed) *Meaning and Context: Quentin Skinner and his Critics* (Cambridge: Polity).

Teichgraeber III, R. (1981) 'Rethinking Das Adam Smith Problem', *The Journal of British Studies*, 20 (2), pp. 106–123.

Teichgraeber III, R. (1986) *'Free Trade' and Moral Philosophy: Rethinking the Sources of Adam Smith's Wealth of Nations* (Durham, NC: Duke University Press).

Thaler, R. H. and Sunstein, C. R. (2008) *Nudge: Improving Decisions About Health, Wealth, and Happiness* (New Haven, CT: Yale University Press).

The Occupied Times of London (2011a) *Issue 1*, October 26.
The Occupied Times of London (2011b) *Issue 2*, November 2.
The Occupied Times of London (2011c) *Issue 3*, November 9.
The Occupied Times of London (2011d) *Issue 4*, November 16.
The Occupied Times of London (2011e) *Issue 5*, November 23.
The Occupied Times of London (2011f) *Issue 6*, November 30.
The Occupied Times of London (2011g) *Issue 7*, December 14.
The Occupied Times of London (2012a) *Issue 8*, January 4.
The Occupied Times of London (2012b) *Issue 9*, January 20.
The Occupied Times of London (2012c) *Issue 10*, February 8.
The Occupied Wall Street Journal (2011a) *Issue 1*, [no date].
The Occupied Wall Street Journal (2011b) *Issue 2*, October 8.
The Occupied Wall Street Journal (2011c) *Issue 5*, November.
Tidal: Occupy Theory, Occupy Strategy (2011) Issue 1. Available online: http://occupytheory.org/ [accessed 27/02/12].
Tobin, J. (1996) *Essays in Economics Volume 4: National and International* (Cambridge, MA: MIT Press).
Tooze, R. (1997) 'Constructive Criticism: Threats, Imperatives, and Opportunities of a Constitutive IPE', in Burch, K. and Denemark, R.A. (eds) *Constituting International Political Economy* (London: Lynne Rienner).
Tormey, S. (2012) 'Occupy Wall Street: From Representation to Post-Representation', *Journal of Critical Globalisation Studies*, 5, pp. 132–137.
Tribe, K. (1999) 'Adam Smith: Critical Theorist?', *Journal of Economic Literature*, 37 (2), pp. 609–632.
Tully, J. (1988) 'The Pen is a Mighty Sword: Quentin Skinner's Analysis of Politics' in Tully, J. (ed) *Meaning and Context: Quentin Skinner and his Critics* (Cambridge: Polity).
UN (2010) *The Stiglitz Report: Reforming the International Monetary and Financial Systems in the Wake of the Global Crisis* (New York: The New Press).
UNCTAD (2009) *The Global Economic Crisis: Systemic Failures and Multilateral Remedies* (New York: United Nations).
Underhill, G.R.D. (2000) 'Introduction: Conceptualizing the Changing Global Order', in Stubbs, R. and Underhill, G.R.D. (eds) *Political Economy and the Changing Global Order Second Edition* (Oxford University Press).
US Senate Permanent Subcommittee on Investigations (2011) *Wall Street and the Financial Crisis: Anatomy of a Financial Collapse* (Washington, DC: Permanent Subcommittee on Investigations).
Vaggi, G. (2004) 'Adam Smith's Socio-Economic Man – and the Macro-Foundations of Microeconomics', in Aspromourgos, T. and Lodewijks, J. (eds) *History and Political Economy: Essays in Honour of P. D. Groenewegen* (London: Routledge).
Versluysen, E. (1981) *The Political Economy of International Finance* (London: Gower).
Vestergaard, J. (2009) *Discipline in the Global Economy? International Finance and the End of Liberalism* (New York: Routledge).
Viner, J. (1989 [1928]) 'Adam Smith and Laissez Faire', in Clark, J.M., Douglas, P.H., Hollander, J.H., Morrow, G.R., Palyi, M. and Viner, J. (eds) *Adam Smith, 1776–1926: Lectures to Commemorate the Sesquicentennial of The Wealth of Nations* (New York: Augustus M. Kelley Publishers).
Volcker, P. (2010) 'How to Reform Our Financial System', *The New York Times*, January 30.
Wade, R. (2008) 'The First World Debt Crisis of 2007–2010 in Global Perspective', *Challenge*, 51 (4), pp. 23–54.

Wainwright, T. (2009) 'Laying the Foundations for a Crisis: Mapping the Historico-Geographical Construction of Residential Mortgage Backed Securitization in the UK', *International Journal of Urban and Regional Research*, 33 (2), pp. 372–388.

Walker, R.B.J. (2010) 'Conclusion: Cultural, Political, Economy', in Best, J. and Paterson, M. (eds) *Cultural Political Economy* (London: Routledge).

Wall Street Watch (2009) *Sold Out: How Wall Street and Washington Betrayed America*, *wallstreetwatch.org*, Available online: http://wallstreetwatch.org/soldoutreport.php [accessed 09/02/12].

Warwick Commission (2009) *The Warwick Commission on International Financial Reform: In Praise of Unlevel Playing Fields* (University of Warwick).

Watson, M. (2005a) *Foundations of International Political Economy* (Basingstoke: Palgrave).

Watson, M. (2005b) 'What Makes a Market Economy? Schumpeter, Smith and Walras on the Coordination Problem', *New Political Economy*, 10 (2), pp. 143–161.

Watson, M. (2007) *The Political Economy of International Capital Mobility* (Basingstoke: Palgrave Macmillan).

Watson, M. (2009a) 'Gordon Brown's Misplaced Smithian Appeal: The Eclipse of Sympathy in Changing British Welfare Norms', *Journal of Social Policy*, 38 (2). pp. 195–210.

Watson, M. (2009b) 'Headlong into the Polanyian Dilemma: The Impact of Middle-Class Moral Panic on the British Government's Response to the Sub-prime Crisis', *British Journal of Politics and International Relations*, 11 (3), pp. 422–437.

Watson, M. (2010) 'House Price Keynesianism and the Contradictions of the Modern Investor Subject', *Housing Studies*, 25 (3), pp. 413–426.

Watson, M. (2013) 'The Eighteenth-century Historiographic Tradition and Contemporary "Everyday IPE"', *Review of International Studies*, 39 (1), pp.1–23.

Wearing, D. (2011) 'Tahrir Square and the Occupy Movement', *The Occupied Times of London, Issue 4*, November 16.

Weinstein, J. (2006) 'Sympathy, Difference, and Education: Social Unity in the Work of Adam Smith', *Economics and Philosophy*, 22, pp. 79–111.

White, M. and Lasn, K. (2011) 'The Call to Occupy Wall Street Resonates Around the World: We Need Deeper Changes to Our Financial System, or Tent Cities of People Angry at Corporate Greed will Keep Appearing', *guardian.co.uk*, September, 19, Available online: http://www.guardian.co.uk/commentisfree/cifamerica/2011/sep/19/occupy-wall-street-financial-system [accessed 09/02/12].

Williams, M.T. (2010) *Uncontrolled Risk: The Lessons of Lehman Brothers and How Systemic Risk Can Bring Down the World Financial System* (New York: McGraw-Hill).

Williamson, J. and Milner, C. (1991) *The World Economy: A Textbook in International Economics Second Edition* (New York: Harvester Wheatsheaf).

Wilson, T. (1976) 'Sympathy and Self-Interest', in Wilson, T. and Skinner, A. S. (eds) *The Market and the State: Essays in Honour of Adam Smith* (Oxford University Press).

Winch, D. (1978) *Adam Smith's Politics: An Essay in Historiographic Revision* (Cambridge University Press).

Winch, D. (1983) 'Adam Smith's "Enduring Particular Result": A Political and Cosmopolitan Perspective' in Hont, I. and Ignatieff, M. (eds) *Wealth and Virtue: The Shaping of Political Economy in the Scottish Enlightenment* (Cambridge University Press).

Winch, D. (1992) 'Adam Smith: Scottish Moral Philosopher as Political Economist', *The Historical Journal*, 35 (1), pp. 91–113.

Winch, D. (1997) 'Adam Smith's Problems and Ours', *Scottish Journal of Political Economy*, 44 (4), pp. 384–402.

Wolf, M. (2014) 'Strip Private Banks of Their Power to Create Money', *The Financial Times*, April 25.

Woo-Cumings, M. (2003) 'Diverse Paths Towards "The Right Institutions": Law, the State, and Economic Reform in East Asia', in Weiss, L. (ed) *States in the Global Economy: Bringing Domestic Institutions Back In* (Cambridge University Press).

Woods, N. (2001) 'International Political Economy in an Age of Globalization', in Baylis, J. and Smith, S. (eds) *The Globalization of World Politics: An Introduction to International Relations Second Edition* (Oxford University Press).

Zandi, M. (2009) *Financial Shock: Global Panic and Government Bailouts – How We Got Here and What Must Be Done to Fix It Updated Edition* (Upper Saddle River, NJ: Pearson Education).

Index